International Seabed Authority

CONSOLIDATED REGULATIONS AND RECOMMENDATIONS ON PROSPECTING AND EXPLORATION

Revised edition

2015

Published in Jamaica 2015 by
The International Seabed Authority

© International Seabed Authority 2015

All rights reserved. No part of this publication may be reproduced, stored in a retrieval system, or transmitted in any form or by any means, electronic, mechanical, photocopy or otherwise, without the prior permission of the copyright owner. Application for such permission with a statement of purpose and extent of reproduction, should be addressed to the International Seabed Authority, 14-20 Port Royal Street, Kingston, Jamaica.

CONTENTS

INTRODUCTION

I. REGULATIONS

1. ISBA/19/A/9 — Decision of the Assembly of the International Seabed Authority regarding the amendments to the Regulations on Prospecting and Exploration for Polymetallic Nodules in the Area

2. ISBA/19/C/17 — Decision of the Council of the International Seabed Authority relating to amendments to the Regulations on Prospecting and Exploration for Polymetallic Nodules in the Area and related matters

3. ISBA/16/A/12/Rev.1 — Decision of the Assembly of the International Seabed Authority relating to the Regulations on Prospecting and Exploration for Polymetallic Sulphides in the Area

4. ISBA/18/A/11 — Decision of the Assembly of the International Seabed Authority relating to the Regulations on Prospecting and Exploration for Cobalt-rich Ferromanganese Crusts in the Area

II. RECOMMENDATIONS AND PROCEDURES

5. ISBA/19/LTC/8 — Recommendations for the guidance of contractors for the assessment of the possible environmental impacts arising from exploration for marine minerals in the Area

6. ISBA/19/LTC/14 — Recommendations for the guidance of contractors and sponsoring States relating to training programmes under plans of work for exploration

7. ISBA/21/LTC/11 — Recommendations for the guidance of contractors for the reporting of actual and direct exploration expenditure

8. ISBA/21/LTC/15 — Recommendations for the guidance of contractors on the content, format and structure of annual reports

9. ISBA/21/C/19* — Decision of the Council of the International Seabed Authority relating to the procedures and criteria for the extension of an approved plan of work for exploration pursuant to section 1, paragraph 9, of the annex to the Agreement relating to the Implementation of Part XI of the United Nations Convention on the Law of the Sea of 10 December 1982

INTRODUCTION

This revised edition of the *Consolidated regulations and recommendations on prospecting and exploration* contains the regulations that the Assembly of the International Seabed Authority has approved to date, and the recommendations on technical and administrative matters that have been issued for the implementation of the rules, regulations and procedures of the Authority.

The first part includes three sets of regulations that relate only to prospecting and exploration for marine mineral resources in the Area. Since the publication of the first edition, the Authority has made further amendments to these Regulations. These are inserted in the appropriate places to provide an unofficial consolidated version of the text. Amendments are in a different font, in bold, and referenced by footnotes. These are:

- The Regulations on Prospecting and Exploration for Polymetallic Nodules in the Area (approved on 13 July 2000, and amended on 25 July 2013 and 24 July 2014);[1]
- The Regulations on Prospecting and Exploration for Polymetallic Sulphides in the Area (approved on 7 May 2010 and amended on 25 July 2013 and 24 July 2014);[2] and
- The Regulations on Prospecting and Exploration for Cobalt-rich Ferromanganese Crusts in the Area (approved on 27 July 2012 and amended on 25 July 2013).[3]

These Regulations are part of the overall legislative regime for the Area which is mostly set out in Part XI and Annexes III and IV of the 1982 United Nations Convention on the Law of the Sea[4] and the 1994 Agreement relating to the Implementation of Part XI.[5]

The second part reproduces the recommendations that the Legal and Technical Commission of the Authority has issued for the guidance of contractors to assist them in the implementation of the rules, regulations and procedures of the Authority. These include:

- Recommendations for the guidance of contractors for the assessment of the possible environmental impacts arising from exploration for marine minerals in the Area;[6]
- Recommendations for the guidance of contractors and sponsoring States relating to training programmes under plans of work for exploration;[7]
- Recommendations for the guidance of contractors for the reporting of actual and direct exploration expenditure;[8]
- Recommendations for the guidance of contractors on the content, format and structure of annual reports;[9]

Also included is the:

- Decision of the Council of the International Seabed Authority relating to the procedures and criteria for the extension of an approved plan of work for exploration.[10]

---

[1] ISBA/6/A/18; ISBA/19/A/9, ISBA/19/A/12 and ISBA/20/A/9.
[2] ISBA/16/A/12/Rev.1, ISBA/19/A/12 and ISBA/20/A/10.
[3] ISBA/18/A/11 and ISBA/19/A/12.
[4] A/CONF.62/122 and Corr. 1-11. *The Law of the Sea: Compendium of Basic Documents* (International Seabed Authority/The Caribbean Law Publishing Company, 2001), p. 1.
[5] A/RES/48/263, Annex. Also reproduced in *The Law of the Sea: Compendium of Basic Documents* (International Seabed Authority/The Caribbean Law Publishing Company, 2001), p. 206.
[6] ISBA/19/LTC/8.
[7] ISBA/19/LTC/14.
[8] ISBA/21/LTC/11.
[9] ISBA/21/LTC/15.
[10] ISBA/21/C/19*.

I. REGULATIONS

International Seabed Authority

Assembly

ISBA/19/A/9

Distr.: General
25 July 2013

Original: English

Nineteenth session
Kingston, Jamaica
15-26 July 2013

Decision of the Assembly of the International Seabed Authority regarding the amendments to the Regulations on Prospecting and Exploration for Polymetallic Nodules in the Area

The Assembly of the International Seabed Authority,

Having considered the amendments to the Regulations on Prospecting and Exploration for Polymetallic Nodules, as provisionally adopted by the Council at its 190th meeting, on 22 July 2013,

Approves the amendments to the Regulations on Prospecting and Exploration for Polymetallic Nodules in the Area, as contained in the annex to the decision of the Council.[1]

142nd meeting
25 July 2013

---

[1] ISBA/19/C/17, annex.

International Seabed Authority

ISBA/19/C/17

Council

Distr.: General
22 July 2013

Original: English

Nineteenth session
Kingston, Jamaica
15-26 July 2013

Decision of the Council of the International Seabed Authority relating to amendments to the Regulations on Prospecting and Exploration for Polymetallic Nodules in the Area and related matters

The Council of the International Seabed Authority,

1. *Adopts* the amendments to the Regulations on Prospecting and Exploration for Polymetallic Nodules in the Area as contained in the annex to the present document;

2. *Decides* to apply the amended Regulations provisionally from the date of their adoption by the Council, pending their approval by the Assembly of the International Seabed Authority;

3. *Requests* the Secretary-General, in the case of a pending application for approval of a plan of work for polymetallic nodules submitted prior to the entry into force of the amendments to the Regulations, to consult the applicant prior to the signature of the contract for exploration, with a view to incorporating any necessary revisions into the standard terms of contract;

4. *Requests* the Legal and Technical Commission of the Authority to make a recommendation for consideration by the Council at its twentieth session to bring regulation 21 of the Regulations on Prospecting and Exploration for Polymetallic Sulphides in the Area[1] into line with regulation 21 of the Regulations on Prospecting and Exploration for Cobalt-rich Ferromanganese Crusts in the Area;[2]

5. *Decides that*, pending the receipt of the recommendation of the Legal and Technical Commission referred to in paragraph 4, regulation 21 (1) (b) of the Regulations on Prospecting and Exploration for Polymetallic Sulphides in the Area shall not apply;

---

[1] ISBA/16/A/12/Rev.1.
[2] ISBA/18/A/11.

13-40403 (E)   230713
1340403

6. *Further requests* the Legal and Technical Commission to review the provisions of the Regulations on Prospecting and Exploration for Polymetallic Nodules in the Area, the Regulations on Prospecting and Exploration for Polymetallic Sulphides and the Regulations on Prospecting and Exploration for Cobalt-rich Ferromanganese Crusts in the Area relating to the monopolization of activities in the Area and the option of offering an equity interest in a joint venture arrangement with a view to possibly aligning all three sets of regulations in this respect and to make a recommendation thereon for consideration by the Council at its twentieth session.

190th meeting
22 July 2013

Annex

Regulations on Prospecting and Exploration for Polymetallic Nodules in the Area

Preamble

In accordance with the United Nations Convention on the Law of the Sea of 10 December 1982 ("the Convention"), the seabed and ocean floor and the subsoil thereof beyond the limits of national jurisdiction, as well as its resources, are the common heritage of mankind, the exploration and exploitation of which shall be carried out for the benefit of mankind as a whole, on whose behalf the International Seabed Authority acts. The objective of this set of Regulations is to provide for prospecting and exploration for polymetallic nodules.

Part I
Introduction

Regulation 1
Use of terms and scope

1. Terms used in the Convention shall have the same meaning in these Regulations.

2. In accordance with the Agreement relating to the Implementation of Part XI of the United Nations Convention on the Law of the Sea of 10 December 1982 ("the Agreement"), the provisions of the Agreement and Part XI of the Convention shall be interpreted and applied together as a single instrument. These Regulations and references in these Regulations to the Convention are to be interpreted and applied accordingly.

3. For the purposes of these Regulations:

    (a) "Exploitation" means the recovery for commercial purposes of polymetallic nodules in the Area and the extraction of minerals therefrom, including the construction and operation of mining, processing and transportation systems, for the production and marketing of metals;

    (b) "Exploration" means the searching for deposits of polymetallic nodules in the Area with exclusive rights, the analysis of such deposits, the use and testing of recovery systems and equipment, processing facilities and transportation systems and the carrying out of studies of the environmental, technical, economic, commercial and other appropriate factors that must be taken into account in exploitation;

    (c) "Marine environment" includes the physical, chemical, geological and biological components, conditions and factors which interact and determine the productivity, state, condition and quality of the marine ecosystem, the waters of the seas and oceans and the airspace above those waters, as well as the seabed and ocean floor and subsoil thereof;

(d) "Polymetallic nodules" means one of the resources of the Area consisting of any deposit or accretion of nodules, on or just below the surface of the deep seabed, which contain manganese, nickel, cobalt and copper;

(e) "Prospecting" means the search for deposits of polymetallic nodules in the Area, including estimation of the composition, sizes and distributions of deposits of polymetallic nodules and their economic values, without any exclusive rights;

(f) "Serious harm to the marine environment" means any effect from activities in the Area on the marine environment which represents a significant adverse change in the marine environment determined according to the rules, regulations and procedures adopted by the Authority on the basis of internationally recognized standards and practices.

4. These Regulations shall not in any way affect the freedom of scientific research, pursuant to article 87 of the Convention, or the right to conduct marine scientific research in the Area pursuant to articles 143 and 256 of the Convention. Nothing in these Regulations shall be construed in such a way as to restrict the exercise by States of the freedom of the high seas as reflected in article 87 of the Convention.

5. These Regulations may be supplemented by further rules, regulations and procedures, in particular on the protection and preservation of the marine environment. These Regulations shall be subject to the provisions of the Convention and the Agreement and other rules of international law not incompatible with the Convention.

Part II
Prospecting

Regulation 2
Prospecting

1. Prospecting shall be conducted in accordance with the Convention and these Regulations and may commence only after the prospector has been informed by the Secretary-General that its notification has been recorded pursuant to regulation 4 (2).

2. Prospectors and the Authority shall apply a precautionary approach, as reflected in principle 15 of the Rio Declaration on Environment and Development.[3] Prospecting shall not be undertaken if substantial evidence indicates the risk of serious harm to the marine environment.

3. Prospecting shall not be undertaken in an area covered by an approved plan of work for exploration for polymetallic nodules or in a reserved area; nor may there be prospecting in an area which the Council has disapproved for exploitation because of the risk of serious harm to the marine environment.

4. Prospecting shall not confer on the prospector any rights with respect to resources. A prospector may, however, recover a reasonable quantity of minerals, being the quantity necessary for testing and not for commercial use.

---

[3] *Report of the United Nations Conference on Environment and Development, Rio de Janeiro, 3-14 June 1992* (United Nations publication, Sales No. E.93.I.8 and corrigendum), vol. I, *Resolutions adopted by the Conference*, resolution 1, annex I.

5. There shall be no time limit on prospecting, except that prospecting in a particular area shall cease upon written notification to the prospector by the Secretary-General that a plan of work for exploration has been approved with regard to that area.

6. Prospecting may be conducted simultaneously by more than one prospector in the same area or areas.

Regulation 3
Notification of prospecting

1. A proposed prospector shall notify the Authority of its intention to engage in prospecting.

2. Each notification of prospecting shall be in the form prescribed in annex I to these Regulations, shall be addressed to the Secretary-General and shall conform to the requirements of these Regulations.

3. Each notification shall be submitted:

  (a) In the case of a State, by the authority designated for that purpose by it;

  (b) In the case of an entity, by its designated representative;

  (c) In the case of the Enterprise, by its competent authority.

4. Each notification shall be in one of the languages of the Authority and shall contain:

  (a) The name, nationality and address of the proposed prospector and its designated representative;

  (b) The coordinates of the broad area or areas within which prospecting is to be conducted, in accordance with the most recent generally accepted international standard used by the Authority;

  (c) A general description of the prospecting programme, including the proposed date of commencement and its approximate duration;

  (d) A satisfactory written undertaking that the proposed prospector will:

  (i) Comply with the Convention and the relevant rules, regulations and procedures of the Authority concerning:

  a. Cooperation in the training programmes in connection with marine scientific research and transfer of technology referred to in articles 143 and 144 of the Convention; and

  b. Protection and preservation of the marine environment;

  (ii) Accept verification by the Authority of compliance therewith; and

  (iii) Make available to the Authority, as far as practicable, such data as may be relevant to the protection and preservation of the marine environment.

Regulation 4
Consideration of notifications

1. The Secretary-General shall acknowledge in writing receipt of each notification submitted under regulation 3, specifying the date of receipt.

2. The Secretary-General shall review and act on the notification within 45 days of its receipt. If the notification conforms with the requirements of the Convention and these Regulations, the Secretary-General shall record the particulars of the notification in a register maintained for that purpose and shall inform the prospector in writing that the notification has been so recorded.

3. The Secretary-General shall, within 45 days of receipt of the notification, inform the proposed prospector in writing if the notification includes any part of an area included in an approved plan of work for exploration or exploitation of any category of resources, or any part of a reserved area, or any part of an area which has been disapproved by the Council for exploitation because of the risk of serious harm to the marine environment, or if the written undertaking is not satisfactory, and shall provide the proposed prospector with a written statement of reasons. In such cases, the proposed prospector may, within 90 days, submit an amended notification. The Secretary-General shall, within 45 days, review and act upon such amended notification.

4. A prospector shall inform the Secretary-General in writing of any change in the information contained in the notification.

5. The Secretary-General shall not release any particulars contained in the notification except with the written consent of the prospector. The Secretary-General shall, however, from time to time inform all members of the Authority of the identity of prospectors and the general areas in which prospecting is being conducted.

Regulation 5
Protection and preservation of the marine environment during prospecting

1. Each prospector shall take necessary measures to prevent, reduce and control pollution and other hazards to the marine environment arising from prospecting, as far as reasonably possible, applying a precautionary approach and best environmental practices. In particular, each prospector shall minimize or eliminate:

   (a) Adverse environmental impacts from prospecting; and

   (b) Actual or potential conflicts or interference with existing or planned marine scientific research activities, in accordance with the relevant future guidelines in this regard.

2. Prospectors shall cooperate with the Authority in the establishment and implementation of programmes for monitoring and evaluating the potential impacts of the exploration for and exploitation of polymetallic nodules on the marine environment.

3. A prospector shall immediately notify the Secretary-General in writing, using the most effective means, of any incident arising from prospecting which has caused, is causing or poses a threat of serious harm to the marine environment.

Upon receipt of such notification the Secretary-General shall act in a manner consistent with regulation 33.

Regulation 6
Annual report

1. A prospector shall, within 90 days of the end of each calendar year, submit a report to the Authority on the status of prospecting. Such reports shall be submitted by the Secretary-General to the Legal and Technical Commission. Each such report shall contain:

 (a) A general description of the status of prospecting and of the results obtained;

 (b) Information on compliance with the undertakings referred to in regulation 3 (4) (d); and

 (c) Information on adherence to the relevant guidelines in this regard.

2. If the prospector intends to claim expenditures for prospecting as part of the development costs incurred prior to the commencement of commercial production, the prospector shall submit an annual statement, in conformity with internationally accepted accounting principles and certified by a duly qualified firm of public accountants, of the actual and direct expenditures incurred by the prospector in carrying out prospecting.

Regulation 7
Confidentiality of data and information from prospecting contained in the annual report

1. The Secretary-General shall ensure the confidentiality of all data and information contained in the reports submitted under regulation 6 applying mutatis mutandis the provisions of regulations 36 and 37, provided that data and information relating to the protection and preservation of the marine environment, in particular those from environmental monitoring programmes, shall not be considered confidential. The prospector may request that such data not be disclosed for up to three years following the date of their submission.

2. The Secretary-General may, at any time, with the consent of the prospector concerned, release data and information relating to prospecting in an area in respect of which a notification has been submitted. If, after having made reasonable efforts for at least two years, the Secretary-General determines that the prospector no longer exists or cannot be located, the Secretary-General may release such data and information.

Regulation 8
Objects of an archaeological or historical nature

A prospector shall immediately notify the Secretary-General in writing of any finding in the Area of an object of actual or potential archaeological or historical nature and its location. The Secretary-General shall transmit such information to the Director General of the United Nations Educational, Scientific and Cultural Organization.

Part III
Applications for approval of plans of work for exploration in the form of contracts

Section 1
General provisions

Regulation 9
General

Subject to the provisions of the Convention, the following may apply to the Authority for approval of plans of work for exploration:

(a) The Enterprise, on its own behalf or in a joint arrangement;

(b) States parties, State enterprises or natural or juridical persons which possess the nationality of States or are effectively controlled by them or their nationals, when sponsored by such States, or any group of the foregoing which meets the requirements of these Regulations.

Section 2
Content of applications

Regulation 10
Form of applications

1. Each application for approval of a plan of work for exploration shall be in the form prescribed in annex II to these Regulations, shall be addressed to the Secretary-General and shall conform to the requirements of these Regulations.

2. Each application shall be submitted:

(a) In the case of a State, by the authority designated for that purpose by it;

(b) In the case of an entity, by its designated representative or the authority designated for that purpose by the sponsoring State or States; and

(c) In the case of the Enterprise, by its competent authority.

3. Each application by a State enterprise or one of the entities referred to in regulation 9 (b) shall also contain:

(a) Sufficient information to determine the nationality of the applicant or the identity of the State or States by which, or by whose nationals, the applicant is effectively controlled; and

(b) The principal place of business or domicile and, if applicable, place of registration of the applicant.

4. Each application submitted by a partnership or consortium of entities shall contain the required information in respect of each member of the partnership or consortium.

Regulation 11
Certificate of sponsorship

1. Each application by a State enterprise or one of the entities referred to in regulation 9 (b) shall be accompanied by a certificate of sponsorship issued by the State of which it is a national or by which or by whose nationals it is effectively controlled. If the applicant has more than one nationality, as in the case of a partnership or consortium of entities from more than one State, each State involved shall issue a certificate of sponsorship.

2. Where the applicant has the nationality of one State but is effectively controlled by another State or its nationals, each State involved shall issue a certificate of sponsorship.

3. Each certificate of sponsorship shall be duly signed on behalf of the State by which it is submitted and shall contain:

   (a) The name of the applicant;

   (b) The name of the sponsoring State;

   (c) A statement that the applicant is:

   (i) A national of the sponsoring State; or

   (ii) Subject to the effective control of the sponsoring State or its nationals;

   (d) A statement by the sponsoring State that it sponsors the applicant;

   (e) The date of deposit by the sponsoring State of its instrument of ratification of, or accession or succession to, the Convention;

   (f) A declaration that the sponsoring State assumes responsibility in accordance with articles 139 and 153 (4) of the Convention and article 4 (4) of annex III to the Convention.

4. States or entities in a joint arrangement with the Enterprise shall also comply with this regulation.

Regulation 12
Financial and technical capabilities

1. Each application for approval of a plan of work for exploration shall contain specific and sufficient information to enable the Council to determine whether the applicant is financially and technically capable of carrying out the proposed plan of work for exploration and of fulfilling its financial obligations to the Authority.

2. An application for approval of a plan of work for exploration submitted on behalf of a State or entity, or any component of such entity, referred to in paragraph 1 (a) (ii) or (iii) of resolution II, other than a registered pioneer investor, which has already undertaken substantial activities in the Area prior to the entry into force of the Convention, or its successor in interest, shall be considered to have met the financial and technical qualifications necessary for approval of a plan of work for exploration if the sponsoring State or States certify that the applicant has expended an amount equivalent to at least 30 million United States dollars in research and exploration activities and has expended no less than 10 per cent of that amount in

the location, survey and evaluation of the area referred to in the plan of work for exploration.

3. An application for approval of a plan of work for exploration by the Enterprise shall include a statement by its competent authority certifying that the Enterprise has the necessary financial resources to meet the estimated costs of the proposed plan of work for exploration.

4. An application for approval of a plan of work for exploration by a State or a State enterprise, other than a registered pioneer investor or an entity referred to in paragraph 1 (a) (ii) or (iii) of resolution II, shall include a statement by the State or the sponsoring State certifying that the applicant has the necessary financial resources to meet the estimated costs of the proposed plan of work for exploration.

5. An application for approval of a plan of work for exploration by an entity, other than a registered pioneer investor or an entity referred to in paragraph 1 (a) (ii) or (iii) of resolution II, shall include copies of its audited financial statements, including balance sheets and profit-and-loss statements, for the most recent three years, in conformity with internationally accepted accounting principles and certified by a duly qualified firm of public accountants.

6. If the applicant is a newly organized entity and a certified balance sheet is not available, the application shall include a pro forma balance sheet certified by an appropriate official of the applicant.

7. If the applicant is a subsidiary of another entity, the application shall include copies of such financial statements of that entity and a statement from that entity, in conformity with internationally accepted accounting principles and certified by a duly qualified firm of public accountants, that the applicant will have the financial resources to carry out the plan of work for exploration.

8. If the applicant is controlled by a State or a State enterprise, the application shall include a statement from the State or State enterprise certifying that the applicant will have the financial resources to carry out the plan of work for exploration.

9. Where an applicant seeking approval of a plan of work for exploration intends to finance the proposed plan of work for exploration by borrowings, its application shall include the amount of such borrowings, the repayment period and the interest rate.

10. Except as provided for in paragraph 2, each application shall include:

(a) A general description of the applicant's previous experience, knowledge, skills, technical qualifications and expertise relevant to the proposed plan of work for exploration;

(b) A general description of the equipment and methods expected to be used in carrying out the proposed plan of work for exploration and other relevant non proprietary information about the characteristics of such technology; and

(c) A general description of the applicant's financial and technical capability to respond to any incident or activity which causes serious harm to the marine environment.

11. Where the applicant is a partnership or consortium of entities in a joint arrangement, each member of the partnership or consortium shall provide the information required by this regulation.

Regulation 13
Previous contracts with the Authority

Where the applicant or, in the case of an application by a partnership or consortium of entities in a joint arrangement, any member of the partnership or consortium, has previously been awarded any contract with the Authority, the application shall include:

(a) The date of the previous contract or contracts;

(b) The date, reference number and title of each report submitted to the Authority in connection with the contract or contracts; and

(c) The date of termination of the contract or contracts, if applicable.

Regulation 14
Undertakings

Each applicant, including the Enterprise, shall, as part of its application for approval of a plan of work for exploration, provide a written undertaking to the Authority that it will:

(a) Accept as enforceable and comply with the applicable obligations created by the provisions of the Convention and the rules, regulations and procedures of the Authority, the decisions of the organs of the Authority and the terms of its contracts with the Authority;

(b) Accept control by the Authority of activities in the Area, as authorized by the Convention; and

(c) Provide the Authority with a written assurance that its obligations under the contract will be fulfilled in good faith.

Regulation 15
Total area covered by the application

Each application for approval of a plan of work for exploration shall define the boundaries of the area under application by a list of coordinates in accordance with the most recent generally accepted international standard used by the Authority. Applications other than those under regulation 17 shall cover a total area, which need not be a single continuous area, sufficiently large and of sufficient estimated commercial value to allow two mining operations. The applicant shall indicate the coordinates dividing the area into two parts of equal estimated commercial value. The area to be allocated to the applicant shall be subject to the provisions of regulation 25.

Regulation 16
Data and information to be submitted before the designation of a reserved area

1. Each application shall contain sufficient data and information, as prescribed in section II of annex II to these Regulations, with respect to the area under application

to enable the Council, on the recommendation of the Legal and Technical Commission, to designate a reserved area based on the estimated commercial value of each part. Such data and information shall consist of data available to the applicant with respect to both parts of the area under application, including the data used to determine their commercial value.

2. The Council, on the basis of the data and information submitted by the applicant pursuant to section II of annex II to these Regulations, if found satisfactory, and taking into account the recommendation of the Legal and Technical Commission, shall designate the part of the area under application which is to be a reserved area. The area so designated shall become a reserved area as soon as the plan of work for exploration for the non-reserved area is approved and the contract is signed. If the Council determines that additional information, consistent with these Regulations and annex II, is needed to designate the reserved area, it shall refer the matter back to the Commission for further consideration, specifying the additional information required.

3. Once the plan of work for exploration is approved and a contract has been issued, the data and information transferred to the Authority by the applicant in respect of the reserved area may be disclosed by the Authority in accordance with article 14 (3) of annex III to the Convention.

Regulation 17
Applications for approval of plans of work with respect to a reserved area

1. Any State which is a developing State or any natural or juridical person sponsored by it and effectively controlled by it or by any other developing State, or any group of the foregoing, may notify the Authority that it wishes to submit a plan of work for exploration with respect to a reserved area. The Secretary-General shall forward such notification to the Enterprise, which shall inform the Secretary-General in writing within six months whether or not it intends to carry out activities in that area. If the Enterprise intends to carry out activities in that area, it shall, pursuant to paragraph 4, also inform in writing the contractor whose application for approval of a plan of work for exploration originally included that area.

2. An application for approval of a plan of work for exploration in respect of a reserved area may be submitted at any time after such an area becomes available following a decision by the Enterprise that it does not intend to carry out activities in that area or where the Enterprise has not, within six months of the notification by the Secretary-General, either taken a decision on whether it intends to carry out activities in that area or notified the Secretary-General in writing that it is engaged in discussions regarding a potential joint venture. In the latter instance, the Enterprise shall have one year from the date of such notification in which to decide whether to conduct activities in that area.

3. If the Enterprise or a developing State or one of the entities referred to in paragraph 1 does not submit an application for approval of a plan of work for exploration for activities in a reserved area within 15 years of the commencement by the Enterprise of its functions independent of the Secretariat of the Authority or within 15 years of the date on which that area is reserved for the Authority, whichever is the later, the contractor whose application for approval of a plan of work for exploration originally included that area shall be entitled to apply for a

plan of work for exploration for that area provided it offers in good faith to include the Enterprise as a joint-venture partner.

4. A contractor has the right of first refusal to enter into a joint venture arrangement with the Enterprise for exploration of the area which was included in its application for approval of a plan of work for exploration and which was designated by the Council as a reserved area.

Regulation 18
Data and information to be submitted for approval of the plan of work for exploration

Each applicant shall submit, with a view to receiving approval of the plan of work for exploration in the form of a contract, the following information:

(a) A general description and a schedule of the proposed exploration programme, including the programme of activities for the immediate five-year period, such as studies to be undertaken in respect of the environmental, technical, economic and other appropriate factors that must be taken into account in exploration;

(b) A description of the programme for oceanographic and environmental baseline studies in accordance with these Regulations and any environmental rules, regulations and procedures established by the Authority that would enable an assessment of the potential environmental impact, including, but not restricted to, the impact on biodiversity, of the proposed exploration activities, taking into account any recommendations issued by the Legal and Technical Commission;

(c) A preliminary assessment of the possible impact of the proposed exploration activities on the marine environment;

(d) A description of proposed measures for the prevention, reduction and control of pollution and other hazards, as well as possible impacts, to the marine environment;

(e) Data necessary for the Council to make the determination it is required to make in accordance with regulation 12 (1); and

(f) A schedule of anticipated yearly expenditures in respect of the programme of activities for the immediate five-year period.

Section 3
Fees

Regulation 19
Fee for applications

1. The fee for processing an application for approval of a plan of work for exploration for polymetallic nodules shall be a fixed amount of 500,000 United States dollars or its equivalent in a freely convertible currency, to be paid in full at the time of the submission of an application.

2. If the administrative costs incurred by the Authority in processing an application are less than the fixed amount indicated in paragraph 1 above, the Authority shall refund the difference to the applicant. If the administrative costs

incurred by the Authority in processing an application are more than the fixed amount indicated in paragraph 1 above, the applicant shall pay the difference to the Authority, provided that any additional amount to be paid by the applicant shall not exceed 10 per cent of the fixed fee referred to in paragraph 1.

3. Taking into account any criteria established for this purpose by the Finance Committee, the Secretary-General shall determine the amount of such differences as indicated in paragraph 2 above and notify the applicant of its amount. The notification shall include a statement of the expenditure incurred by the Authority. The amount due shall be paid by the applicant or reimbursed by the Authority within three months of the signing of the contract referred to in regulation 23 below.

4. The fixed amount referred to in paragraph 1 above shall be reviewed on a regular basis by the Council in order to ensure that it covers the expected administrative costs of processing applications and to avoid the need for applicants to pay additional amounts in accordance with paragraph 2 above.

Section 4
Processing of applications

Regulation 20
Receipt, acknowledgement and safe custody of applications

1. The Secretary-General shall:

    (a) Acknowledge in writing within 30 days receipt of every application for approval of a plan of work for exploration submitted under this Part, specifying the date of receipt;

    (b) Place the application together with the attachments and annexes thereto in safe custody and ensure the confidentiality of all confidential data and information contained in the application; and

    (c) Notify the members of the Authority of the receipt of such application and circulate to them information of a general nature which is not confidential regarding the application.

Regulation 21
Consideration by the Legal and Technical Commission

1. Upon receipt of an application for approval of a plan of work for exploration, the Secretary-General shall notify the members of the Legal and Technical Commission and place consideration of the application as an item on the agenda for the next meeting of the Commission. The Commission shall consider only applications in respect of which notification and information has been circulated by the Secretary-General in accordance with regulation 20 (c) at least 30 days prior to the commencement of the meeting of the Commission at which they are to be considered.

2. The Commission shall examine applications in the order in which they are received.

3. The Commission shall determine if the applicant:

    (a) Has complied with the provisions of these Regulations;

(b) Has given the undertakings and assurances specified in regulation 14;

(c) Possesses the financial and technical capability to carry out the proposed plan of work for exploration and has provided details as to its ability to comply promptly with emergency orders; and

(d) Has satisfactorily discharged its obligations in relation to any previous contract with the Authority.

4. The Commission shall, in accordance with the requirements set forth in these Regulations and its procedures, determine whether the proposed plan of work for exploration will:

(a) Provide for effective protection of human health and safety;

(b) Provide for effective protection and preservation of the marine environment including, but not restricted to, the impact on biodiversity;

(c) Ensure that installations are not established where interference may be caused to the use of recognized sea lanes essential to international navigation or in areas of intense fishing activity.

5. If the Commission makes the determinations specified in paragraph 3 and determines that the proposed plan of work for exploration meets the requirements of paragraph 4, the Commission shall recommend approval of the plan of work for exploration to the Council.

6. The Commission shall not recommend approval of the plan of work for exploration if part or all of the area covered by the proposed plan of work for exploration is included in:

(a) A plan of work for exploration approved by the Council for polymetallic nodules; or

(b) A plan of work approved by the Council for exploration for or exploitation of other resources if the proposed plan of work for exploration for polymetallic nodules might cause undue interference with activities under such approved plan of work for other resources; or

(c) An area disapproved for exploitation by the Council in cases where substantial evidence indicates the risk of serious harm to the marine environment; or

(d) If the proposed plan of work for exploration has been submitted or sponsored by a State that already holds:

(i) Plans of work for exploration and exploitation or exploitation only in non-reserved areas that, together with either part of the area covered by the application, exceed in size 30 per cent of a circular area of 400,000 square kilometres surrounding the centre of either part of the area covered by the proposed plan of work;

(ii) Plans of work for exploration and exploitation or exploitation only in non-reserved areas which, taken together, constitute 2 per cent of that part of the Area which is not reserved or disapproved for exploitation pursuant to article 162 (2) (x) of the Convention.

> 7. The Legal and Technical Commission may recommend approval of a plan of work if it determines that such approval would not permit a State Party or entities sponsored by it to monopolize the conduct of activities in the Area with regard to polymetallic nodules or to preclude other States parties from activities in the Area with regard to polymetallic nodules.[4]

8. Except in the case of applications by the Enterprise, on its own behalf or in a joint venture, and applications under regulation 17, the Commission shall not recommend approval of the plan of work for exploration if part or all of the area covered by the proposed plan of work for exploration is included in a reserved area or an area designated by the Council to be a reserved area.

9. If the Commission finds that an application does not comply with these Regulations, it shall notify the applicant in writing, through the Secretary-General, indicating the reasons. The applicant may, within 45 days of such notification, amend its application. If the Commission after further consideration is of the view that it should not recommend approval of the plan of work for exploration, it shall so inform the applicant and provide the applicant with a further opportunity to make representations within 30 days of such information. The Commission shall consider any such representations made by the applicant in preparing its report and recommendation to the Council.

10. In considering a proposed plan of work for exploration, the Commission shall have regard to the principles, policies and objectives relating to activities in the Area as provided for in Part XI and annex III of the Convention and the Agreement.

11. The Commission shall consider applications expeditiously and shall submit its report and recommendations to the Council on the designation of the areas and on the plan of work for exploration at the first possible opportunity, taking into account the schedule of meetings of the Authority.

12. In discharging its duties, the Commission shall apply these Regulations and the rules, regulations and procedures of the Authority in a uniform and non-discriminatory manner.

Regulation 22
Consideration and approval of plans of work for exploration by the Council

The Council shall consider the reports and recommendations of the Commission relating to approval of plans of work for exploration in accordance with paragraphs 11 and 12 of section 3 of the annex to the Agreement.

---

[4] ISBA/20/A/9, dated 24 July 2014, Amendments.

Part IV
Contracts for exploration

Regulation 23
The contract

1. After a plan of work for exploration has been approved by the Council, it shall be prepared in the form of a contract between the Authority and the applicant as prescribed in annex III to these Regulations. Each contract shall incorporate the standard clauses set out in annex IV in effect at the date of entry into force of the contract.

2. The contract shall be signed by the Secretary-General on behalf of the Authority and by the applicant. The Secretary-General shall notify all members of the Authority in writing of the conclusion of each contract.

3. In accordance with the principle of non-discrimination, a contract with a State or entity or any component of such entity referred to in paragraph 6 (a) (i) of section 1 of the annex to the Agreement shall include arrangements that shall be similar to and no less favourable than those agreed with any registered pioneer investor. If any of the States or entities or any components of such entities referred to in paragraph 6 (a) (i) of section 1 of the annex to the Agreement are granted more favourable arrangements, the Council shall make similar and no less favourable arrangements with regard to the rights and obligations assumed by the registered pioneer investors, provided that such arrangements do not affect or prejudice the interests of the Authority.

Regulation 24
Rights of the contractor

1. The contractor shall have the exclusive right to explore an area covered by a plan of work for exploration in respect of polymetallic nodules. The Authority shall ensure that no other entity operates in the same area for other resources in a manner that might interfere with the operations of the contractor.

2. A contractor who has an approved plan of work for exploration only shall have a preference and a priority among applicants submitting plans of work for exploitation of the same area and resources. Such preference or priority may be withdrawn by the Council if the contractor has failed to comply with the requirements of its approved plan of work for exploration within the time period specified in a written notice or notices from the Council to the contractor indicating which requirements have not been complied with by the contractor. The time period specified in any such notice shall not be unreasonable. The contractor shall be accorded a reasonable opportunity to be heard before the withdrawal of such preference or priority becomes final. The Council shall provide the reasons for its proposed withdrawal of preference or priority and shall consider any contractor's response. The decision of the Council shall take account of that response and shall be based on substantial evidence.

3. A withdrawal of preference or priority shall not become effective until the contractor has been accorded a reasonable opportunity to exhaust the judicial remedies available to it pursuant to Part XI, section 5, of the Convention.

Regulation 25
Size of area and relinquishment

1. The total area allocated to the contractor under the contract shall not exceed 150,000 square kilometres. The contractor shall relinquish portions of the area allocated to it to revert to the Area. By the end of the third year from the date of the contract, the contractor shall have relinquished 20 per cent of the area allocated to it; by the end of the fifth year from the date of the contract, the contractor shall have relinquished an additional 10 per cent of the area allocated to it; and, after eight years from the date of the contract, the contractor shall have relinquished an additional 20 per cent of the area allocated to it, or such larger amount as would exceed the exploitation area decided upon by the Authority, provided that a contractor shall not be required to relinquish any portion of such area when the total area allocated to it does not exceed 75,000 square kilometres.

2. The Council may, at the request of the contractor, and on the recommendation of the Commission, in exceptional circumstances, defer the schedule of relinquishment. Such exceptional circumstances shall be determined by the Council and shall include, inter alia, consideration of prevailing economic circumstances or other unforeseen exceptional circumstances arising in connection with the operational activities of the contractor.

Regulation 26
Duration of contracts

1. A plan of work for exploration shall be approved for a period of 15 years. Upon expiration of a plan of work for exploration, the contractor shall apply for a plan of work for exploitation unless the contractor has already done so, has obtained an extension for the plan of work for exploration or decides to renounce its rights in the area covered by the plan of work for exploration.

2. Not later than six months before the expiration of a plan of work for exploration, a contractor may apply for extensions for the plan of work for exploration for periods of not more than five years each. Such extensions shall be approved by the Council, on the recommendation of the Commission, if the contractor has made efforts in good faith to comply with the requirements of the plan of work but for reasons beyond the contractor's control has been unable to complete the necessary preparatory work for proceeding to the exploitation stage or if the prevailing economic circumstances do not justify proceeding to the exploitation stage.

Regulation 27
Training

Pursuant to article 15 of annex III to the Convention, each contract shall include as a schedule a practical programme for the training of personnel of the Authority and developing States and drawn up by the contractor in cooperation with the Authority and the sponsoring State or States. Training programmes shall focus on training in the conduct of exploration, and shall provide for full participation by such personnel in all activities covered by the contract. Such training programmes may be revised and developed from time to time as necessary by mutual agreement.

Regulation 28
Periodic review of the implementation of the plan of work for exploration

1. The contractor and the Secretary-General shall jointly undertake a periodic review of the implementation of the plan of work for exploration at intervals of five years. The Secretary-General may request the contractor to submit such additional data and information as may be necessary for the purposes of the review.

2. In the light of the review, the contractor shall indicate its programme of activities for the following five-year period, making such adjustments to its previous programme of activities as are necessary.

3. The Secretary-General shall report on the review to the Commission and to the Council. The Secretary-General shall indicate in the report whether any observations transmitted to him by States parties to the Convention concerning the manner in which the contractor has discharged its obligations under these Regulations relating to the protection and preservation of the marine environment were taken into account in the review.

Regulation 29
Termination of sponsorship

1. Each contractor shall have the required sponsorship throughout the period of the contract.

2. If a State terminates its sponsorship it shall promptly notify the Secretary-General in writing. The sponsoring State should also inform the Secretary-General of the reasons for terminating its sponsorship. Termination of sponsorship shall take effect six months after the date of receipt of the notification by the Secretary-General, unless the notification specifies a later date.

3. In the event of termination of sponsorship the contractor shall, within the period referred to in paragraph 2, obtain another sponsor. Such sponsor shall submit a certificate of sponsorship in accordance with regulation 11. Failure to obtain a sponsor within the required period shall result in the termination of the contract.

4. A sponsoring State shall not be discharged by reason of the termination of its sponsorship from any obligations accrued while it was a sponsoring State, nor shall such termination affect any legal rights and obligations created during such sponsorship.

5. The Secretary-General shall notify the members of the Authority of the termination or change of sponsorship.

Regulation 30
Responsibility and liability

Responsibility and liability of the contractor and of the Authority shall be in accordance with the Convention. The contractor shall continue to have responsibility for any damage arising out of wrongful acts in the conduct of its operations, in particular damage to the marine environment, after the completion of the exploration phase.

Part V
Protection and preservation of the marine environment

Regulation 31
Protection and preservation of the marine environment

1. The Authority shall, in accordance with the Convention and the Agreement, establish and keep under periodic review environmental rules, regulations and procedures to ensure effective protection for the marine environment from harmful effects which may arise from activities in the Area.

2. In order to ensure effective protection for the marine environment from harmful effects which may arise from activities in the Area, the Authority and sponsoring States shall apply a precautionary approach, as reflected in principle 15 of the Rio Declaration, and best environmental practices.

3. The Legal and Technical Commission shall make recommendations to the Council on the implementation of paragraphs 1 and 2 above.

4. The Commission shall develop and implement procedures for determining, on the basis of the best available scientific and technical information, including information provided pursuant to regulation 18, whether proposed exploration activities in the Area would have serious harmful effects on vulnerable marine ecosystems and ensure that, if it is determined that certain proposed exploration activities would have serious harmful effects on vulnerable marine ecosystems, those activities are managed to prevent such effects or not authorized to proceed.

5. Pursuant to article 145 of the Convention and paragraph 2 of this regulation, each contractor shall take necessary measures to prevent, reduce and control pollution and other hazards to the marine environment arising from its activities in the Area as far as reasonably possible, applying a precautionary approach and best environmental practices.

6. Contractors, sponsoring States and other interested States or entities shall cooperate with the Authority in the establishment and implementation of programmes for monitoring and evaluating the impacts of deep seabed mining on the marine environment. When required by the Council, such programmes shall include proposals for areas to be set aside and used exclusively as impact reference zones and preservation reference zones. "Impact reference zones" means areas to be used for assessing the effect of activities in the Area on the marine environment and which are representative of the environmental characteristics of the Area. "Preservation reference zones" means areas in which no mining shall occur to ensure representative and stable biota of the seabed in order to assess any changes in the biodiversity of the marine environment.

Regulation 32
Environmental baselines and monitoring

1. Each contract shall require the contractor to gather environmental baseline data and to establish environmental baselines, taking into account any recommendations issued by the Legal and Technical Commission pursuant to regulation 39, against which to assess the likely effects of its programme of activities under the plan of work for exploration on the marine environment and a programme to monitor and report on such effects. The recommendations issued by

the Commission may, inter alia, list those exploration activities which may be considered to have no potential for causing harmful effects on the marine environment. The contractor shall cooperate with the Authority and the sponsoring State or States in the establishment and implementation of such monitoring programme.

2. The contractor shall report annually in writing to the Secretary-General on the implementation and results of the monitoring programme referred to in paragraph 1 and shall submit data and information, taking into account any recommendations issued by the Commission pursuant to regulation 39. The Secretary-General shall transmit such reports to the Commission for its consideration pursuant to article 165 of the Convention.

Regulation 33
Emergency orders

1. A contractor shall promptly report to the Secretary-General in writing, using the most effective means, any incident arising from activities which have caused, are causing or pose a threat of serious harm to the marine environment.

2. When the Secretary-General has been notified by a contractor or otherwise becomes aware of an incident resulting from or caused by a contractor's activities in the Area that has caused, is causing or poses a threat of serious harm to the marine environment, the Secretary-General shall cause a general notification of the incident to be issued, shall notify in writing the contractor and the sponsoring State or States, and shall report immediately to the Legal and Technical Commission, to the Council and to all other members of the Authority. A copy of the report shall be circulated to competent international organizations and to concerned subregional, regional and global organizations and bodies. The Secretary-General shall monitor developments with respect to all such incidents and shall report on them as appropriate to the Commission, the Council and all other members of the Authority.

3. Pending any action by the Council, the Secretary-General shall take such immediate measures of a temporary nature as are practical and reasonable in the circumstances to prevent, contain and minimize serious harm or the threat of serious harm to the marine environment. Such temporary measures shall remain in effect for no longer than 90 days, or until the Council decides at its next regular session or a special session, what measures, if any, to take pursuant to paragraph 6 of this regulation.

4. After having received the report of the Secretary-General, the Commission shall determine, based on the evidence provided to it and taking into account the measures already taken by the contractor, which measures are necessary to respond effectively to the incident in order to prevent, contain and minimize serious harm or the threat of serious harm to the marine environment, and shall make its recommendations to the Council.

5. The Council shall consider the recommendations of the Commission.

6. The Council, taking into account the recommendations of the Commission, the report of the Secretary-General, any information provided by the contractor and any other relevant information, may issue emergency orders, which may include orders for the suspension or adjustment of operations, as may be reasonably necessary to

prevent, contain and minimize serious harm or the threat of serious harm to the marine environment arising out of activities in the Area.

7. If a contractor does not promptly comply with an emergency order to prevent, contain and minimize serious harm or the threat of serious harm to the marine environment arising out of its activities in the Area, the Council shall take by itself or through arrangements with others on its behalf, such practical measures as are necessary to prevent, contain and minimize any such serious harm or threat of serious harm to the marine environment.

8. In order to enable the Council, when necessary, to take immediately the practical measures to prevent, contain and minimize the serious harm or threat of serious harm to the marine environment referred to in paragraph 7, the contractor, prior to the commencement of testing of collecting systems and processing operations, will provide the Council with a guarantee of its financial and technical capability to comply promptly with emergency orders or to assure that the Council can take such emergency measures. If the contractor does not provide the Council with such a guarantee, the sponsoring State or States shall, in response to a request by the Secretary-General and pursuant to articles 139 and 235 of the Convention, take necessary measures to ensure that the contractor provides such a guarantee or shall take measures to ensure that assistance is provided to the Authority in the discharge of its responsibilities under paragraph 7.

Regulation 34
Rights of coastal States

1. Nothing in these Regulations shall affect the rights of coastal States in accordance with article 142 and other relevant provisions of the Convention.

2. Any coastal State which has grounds for believing that any activity in the Area by a contractor is likely to cause serious harm or a threat of serious harm to the marine environment under its jurisdiction or sovereignty may notify the Secretary-General in writing of the grounds upon which such belief is based. The Secretary-General shall provide the contractor and its sponsoring State or States with a reasonable opportunity to examine the evidence, if any, provided by the coastal State as the basis for its belief. The contractor and its sponsoring State or States may submit their observations thereon to the Secretary-General within a reasonable time.

3. If there are clear grounds for believing that serious harm to the marine environment is likely to occur, the Secretary-General shall act in accordance with regulation 33 and, if necessary, shall take immediate measures of a temporary nature as provided for in regulation 33 (3).

4. Contractors shall take all measures necessary to ensure that their activities are conducted so as not to cause serious harm to the marine environment, including, but not restricted to, pollution, under the jurisdiction or sovereignty of coastal States, and that such serious harm or pollution arising from incidents or activities in its exploration area does not spread beyond such area.

Regulation 35
Human remains and objects and sites of an archaeological or historical nature

The contractor shall immediately notify the Secretary-General in writing of any finding in the exploration area of any human remains of an archaeological or historical nature, or any object or site of a similar nature and its location, including the preservation and protection measures taken. The Secretary-General shall transmit such information to the Director General of the United Nations Educational, Scientific and Cultural Organization and any other competent international organization. Following the finding of any such human remains, object or site in the exploration area, and in order to avoid disturbing such human remains, object or site, no further prospecting or exploration shall take place, within a reasonable radius, until such time as the Council decides otherwise after taking account of the views of the Director General of the United Nations Educational, Scientific and Cultural Organization or any other competent international organization.

Part VI
Confidentiality

Regulation 36
Confidentiality of data and information

1. Data and information submitted or transferred to the Authority or to any person participating in any activity or programme of the Authority pursuant to these Regulations or a contract issued under these Regulations, and designated by the contractor, in consultation with the Secretary-General, as being of a confidential nature, shall be considered confidential unless it is data and information which:

 (a) Is generally known or publicly available from other sources;

 (b) Has been previously made available by the owner to others without an obligation concerning its confidentiality; or

 (c) Is already in the possession of the Authority with no obligation concerning its confidentiality.

2. Data and information that is necessary for the formulation by the Authority of rules, regulations and procedures concerning protection and preservation of the marine environment and safety, other than proprietary equipment design data, shall not be deemed confidential.

3. Confidential data and information may only be used by the Secretary-General and staff of the Secretariat, as authorized by the Secretary-General, and by the members of the Legal and Technical Commission as necessary for and relevant to the effective exercise of their powers and functions. The Secretary-General shall authorize access to such data and information only for limited use in connection with the functions and duties of the staff of the Secretariat and the functions and duties of the Legal and Technical Commission.

4. Ten years after the date of submission of confidential data and information to the Authority or the expiration of the contract for exploration, whichever is the later, and every five years thereafter, the Secretary-General and the contractor shall review such data and information to determine whether they should remain

confidential. Such data and information shall remain confidential if the contractor establishes that there would be a substantial risk of serious and unfair economic prejudice if the data and information were to be released. No such data and information shall be released until the contractor has been accorded a reasonable opportunity to exhaust the judicial remedies available to it pursuant to Part XI, section 5, of the Convention.

5. If, at any time following the expiration of the contract for exploration, the contractor enters into a contract for exploitation in respect of any part of the exploration area, confidential data and information relating to that part of the area shall remain confidential in accordance with the contract for exploitation.

6. The contractor may at any time waive confidentiality of data and information.

Regulation 37
Procedures to ensure confidentiality

1. The Secretary-General shall be responsible for maintaining the confidentiality of all confidential data and information and shall not, except with the prior written consent of the contractor, release such data and information to any person external to the Authority. To ensure the confidentiality of such data and information, the Secretary-General shall establish procedures, consistent with the provisions of the Convention, governing the handling of confidential information by members of the Secretariat, members of the Legal and Technical Commission and any other person participating in any activity or programme of the Authority. Such procedures shall include:

(a) Maintenance of confidential data and information in secure facilities and development of security procedures to prevent unauthorized access to or removal of such data and information;

(b) Development and maintenance of a classification, log and inventory system of all written data and information received, including its type and source and routing from the time of receipt until final disposition.

2. A person who is authorized pursuant to these Regulations to have access to confidential data and information shall not disclose such data and information except as permitted under the Convention and these Regulations. The Secretary-General shall require any person who is authorized to have access to confidential data and information to make a written declaration witnessed by the Secretary-General or his or her authorized representative to the effect that the person so authorized:

(a) Acknowledges his or her legal obligation under the Convention and these Regulations with respect to the non-disclosure of confidential data and information;

(b) Agrees to comply with the applicable regulations and procedures established to ensure the confidentiality of such data and information.

3. The Legal and Technical Commission shall protect the confidentiality of confidential data and information submitted to it pursuant to these Regulations or a contract issued under these Regulations. In accordance with the provisions of article 163 (8) of the Convention, members of the Commission shall not disclose, even after the termination of their functions, any industrial secret, proprietary data which are transferred to the Authority in accordance with article 14 of annex III to the

Convention, or any other confidential information coming to their knowledge by reason of their duties for the Authority.

4. The Secretary-General and staff of the Authority shall not disclose, even after the termination of their functions with the Authority, any industrial secret, proprietary data which are transferred to the Authority in accordance with article 14 of annex III to the Convention, or any other confidential information coming to their knowledge by reason of their employment with the Authority.

5. Taking into account the responsibility and liability of the Authority pursuant to article 22 of annex III to the Convention, the Authority may take such action as may be appropriate against any person who, by reason of his or her duties for the Authority, has access to any confidential data and information and who is in breach of the obligations relating to confidentiality contained in the Convention and these Regulations.

Part VII
General procedures

Regulation 38
Notice and general procedures

1. Any application, request, notice, report, consent, approval, waiver, direction or instruction hereunder shall be made by the Secretary-General or by the designated representative of the prospector, applicant or contractor, as the case may be, in writing. Service shall be by hand, or by telex, fax, registered airmail or e-mail containing an authorized electronic signature to the Secretary-General at the headquarters of the Authority or to the designated representative.

2. Delivery by hand shall be effective when made. Delivery by telex shall be deemed to be effective on the business day following the day when the "answer back" appears on the sender's telex machine. Delivery by fax shall be effective when the "transmit confirmation report" confirming the transmission to the recipient's published fax number is received by the transmitter. Delivery by registered airmail shall be deemed to be effective 21 days after posting. An e-mail is presumed to be received by the addressee when it enters an information system designated or used by the addressee for the purpose of receiving documents of the type sent and is capable of being retrieved and processed by the addressee.

3. Notice to the designated representative of the prospector, applicant or contractor shall constitute effective notice to the prospector, applicant or contractor for all purposes under these Regulations, and the designated representative shall be the agent of the prospector, applicant or contractor for the service of process or notification in any proceeding of any court or tribunal having jurisdiction.

4. Notice to the Secretary-General shall constitute effective notice to the Authority for all purposes under these Regulations, and the Secretary-General shall be the Authority's agent for the service of process or notification in any proceeding of any court or tribunal having jurisdiction.

Regulation 39
Recommendations for the guidance of contractors

1. The Legal and Technical Commission may from time to time issue recommendations of a technical or administrative nature for the guidance of contractors to assist them in the implementation of the rules, regulations and procedures of the Authority.

2. The full text of such recommendations shall be reported to the Council. Should the Council find that a recommendation is inconsistent with the intent and purpose of these Regulations, it may request that the recommendation be modified or withdrawn.

Part VIII
Settlement of disputes

Regulation 40
Disputes

1. Disputes concerning the interpretation or application of these Regulations shall be settled in accordance with Part XI, section 5, of the Convention.

2. Any final decision rendered by a court or tribunal having jurisdiction under the Convention relating to the rights and obligations of the Authority and of the contractor shall be enforceable in the territory of each State party to the Convention.

Part IX
Resources other than polymetallic nodules

Regulation 41
Resources other than polymetallic nodules

If a prospector or contractor finds resources in the Area other than polymetallic nodules, the prospecting and exploration for and exploitation of such resources shall be subject to the rules, regulations and procedures of the Authority relating to such resources in accordance with the Convention and the Agreement. The prospector or contractor shall notify the Authority of its find.

Part X
Review

Regulation 42
Review

1. Five years following the approval of these revised Regulations by the Assembly, or at any time thereafter, the Council shall undertake a review of the manner in which the Regulations have operated in practice.

2. If, in the light of improved knowledge or technology, it becomes apparent that the Regulations are not adequate, any State party, the Legal and Technical Commission or any contractor through its sponsoring State may at any time request the Council to consider, at its next ordinary session, revisions to these Regulations.

3. In the light of the review, the Council may adopt and apply provisionally, pending approval by the Assembly, amendments to the provisions of these Regulations, taking into account the recommendations of the Legal and Technical Commission or other subordinate organs concerned. Any such amendments shall be without prejudice to the rights conferred on any contractor with the Authority under the provisions of a contract entered into pursuant to these Regulations in force at the time of any such amendment.

4. In the event that any provisions of these Regulations are amended, the contractor and the Authority may revise the contract in accordance with section 24 of annex IV.

Annex I

Notification of intention to engage in prospecting

1. Name of prospector:

2. Street address of prospector:

3. Postal address (if different from above):

4. Telephone number:

5. Fax number:

6. E-mail address:

7. Nationality of prospector:

8. If prospector is a juridical person:

    (a) Identify prospector's place of registration;

    (b) Identify prospector's principal place of business/domicile;

    (c) Attach a copy of prospector's certificate of registration.

9. Name of prospector's designated representative:

10. Street address of prospector's designated representative (if different from above):

11. Postal address (if different from above):

12. Telephone number:

13. Fax number:

14. E-mail address:

15. Attach the coordinates of the broad area or areas in which prospecting is to be conducted (in accordance with the World Geodetic System WGS 84).

16. Attach a general description of the prospecting programme, including the date of commencement and the approximate duration of the programme.

17. Attach a written undertaking that the prospector will:

    (a) Comply with the Convention and the relevant rules, regulations and procedures of the Authority concerning:

       (i) Cooperation in the training programmes in connection with marine scientific research and transfer of technology referred to in articles 143 and 144 of the Convention; and

       (ii) Protection and preservation of the marine environment; and

    (b) Accept verification by the Authority of compliance therewith.

18. List hereunder all the attachments and annexes to this notification (all data and information should be submitted in hard copy and in a digital format specified by the Authority).

Date: _____   _____
                                        Signature of prospector's designated
                                        representative

Attestation:

_____
Signature of person attesting

_____
Name of person attesting

_____
Title of person attesting

Annex II

Application for approval of a plan of work for exploration to obtain a contract

Section I
Information concerning the applicant

1. Name of applicant:
2. Street address of applicant:
3. Postal address (if different from above):
4. Telephone number:
5. Fax number:
6. E-mail address:
7. Name of applicant's designated representative:
8. Street address of applicant's designated representative (if different from above):
9. Postal address (if different from above):
10. Telephone number:
11. Fax number:
12. E-mail address:
13. If the applicant is a juridical person:
    (a) Identify applicant's place of registration;
    (b) Identify applicant's principal place of business/domicile;
    (c) Attach a copy of applicant's certificate of registration.
14. Identify the sponsoring State or States.

15. In respect of each sponsoring State, provide the date of deposit of its instrument of ratification of, or accession or succession to, the United Nations Convention on the Law of the Sea of 10 December 1982 and the date of its consent to be bound by the Agreement relating to the Implementation of Part XI of the Convention.

16. A certificate of sponsorship issued by the sponsoring State must be attached with this application. If the applicant has more than one nationality, as in the case of a partnership or consortium of entities from more than one State, certificates of sponsorship issued by each of the States involved must be attached.

Section II
Information relating to the area under application

17. Define the boundaries of the area under application by attaching a list of geographical coordinates (in accordance with the World Geodetic System WGS 84).

18. Attach a chart (on a scale and projection specified by the Authority) and a list of the coordinates dividing the total area into two parts of equal estimated commercial value.

19. Include in an attachment sufficient information to enable the Council to designate a reserved area based on the estimated commercial value of each part of the area under application. Such attachment must include the data available to the applicant with respect to both parts of the area under application, including:

    (a) Data on the location, survey and evaluation of the polymetallic nodules in the areas, including:

    (i) A description of the technology related to the recovery and processing of polymetallic nodules that is necessary for making the designation of a reserved area;

    (ii) A map of the physical and geological characteristics, such as seabed topography, bathymetry and bottom currents and information on the reliability of such data;

    (iii) Data showing the average density (abundance) of polymetallic nodules in kg/m^2 and an associated abundance map showing the location of sampling sites;

    (iv) Data showing the average elemental content of metals of economic interest (grade) based on chemical assays in (dry) weight per cent and an associated grade map;

    (v) Combined maps of abundance and grade of polymetallic nodules;

    (vi) A calculation based on standard procedures, including statistical analysis, using the data submitted and assumptions made in the calculations that the two areas could be expected to contain polymetallic nodules of equal estimated commercial value expressed as recoverable metals in mineable areas;

    (vii) A description of the techniques used by the applicant.

    (b) Information concerning environmental parameters (seasonal and during test period) including, inter alia, wind speed and direction, water salinity, temperature and biological communities.

20. If the area under application includes any part of a reserved area, attach a list of coordinates of the area which forms part of the reserved area and indicate the applicant's qualifications in accordance with regulation 17 of the Regulations.

Section III
Financial and technical information[a]

21. Attach sufficient information to enable the Council to determine whether the applicant is financially capable of carrying out the proposed plan of work for exploration and of fulfilling its financial obligations to the Authority:

(a) If the application is made by the Enterprise, attach certification by its competent authority that the Enterprise has the necessary financial resources to meet the estimated costs of the proposed plan of work for exploration;

(b) If the application is made by a State or a State enterprise, attach a statement by the State or the sponsoring State certifying that the applicant has the necessary financial resources to meet the estimated costs of the proposed plan of work for exploration;

(c) If the application is made by an entity, attach copies of the applicant's audited financial statements, including balance sheets and profit-and-loss statements, for the most recent three years in conformity with internationally accepted accounting principles and certified by a duly qualified firm of public accountants; and

(i) If the applicant is a newly organized entity and a certified balance sheet is not available, a pro forma balance sheet certified by an appropriate official of the applicant;

(ii) If the applicant is a subsidiary of another entity, copies of such financial statements of that entity and a statement from that entity in conformity with internationally accepted accounting practices and certified by a duly qualified firm of public accountants that the applicant will have the financial resources to carry out the plan of work for exploration;

(iii) If the applicant is controlled by a State or a State enterprise, a statement from the State or State enterprise certifying that the applicant will have the financial resources to carry out the plan of work for exploration.

22. If it is intended to finance the proposed plan of work for exploration by borrowings, attach a statement of the amount of such borrowings, the repayment period and the interest rate.

23. Attach sufficient information to enable the Council to determine whether the applicant is technically capable of carrying out the proposed plan of work for exploration, including:

(a) A general description of the applicant's previous experience, knowledge, skills, technical qualifications and expertise relevant to the proposed plan of work for exploration;

---

[a] An application for approval of a plan of work for exploration submitted on behalf of a State or entity, or any component of such entity, referred to in paragraph 1 (a) (ii) or (iii) of resolution II, other than a registered pioneer investor, which has already undertaken substantial activities in the Area prior to the entry into force of the Convention, or its successor in interest, shall be considered to have met the financial and technical qualifications necessary for approval of a plan of work if the sponsoring State or States certify that the applicant has expended an amount equivalent to at least 30 million United States dollars in research and exploration activities and has expended no less than 10 per cent of that amount in the location, survey and evaluation of the area referred to in the plan of work.

(b) A general description of the equipment and methods expected to be used in carrying out the proposed plan of work for exploration and other relevant non-proprietary information about the characteristics of such technology; and

(c) A general description of the applicant's financial and technical capability to respond to any incident or activity which causes serious harm to the marine environment.

Section IV
The plan of work for exploration

24. Attach the following information relating to the plan of work for exploration:

(a) A general description and a schedule of the proposed exploration programme, including the programme of activities for the immediate five-year period, such as studies to be undertaken in respect of the environmental, technical, economic and other appropriate factors which must be taken into account in exploration;

(b) A description of a programme for oceanographic and environmental baseline studies in accordance with the Regulations and any environmental rules, regulations and procedures established by the Authority that would enable an assessment of the potential environmental impact including, but not restricted to, the impact on biodiversity, of the proposed exploration activities, taking into account any recommendations issued by the Legal and Technical Commission;

(c) A preliminary assessment of the possible impact of the proposed exploration activities on the marine environment;

(d) A description of proposed measures for the prevention, reduction and control of pollution and other hazards, as well as possible impacts, to the marine environment;

(e) A schedule of anticipated yearly expenditures in respect of the programme of activities for the immediate five-year period.

Section V
Undertakings

25. Attach a written undertaking that the applicant will:

(a) Accept as enforceable and comply with the applicable obligations created by the provisions of the Convention and the rules, regulations and procedures of the Authority, the decisions of the relevant organs of the Authority and the terms of its contracts with the Authority;

(b) Accept control by the Authority of activities in the Area as authorized by the Convention;

(c) Provide the Authority with a written assurance that its obligations under the contract will be fulfilled in good faith.

Section VI
Previous contracts

26. If the applicant or, in the case of an application by a partnership or consortium of entities in a joint arrangement, any member of the partnership or consortium has previously been awarded any contract with the Authority, the application must include:

   (a) The date of the previous contract or contracts;

   (b) The date, reference number and title of each report submitted to the Authority in connection with the contract or contracts; and

   (c) The date of termination of the contract or contracts, if applicable.

Section VII
Attachments

27. List all the attachments and annexes to this application (all data and information should be submitted in hard copy and in a digital format specified by the Authority).

Date: _____   _____
                                      Signature of applicant's designated
                                      representative

Attestation:

_____
Signature of person attesting

_____
Name of person attesting

_____
Title of person attesting

Annex III

Contract for exploration

THIS CONTRACT made the ... day of ... between the **INTERNATIONAL SEABED AUTHORITY** represented by its **SECRETARY-GENERAL** (hereinafter referred to as "the Authority") and ... represented by ... (hereinafter referred to as "the Contractor") **WITNESSETH** as follows:

Incorporation of clauses

1. The standard clauses set out in annex IV to the Regulations on Prospecting and Exploration for Polymetallic Nodules in the Area shall be incorporated herein and shall have effect as if herein set out at length.

Exploration area

2. For the purposes of this contract, the "exploration area" means that part of the Area allocated to the Contractor for exploration, defined by the coordinates listed in schedule 1 hereto, as reduced from time to time in accordance with the standard clauses and the Regulations.

Grant of rights

3. In consideration of (a) their mutual interest in the conduct of exploration activities in the exploration area pursuant to the United Nations Convention on the Law of the Sea of 10 December 1982 and the Agreement relating to the Implementation of Part XI of the Convention, (b) the responsibility of the Authority to organize and control activities in the Area, particularly with a view to administering the resources of the Area, in accordance with the legal regime established in Part XI of the Convention and the Agreement and Part XII of the Convention, respectively, and (c) the interest and financial commitment of the Contractor in conducting activities in the exploration area and the mutual covenants made herein, the Authority hereby grants to the Contractor the exclusive right to explore for polymetallic nodules in the exploration area in accordance with the terms and conditions of this contract.

Entry into force and contract term

4. This contract shall enter into force on signature by both parties and, subject to the standard clauses, shall remain in force for a period of fifteen years thereafter unless:

(a) The Contractor obtains a contract for exploitation in the exploration area which enters into force before the expiration of such period of fifteen years; or

(b) The contract is sooner terminated, provided that the term of the contract may be extended in accordance with standard clauses 3.2 and 17.2.

Schedules

5. The schedules referred to in the standard clauses, namely section 4 and section 8, are for the purposes of this contract schedules 2 and 3 respectively.

Entire agreement

6. This contract expresses the entire agreement between the parties, and no oral understanding or prior writing shall modify the terms hereof.

IN WITNESS WHEREOF the undersigned, being duly authorized thereto by the respective parties, have signed this contract at ..., this ... day of ... .

Schedule 1

[Coordinates and illustrative chart of the exploration area]

Schedule 2

[The current five-year programme of activities as revised from time to time]

Schedule 3

[The training programme shall become a schedule to the contract when approved by the Authority in accordance with section 8 of the standard clauses]

Annex IV

Standard clauses for exploration contract

Section 1
Definitions

1.1 In the following clauses:

(a) "Exploration area" means that part of the Area allocated to the Contractor for exploration, described in schedule 1 hereto, as the same may be reduced from time to time in accordance with this contract and the Regulations;

(b) "Programme of activities" means the programme of activities which is set out in schedule 2 hereto as the same may be adjusted from time to time in accordance with sections 4.3 and 4.4 hereof;

(c) "Regulations" means the Regulations on Prospecting and Exploration for Polymetallic Nodules in the Area, adopted by the Authority.

1.2 Terms and phrases defined in the Regulations shall have the same meaning in these standard clauses.

1.3 In accordance with the Agreement relating to the Implementation of Part XI of the United Nations Convention on the Law of the Sea of 10 December 1982, its provisions and Part XI of the Convention are to be interpreted and applied together as a single instrument; this contract and references in this contract to the Convention are to be interpreted and applied accordingly.

1.4 This contract includes the schedules to this contract, which shall be an integral part hereof.

Section 2
Security of tenure

2.1 The Contractor shall have security of tenure and this contract shall not be suspended, terminated or revised except in accordance with sections 20, 21 and 24 hereof.

2.2 The Contractor shall have the exclusive right to explore for polymetallic nodules in the exploration area in accordance with the terms and conditions of this contract. The Authority shall ensure that no other entity operates in the exploration area for a different category of resources in a manner that might unreasonably interfere with the operations of the Contractor.

2.3 The Contractor, by notice to the Authority, shall have the right at any time to renounce without penalty the whole or part of its rights in the exploration area, provided that the Contractor shall remain liable for all obligations accrued prior to the date of such renunciation in respect of the area renounced.

2.4 Nothing in this contract shall be deemed to confer any right on the Contractor other than those rights expressly granted herein. The Authority reserves the right to enter into contracts with respect to resources other than polymetallic nodules with third parties in the area covered by this contract.

Section 3
Contract term

3.1 This contract shall enter into force on signature by both parties and shall remain in force for a period of fifteen years thereafter unless:

(a) The Contractor obtains a contract for exploitation in the exploration area which enters into force before the expiration of such period of fifteen years; or

(b) The contract is sooner terminated, provided that the term of the contract may be extended in accordance with sections 3.2 and 17.2 hereof.

3.2 Upon application by the Contractor, not later than six months before the expiration of this contract, this contract may be extended for periods of not more than five years each on such terms and conditions as the Authority and the Contractor may then agree in accordance with the Regulations. Such extensions shall be approved if the Contractor has made efforts in good faith to comply with the requirements of this contract but for reasons beyond the Contractor's control has been unable to complete the necessary preparatory work for proceeding to the exploitation stage or if the prevailing economic circumstances do not justify proceeding to the exploitation stage.

3.3 Notwithstanding the expiration of this contract in accordance with section 3.1 hereof, if the Contractor has, at least 90 days prior to the date of expiration, applied for a contract for exploitation, the Contractor's rights and obligations under this contract shall continue until such time as the application has been considered and a contract for exploitation has been issued or refused.

Section 4
Exploration

4.1 The Contractor shall commence exploration in accordance with the time schedule stipulated in the programme of activities set out in schedule 2 hereto and shall adhere to such time periods or any modification thereto as provided for by this contract.

4.2 The Contractor shall carry out the programme of activities set out in schedule 2 hereto. In carrying out such activities the Contractor shall spend in each contract year not less than the amount specified in such programme, or any agreed review thereof, in actual and direct exploration expenditures.

4.3 The Contractor, with the consent of the Authority, which consent shall not be unreasonably withheld, may from time to time make such changes in the programme of activities and the expenditures specified therein as may be necessary and prudent in accordance with good mining industry practice, and taking into account the market conditions for the metals contained in polymetallic nodules and other relevant global economic conditions.

4.4 Not later than 90 days prior to the expiration of each five-year period from the date on which this contract enters into force in accordance with section 3 hereof, the Contractor and the Secretary-General shall jointly undertake a review of the implementation of the plan of work for exploration under this contract. The Secretary-General may require the Contractor to submit such additional data and information as may be necessary for the purposes of the review. In the light of the review, the Contractor shall make such adjustments to its plan of work as are necessary and shall indicate its programme of activities for the following five-year period, including a revised schedule of anticipated yearly expenditures. Schedule 2 hereto shall be adjusted accordingly.

Section 5
Environmental monitoring

5.1 The Contractor shall take necessary measures to prevent, reduce and control pollution and other hazards to the marine environment arising from its activities in the Area as far as reasonably possible applying a precautionary approach and best environmental practices.

5.2 Prior to the commencement of exploration activities, the Contractor shall submit to the Authority:

(a) An impact assessment of the potential effects on the marine environment of the proposed activities;

(b) A proposal for a monitoring programme to determine the potential effect on the marine environment of the proposed activities; and

(c) Data that could be used to establish an environmental baseline against which to assess the effect of the proposed activities.

5.3 The Contractor shall, in accordance with the Regulations, gather environmental baseline data as exploration activities progress and develop and shall establish environmental baselines against which to assess the likely effects of the Contractor's activities on the marine environment.

5.4 The Contractor shall, in accordance with the Regulations, establish and carry out a programme to monitor and report on such effects on the marine environment. The Contractor shall cooperate with the Authority in the implementation of such monitoring.

5.5 The Contractor shall, within 90 days of the end of each calendar year, report to the Secretary-General on the implementation and results of the monitoring programme referred to in section 5.4 hereof and shall submit data and information in accordance with the Regulations.

Section 6
Contingency plans and emergencies

6.1 The Contractor shall, prior to the commencement of its programme of activities under this contract, submit to the Secretary-General a contingency plan to respond effectively to incidents that are likely to cause serious harm or a threat of serious harm to the marine environment arising from the Contractor's activities at sea in the exploration area. Such contingency plan shall establish special procedures and provide for adequate and appropriate equipment to deal with such incidents and, in particular, shall include arrangements for:

(a) The immediate raising of a general alarm in the area of the exploration activities;

(b) Immediate notification to the Secretary-General;

(c) The warning of ships which might be about to enter the immediate vicinity;

(d) A continuing flow of full information to the Secretary-General relating to particulars of the contingency measures already taken and further actions required;

(e) The removal, as appropriate, of polluting substances;

(f) The reduction and, so far as reasonably possible, prevention of serious harm to the marine environment, as well as mitigation of such effects;

(g) As appropriate, cooperation with other contractors with the Authority to respond to an emergency; and

(h) Periodic emergency response exercises.

6.2 The Contractor shall promptly report to the Secretary-General any incident arising from its activities that has caused, is causing or poses a threat of serious harm to the marine environment. Each such report shall contain the details of such incident, including, inter alia:

(a) The coordinates of the area affected or which can reasonably be anticipated to be affected;

(b) The description of the action being taken by the Contractor to prevent, contain, minimize and repair the serious harm or threat of serious harm to the marine environment;

(c) A description of the action being taken by the Contractor to monitor the effects of the incident on the marine environment; and

(d) Such supplementary information as may reasonably be required by the Secretary-General.

6.3 The Contractor shall comply with emergency orders issued by the Council and immediate measures of a temporary nature issued by the Secretary-General in accordance with the Regulations, to prevent, contain, minimize or repair serious harm or the threat of serious harm to the marine environment, which may include orders to the Contractor to immediately suspend or adjust any activities in the exploration area.

6.4 If the Contractor does not promptly comply with such emergency orders or immediate measures of a temporary nature, the Council may take such reasonable measures as are necessary to prevent, contain, minimize or repair any such serious harm or the threat of serious harm to the marine environment at the Contractor's expense. The Contractor shall promptly reimburse the Authority the amount of such expenses. Such expenses shall be in addition to any monetary penalties which may be imposed on the Contractor pursuant to the terms of this contract or the Regulations.

Section 7
Human remains and objects and sites of an archaeological or historical nature

The Contractor shall immediately notify the Secretary-General in writing of any finding in the exploration area of any human remains of an archaeological or historical nature, or any object or site of a similar nature and its location, including the preservation and protection measures taken. The Secretary-General shall

transmit such information to the Director General of the United Nations Educational, Scientific and Cultural Organization and any other competent international organization. Following the finding of any such human remains, object or site in the exploration area, and in order to avoid disturbing such human remains, object or site, no further prospecting or exploration shall take place, within a reasonable radius, until such time as the Council decides otherwise after taking account of the views of the Director General of the United Nations Educational, Scientific and Cultural Organization or any other competent international organization.

Section 8
Training

8.1 In accordance with the Regulations, the Contractor shall, prior to the commencement of exploration under this contract, submit to the Authority for approval proposed training programmes for the training of personnel of the Authority and developing States, including the participation of such personnel in all of the Contractor's activities under this contract.

8.2 The scope and financing of the training programme shall be subject to negotiation between the Contractor, the Authority and the sponsoring State or States.

8.3 The Contractor shall conduct training programmes in accordance with the specific programme for the training of personnel referred to in section 8.1 hereof approved by the Authority in accordance with the Regulations, which programme, as revised and developed from time to time, shall become a part of this contract as schedule 3.

Section 9
Books and records

The Contractor shall keep a complete and proper set of books, accounts and financial records, consistent with internationally accepted accounting principles. Such books, accounts and financial records shall include information which will fully disclose the actual and direct expenditures for exploration and such other information as will facilitate an effective audit of such expenditures.

Section 10
Annual reports

10.1 The Contractor shall, within 90 days of the end of each calendar year, submit a report to the Secretary-General in such format as may be recommended from time to time by the Legal and Technical Commission covering its programme of activities in the exploration area and containing, as applicable, information in sufficient detail on:

(a) The exploration work carried out during the calendar year, including maps, charts and graphs illustrating the work that has been done and the results obtained;

(b) The equipment used to carry out the exploration work, including the results of tests conducted of proposed mining technologies, but not equipment design data; and

(c) The implementation of training programmes, including any proposed revisions to or developments of such programmes.

10.2 Such reports shall also contain:

(a) The results obtained from environmental monitoring programmes, including observations, measurements, evaluations and analyses of environmental parameters;

(b) A statement of the quantity of polymetallic nodules recovered as samples or for the purpose of testing;

(c) A statement, in conformity with internationally accepted accounting principles and certified by a duly qualified firm of public accountants, or, where the Contractor is a State or a State enterprise, by the sponsoring State, of the actual and direct exploration expenditures of the Contractor in carrying out the programme of activities during the Contractor's accounting year. Such expenditures may be claimed by the contractor as part of the contractor's development costs incurred prior to the commencement of commercial production; and

(d) Details of any proposed adjustments to the programme of activities and the reasons for such adjustments.

10.3 The Contractor shall also submit such additional information to supplement the reports referred to in sections 10.1 and 10.2 hereof as the Secretary-General may from time to time reasonably require in order to carry out the Authority's functions under the Convention, the Regulations and this contract.

10.4 The Contractor shall keep, in good condition, a representative portion of samples of the polymetallic nodules obtained in the course of exploration until the expiration of this contract. The Authority may request the Contractor in writing to deliver to it for analysis a portion of any such sample obtained during the course of exploration.

10.5 The contractor shall pay at the time of submission of the annual report an annual overhead charge of $47,000 (or such sum as may be fixed in accordance with section 10.6 hereof) to cover the Authority's costs of the administration and supervision of this contract and of reviewing the reports submitted in accordance with section 10.1 hereof.

10.6 The amount of the annual overhead charge may be revised by the Authority to reflect its costs actually and reasonably incurred.[5]

---

[5] ISBA/19/A/12, dated 25 July 2013, Amendments.

Section 11
Data and information to be submitted on expiration of the contract

11.1 The Contractor shall transfer to the Authority all data and information that are both necessary for and relevant to the effective exercise of the powers and functions of the Authority in respect of the exploration area in accordance with the provisions of this section.

11.2 Upon expiration or termination of this contract the Contractor, if it has not already done so, shall submit the following data and information to the Secretary-General:

(a) Copies of geological, environmental, geochemical and geophysical data acquired by the Contractor in the course of carrying out the programme of activities that are necessary for and relevant to the effective exercise of the powers and functions of the Authority in respect of the exploration area;

(b) The estimation of mineable areas, when such areas have been identified, which shall include details of the grade and quantity of the proven, probable and possible polymetallic nodule reserves and the anticipated mining conditions;

(c) Copies of geological, technical, financial and economic reports made by or for the Contractor that are necessary for and relevant to the effective exercise of the powers and functions of the Authority in respect of the exploration area;

(d) Information in sufficient detail on the equipment used to carry out the exploration work, including the results of tests conducted of proposed mining technologies, but not equipment design data;

(e) A statement of the quantity of polymetallic nodules recovered as samples or for the purpose of testing; and

(f) A statement on how and where samples are archived and their availability to the Authority.

11.3 The data and information referred to in section 11.2 hereof shall also be submitted to the Secretary-General if, prior to the expiration of this contract, the Contractor applies for approval of a plan of work for exploitation or if the Contractor renounces its rights in the exploration area to the extent that such data and information relates to the renounced area.

Section 12
Confidentiality

Data and information transferred to the Authority in accordance with this contract shall be treated as confidential in accordance with the provisions of the Regulations.

Section 13
Undertakings

13.1 The Contractor shall carry out exploration in accordance with the terms and conditions of this contract, the Regulations, Part XI of the Convention, the Agreement and other rules of international law not incompatible with the Convention.

13.2 The Contractor undertakes:

(a) To accept as enforceable and comply with the terms of this contract;

(b) To comply with the applicable obligations created by the provisions of the Convention, the rules, regulations and procedures of the Authority and the decisions of the relevant organs of the Authority;

(c) To accept control by the Authority of activities in the Area as authorized by the Convention;

(d) To fulfil its obligations under this contract in good faith; and

(e) To observe, as far as reasonably practicable, any recommendations which may be issued from time to time by the Legal and Technical Commission.

13.3 The Contractor shall actively carry out the programme of activities:

(a) With due diligence, efficiency and economy;

(b) With due regard to the impact of its activities on the marine environment; and

(c) With reasonable regard for other activities in the marine environment.

13.4 The Authority undertakes to fulfil in good faith its powers and functions under the Convention and the Agreement in accordance with article 157 of the Convention.

Section 14
Inspection

14.1 The Contractor shall permit the Authority to send its inspectors on board vessels and installations used by the Contractor to carry out activities in the exploration area to:

(a) Monitor the Contractor's compliance with the terms and conditions of this contract and the Regulations; and

(b) Monitor the effects of such activities on the marine environment.

14.2 The Secretary-General shall give reasonable notice to the Contractor of the projected time and duration of inspections, the name of the inspectors and any activities the inspectors are to perform that are likely to require the availability of special equipment or special assistance from personnel of the Contractor.

14.3 Such inspectors shall have the authority to inspect any vessel or installation, including its log, equipment, records, facilities, all other recorded data and any relevant documents which are necessary to monitor the Contractor's compliance.

14.4 The Contractor, its agents and employees shall assist the inspectors in the performance of their duties and shall:

(a) Accept and facilitate prompt and safe boarding of vessels and installations by inspectors;

(b) Cooperate with and assist in the inspection of any vessel or installation conducted pursuant to these procedures;

(c) Provide access to all relevant equipment, facilities and personnel on vessels and installations at all reasonable times;

(d) Not obstruct, intimidate or interfere with inspectors in the performance of their duties;

(e) Provide reasonable facilities, including, where appropriate, food and accommodation, to inspectors; and

(f) Facilitate safe disembarkation by inspectors.

14.5 Inspectors shall avoid interference with the safe and normal operations on board vessels and installations used by the Contractor to carry out activities in the area visited and shall act in accordance with the Regulations and the measures adopted to protect confidentiality of data and information.

14.6 The Secretary-General and any duly authorized representatives of the Secretary-General, shall have access, for purposes of audit and examination, to any books, documents, papers and records of the Contractor which are necessary and directly pertinent to verify the expenditures referred to in section 10.2 (c).

14.7 The Secretary-General shall provide relevant information contained in the reports of inspectors to the Contractor and its sponsoring State or States where action is necessary.

14.8 If for any reason the Contractor does not pursue exploration and does not request a contract for exploitation, it shall, before withdrawing from the exploration area, notify the Secretary-General in writing in order to permit the Authority, if it so decides, to carry out an inspection pursuant to this section.

Section 15
Safety, labour and health standards

15.1 The Contractor shall comply with the generally accepted international rules and standards established by competent international organizations or general diplomatic conferences concerning the safety of life at sea, and the prevention of collisions and such rules, regulations and procedures as may be adopted by the Authority relating to safety at sea. Each vessel used for carrying out activities in the Area shall possess current valid certificates required by and issued pursuant to such international rules and standards.

15.2 The Contractor shall, in carrying out exploration under this contract, observe and comply with such rules, regulations and procedures as may be adopted by the Authority relating to protection against discrimination in employment, occupational safety and health, labour relations, social security, employment security and living conditions at the work site. Such rules, regulations and procedures shall take into account conventions and recommendations of the International Labour Organization and other competent international organizations.

Section 16
Responsibility and liability

16.1 The Contractor shall be liable for the actual amount of any damage, including damage to the marine environment, arising out of its wrongful acts or omissions, and those of its employees, subcontractors, agents and all persons engaged in working or acting for them in the conduct of its operations under this contract, including the costs of reasonable measures to prevent or limit damage to the marine environment, account being taken of any contributory acts or omissions by the Authority.

16.2 The Contractor shall indemnify the Authority, its employees, subcontractors and agents against all claims and liabilities of any third party arising out of any wrongful acts or omissions of the Contractor and its employees, agents and subcontractors, and all persons engaged in working or acting for them in the conduct of its operations under this contract.

16.3 The Authority shall be liable for the actual amount of any damage to the Contractor arising out of its wrongful acts in the exercise of its powers and functions, including violations under article 168 (2) of the Convention, account being taken of contributory acts or omissions by the Contractor, its employees, agents and subcontractors, and all persons engaged in working or acting for them in the conduct of its operations under this contract.

16.4 The Authority shall indemnify the Contractor, its employees, subcontractors, agents and all persons engaged in working or acting for them in the conduct of its operations under this contract, against all claims and liabilities of any third party arising out of any wrongful acts or omissions in the exercise of its powers and functions hereunder, including violations under article 168 (2) of the Convention.

16.5 The Contractor shall maintain appropriate insurance policies with internationally recognized carriers, in accordance with generally accepted international maritime practice.

Section 17
Force majeure

17.1 The Contractor shall not be liable for an unavoidable delay or failure to perform any of its obligations under this contract due to force majeure. For the purposes of this contract, force majeure shall mean an event or condition that the Contractor could not reasonably be expected to prevent or control; provided that the event or condition was not caused by negligence or by a failure to observe good mining industry practice.

17.2 The Contractor shall, upon request, be granted a time extension equal to the period by which performance was delayed hereunder by force majeure and the term of this contract shall be extended accordingly.

17.3 In the event of force majeure, the Contractor shall take all reasonable measures to remove its inability to perform and comply with the terms and conditions of this contract with a minimum of delay.

17.4 The Contractor shall give notice to the Authority of the occurrence of an event of force majeure as soon as reasonably possible, and similarly give notice to the Authority of the restoration of normal conditions.

Section 18
Disclaimer

Neither the Contractor nor any affiliated company or subcontractor shall in any manner claim or suggest, whether expressly or by implication, that the Authority or any official thereof has, or has expressed, any opinion with respect to polymetallic nodules in the exploration area and a statement to that effect shall not be included in or endorsed on any prospectus, notice, circular, advertisement, press release or similar document issued by the Contractor, any affiliated company or any subcontractor that refers directly or indirectly to this contract. For the purposes of this section, an "affiliated company" means any person, firm or company or State-owned entity controlling, controlled by, or under common control with, the Contractor.

Section 19
Renunciation of rights

The Contractor, by notice to the Authority, shall have the right to renounce its rights and terminate this contract without penalty, provided that the Contractor shall remain liable for all obligations accrued prior to the date of such renunciation and those obligations required to be fulfilled after termination in accordance with the Regulations.

Section 20
Termination of sponsorship

20.1 If the nationality or control of the Contractor changes or the Contractor's sponsoring State, as defined in the Regulations, terminates its sponsorship, the Contractor shall promptly notify the Authority forthwith.

20.2 In either such event, if the Contractor does not obtain another sponsor meeting the requirements prescribed in the Regulations which submits to the Authority a certificate of sponsorship for the Contractor in the prescribed form within the time specified in the Regulations, this contract shall terminate forthwith.

Section 21
Suspension and termination of contract and penalties

21.1 The Council may suspend or terminate this contract, without prejudice to any other rights that the Authority may have, if any of the following events should occur:

(a) If, in spite of written warnings by the Authority, the Contractor has conducted its activities in such a way as to result in serious persistent and wilful violations of the fundamental terms of this contract, Part XI of the Convention, the Agreement and the rules, regulations and procedures of the Authority; or

(b) If the Contractor has failed to comply with a final binding decision of the dispute settlement body applicable to it; or

(c) If the Contractor becomes insolvent or commits an act of bankruptcy or enters into any agreement for composition with its creditors or goes into liquidation or receivership, whether compulsory or voluntary, or petitions or applies to any tribunal for the appointment of a receiver or a trustee or receiver for itself or commences any proceedings relating to itself under any bankruptcy, insolvency or readjustment of debt law, whether now or hereafter in effect, other than for the purpose of reconstruction.

21.2 The Council may, without prejudice to section 17, after consultation with the Contractor, suspend or terminate this contract, without prejudice to any other rights that the Authority may have, if the Contractor is prevented from performing its obligations under this contract by reason of an event or condition of force majeure, as described in section 17.1, which has persisted for a continuous period exceeding two years, despite the Contractor having taken all reasonable measures to overcome its inability to perform and comply with the terms and conditions of this contract with minimum delay.

21.3 Any suspension or termination shall be by notice, through the Secretary-General, which shall include a statement of the reasons for taking such action. The suspension or termination shall be effective 60 days after such notice, unless the Contractor within such period disputes the Authority's right to suspend or terminate this contract in accordance with Part XI, section 5, of the Convention.

21.4 If the Contractor takes such action, this contract shall only be suspended or terminated in accordance with a final binding decision in accordance with Part XI, section 5, of the Convention.

21.5 If the Council has suspended this contract, the Council may by notice require the Contractor to resume its operations and comply with the terms and conditions of this contract, not later than 60 days after such notice.

21.6 In the case of any violation of this contract not covered by section 21.1 (a) hereof, or in lieu of suspension or termination under section 21.1 hereof, the Council may impose upon the Contractor monetary penalties proportionate to the seriousness of the violation.

21.7 The Council may not execute a decision involving monetary penalties until the Contractor has been accorded a reasonable opportunity to exhaust the judicial remedies available to it pursuant to Part XI, section 5, of the Convention.

21.8 In the event of termination or expiration of this contract, the Contractor shall comply with the Regulations and shall remove all installations, plant, equipment and materials in the exploration area and shall make the area safe so as not to constitute a danger to persons, shipping or to the marine environment.

Section 22
Transfer of rights and obligations

22.1 The rights and obligations of the Contractor under this contract may be transferred in whole or in part only with the consent of the Authority and in accordance with the Regulations.

22.2 The Authority shall not unreasonably withhold consent to the transfer if the proposed transferee is in all respects a qualified applicant in accordance with the Regulations and assumes all of the obligations of the Contractor and if the transfer does not confer to the transferee a plan of work, the approval of which would be forbidden by article 6, paragraph 3 (c), of annex III to the Convention.

22.3 The terms, undertakings and conditions of this contract shall inure to the benefit of and be binding upon the parties hereto and their respective successors and assigns.

Section 23
No waiver

No waiver by either party of any rights pursuant to a breach of the terms and conditions of this contract to be performed by the other party shall be construed as a waiver by the party of any succeeding breach of the same or any other term or condition to be performed by the other party.

Section 24
Revision

24.1 When circumstances have arisen or are likely to arise which, in the opinion of the Authority or the Contractor, would render this contract inequitable or make it impracticable or impossible to achieve the objectives set out in this contract or in Part XI of the Convention or the Agreement, the parties shall enter into negotiations to revise it accordingly.

24.2 This contract may also be revised by agreement between the Contractor and the Authority to facilitate the application of any rules, regulations and procedures adopted by the Authority subsequent to the entry into force of this contract.

24.3 This contract may be revised, amended or otherwise modified only with the consent of the Contractor and the Authority by an appropriate instrument signed by the authorized representatives of the parties.

Section 25
Disputes

25.1 Any dispute between the parties concerning the interpretation or application of this contract shall be settled in accordance with Part XI, section 5, of the Convention.

25.2 In accordance with article 21 (2) of Annex III to the Convention, any final decision rendered by a court or tribunal having jurisdiction under the Convention relating to the rights and obligations of the Authority and of the Contractor shall be enforceable in the territory of any State party to the Convention affected thereby.

Section 26
Notice

26.1 Any application, request, notice, report, consent, approval, waiver, direction or instruction hereunder shall be made by the Secretary-General or by the designated representative of the Contractor, as the case may be, in writing. Service shall be by hand, or by telex, fax, registered airmail or e-mail containing an authorized signature to the Secretary-General at the headquarters of the Authority or to the designated representative. The requirement to provide any information in writing under these Regulations is satisfied by the provision of the information in an e-mail containing a digital signature.

26.2 Either party shall be entitled to change any such address to any other address by not less than ten days' notice to the other party.

26.3 Delivery by hand shall be effective when made. Delivery by telex shall be deemed to be effective on the business day following the day when the "answer back" appears on the sender's telex machine. Delivery by fax shall be effective when the "transmit confirmation report" confirming the transmission to the recipient's published fax number is received by the transmitter. Delivery by registered airmail shall be deemed to be effective 21 days after posting. An e-mail is presumed to have been received by the addressee when it enters an information system designated or used by the addressee for the purpose of receiving documents of the type sent and it is capable of being retrieved and processed by the addressee.

26.4   Notice to the designated representative of the Contractor shall constitute effective notice to the Contractor for all purposes under this contract, and the designated representative shall be the Contractor's agent for the service of process or notification in any proceeding of any court or tribunal having jurisdiction.

26.5   Notice to the Secretary-General shall constitute effective notice to the Authority for all purposes under this contract, and the Secretary-General shall be the Authority's agent for the service of process or notification in any proceeding of any court or tribunal having jurisdiction.

Section 27
Applicable law

27.1   This contract shall be governed by the terms of this contract, the rules, regulations and procedures of the Authority, Part XI of the Convention, the Agreement and other rules of international law not incompatible with the Convention.

27.2   The Contractor, its employees, subcontractors, agents and all persons engaged in working or acting for them in the conduct of its operations under this contract shall observe the applicable law referred to in section 27.1 hereof and shall not engage in any transaction, directly or indirectly, prohibited by the applicable law.

27.3   Nothing contained in this contract shall be deemed an exemption from the necessity of applying for and obtaining any permit or authority that may be required for any activities under this contract.

Section 28
Interpretation

The division of this contract into sections and subsections and the insertion of headings are for convenience of reference only and shall not affect the construction or interpretation hereof.

Section 29
Additional documents

Each party hereto agrees to execute and deliver all such further instruments, and to do and perform all such further acts and things as may be necessary or expedient to give effect to the provisions of this contract.

International Seabed Authority

ISBA/16/A/12/Rev.1

Assembly

Distr.: General
15 November 2010

Original: English

Sixteenth session
Kingston, Jamaica
26 April-7 May 2010

Decision of the Assembly of the International Seabed Authority relating to the regulations on prospecting and exploration for polymetallic sulphides in the Area

The Assembly of the International Seabed Authority,

Having considered the Regulations on prospecting and exploration for polymetallic sulphides in the Area, as provisionally adopted by the Council at its 161st meeting, on 6 May 2010 (ISBA/16/C/L.5),

Approves the Regulations on prospecting and exploration for polymetallic sulphides in the Area as contained in the annex to the present document.

130th meeting
7 May 2010

Annex

Regulations on prospecting and exploration for polymetallic sulphides in the Area

Preamble

In accordance with the United Nations Convention on the Law of the Sea ("the Convention"), the seabed and ocean floor and the subsoil thereof beyond the limits of national jurisdiction, as well as its resources, are the common heritage of mankind, the exploration and exploitation of which shall be carried out for the benefit of mankind as a whole, on whose behalf the International Seabed Authority acts. The objective of this set of Regulations is to provide for prospecting and exploration for polymetallic sulphides.

Part I
Introduction

Regulation 1
Use of terms and scope

1. Terms used in the Convention shall have the same meaning in these Regulations.

2. In accordance with the Agreement relating to the Implementation of Part XI of the United Nations Convention on the Law of the Sea of 10 December 1982 ("the Agreement"), the provisions of the Agreement and Part XI of the United Nations Convention on the Law of the Sea of 10 December 1982 shall be interpreted and applied together as a single instrument. These Regulations and references in these Regulations to the Convention are to be interpreted and applied accordingly.

3. For the purposes of these Regulations:

(a) "exploitation" means the recovery for commercial purposes of polymetallic sulphides in the Area and the extraction of minerals therefrom, including the construction and operation of mining, processing and transportation systems, for the production and marketing of metals;

(b) "exploration" means searching for deposits of polymetallic sulphides in the Area with exclusive rights, the analysis of such deposits, the use and testing of recovery systems and equipment, processing facilities and transportation systems, and the carrying out of studies of the environmental, technical, economic, commercial and other appropriate factors that must be taken into account in exploitation;

(c) "marine environment" includes the physical, chemical, geological and biological components, conditions and factors which interact and determine the productivity, state, condition and quality of the marine ecosystem, the waters of the seas and oceans and the airspace above those waters, as well as the seabed and ocean floor and subsoil thereof;

(d) "polymetallic sulphides" means hydrothermally formed deposits of sulphides and accompanying mineral resources in the Area which contain concentrations of metals including, inter alia, copper, lead, zinc, gold and silver;

(e) "prospecting" means the search for deposits of polymetallic sulphides in the Area, including estimation of the composition, size and distribution of deposits of polymetallic sulphides and their economic values, without any exclusive rights;

(f) "serious harm to the marine environment" means any effect from activities in the Area on the marine environment which represents a significant adverse change in the marine environment determined according to the rules, regulations and procedures adopted by the Authority on the basis of internationally recognized standards and practices.

4. These Regulations shall not in any way affect the freedom of scientific research, pursuant to article 87 of the Convention, or the right to conduct marine scientific research in the Area pursuant to articles 143 and 256 of the Convention. Nothing in these Regulations shall be construed in such a way as to restrict the exercise by States of the freedom of the high seas as reflected in article 87 of the Convention.

5. These Regulations may be supplemented by further rules, regulations and procedures, in particular on the protection and preservation of the marine environment. These Regulations shall be subject to the provisions of the Convention and the Agreement and other rules of international law not incompatible with the Convention.

Part II
Prospecting

Regulation 2
Prospecting

1. Prospecting shall be conducted in accordance with the Convention and these Regulations and may commence only after the prospector has been informed by the Secretary-General that its notification has been recorded pursuant to regulation 4, paragraph 2.

2. Prospectors and the Secretary-General shall apply a precautionary approach, as reflected in principle 15 of the Rio Declaration.[1] Prospecting shall not be undertaken if substantial evidence indicates the risk of serious harm to the marine environment.

3. Prospecting shall not be undertaken in an area covered by an approved plan of work for exploration for polymetallic sulphides or in a reserved area; nor may there be prospecting in an area which the Council has disapproved for exploitation because of the risk of serious harm to the marine environment.

---

[1] *Report of the United Nations Conference on Environment and Development, Rio de Janeiro, 3-14 June 1991* (United Nations publication, Sales No. E.91.I.8 and corrigenda), vol. 1: *Resolutions adopted by the Conference*, resolution 1, annex 1.

4. Prospecting shall not confer on the prospector any rights with respect to resources. A prospector may, however, recover a reasonable quantity of minerals, being the quantity necessary for testing and not for commercial use.

5. There shall be no time limit on prospecting, except that prospecting in a particular area shall cease upon written notification to the prospector by the Secretary-General that a plan of work for exploration has been approved with regard to that area.

6. Prospecting may be conducted simultaneously by more than one prospector in the same area or areas.

Regulation 3
Notification of prospecting

1. A proposed prospector shall notify the Authority of its intention to engage in prospecting.

2. Each notification of prospecting shall be in the form prescribed in annex 1 to these Regulations, addressed to the Secretary-General, and shall conform to the requirements of these Regulations.

3. Each notification shall be submitted:

   (a) In the case of a State, by the authority designated for that purpose by it;

   (b) In the case of an entity, by its designated representative;

   (c) In the case of the Enterprise, by its competent authority.

4. Each notification shall be in one of the languages of the Authority and shall contain:

   (a) The name, nationality and address of the proposed prospector and its designated representative;

   (b) The coordinates of the broad area or areas within which prospecting is to be conducted, in accordance with the most recent generally accepted international standard used by the Authority;

   (c) A general description of the prospecting programme, including the proposed date of commencement and its approximate duration;

   (d) A satisfactory written undertaking that the proposed prospector will:

   (i) Comply with the Convention and the relevant rules, regulations and procedures of the Authority concerning:

   a. Cooperation in the training programmes in connection with marine scientific research and transfer of technology referred to in articles 143 and 144 of the Convention; and

   b. Protection and preservation of the marine environment;

   (ii) Accept verification by the Authority of compliance therewith; and

   (iii) Make available to the Authority, as far as practicable, such data as may be relevant to the protection and preservation of the marine environment.

Regulation 4
Consideration of notifications

1. The Secretary-General shall acknowledge in writing receipt of each notification submitted under regulation 3, specifying the date of receipt.

2. The Secretary-General shall review and act on the notification within 45 days of its receipt. If the notification conforms with the requirements of the Convention and these Regulations, the Secretary-General shall record the particulars of the notification in a register maintained for that purpose and shall inform the prospector in writing that the notification has been so recorded.

3. The Secretary-General shall, within 45 days of receipt of the notification, inform the proposed prospector in writing if the notification includes any part of an area included in an approved plan of work for exploration or exploitation of any category of resources, or any part of a reserved area, or any part of an area which has been disapproved by the Council for exploitation because of the risk of serious harm to the marine environment, or if the written undertaking is not satisfactory, and shall provide the proposed prospector with a written statement of reasons. In such cases, the proposed prospector may, within 90 days, submit an amended notification. The Secretary-General shall, within 45 days, review and act upon such amended notification.

4. A prospector shall inform the Secretary-General in writing of any change in the information contained in the notification.

5. The Secretary-General shall not release any particulars contained in the notification except with the written consent of the prospector. The Secretary-General shall, however, from time to time inform all members of the Authority of the identity of prospectors and the general areas in which prospecting is being conducted.

Regulation 5
Protection and preservation of the marine environment during prospecting

1. Each prospector shall take necessary measures to prevent, reduce and control pollution and other hazards to the marine environment arising from prospecting, as far as reasonably possible, applying a precautionary approach and best environmental practices. In particular, each prospector shall minimize or eliminate:

   (a) Adverse environmental impacts from prospecting; and

   (b) Actual or potential conflicts or interference with existing or planned marine scientific research activities, in accordance with the relevant future guidelines in this regard.

2. Prospectors shall cooperate with the Authority in the establishment and implementation of programmes for monitoring and evaluating the potential impacts of the exploration for and exploitation of polymetallic sulphides on the marine environment.

3. A prospector shall immediately notify the Secretary-General in writing, using the most effective means, of any incident arising from prospecting which has caused, is causing or poses a threat of serious harm to the marine environment.

Upon receipt of such notification the Secretary-General shall act in a manner consistent with regulation 35.

Regulation 6
Annual report

1. A prospector shall, within 90 days of the end of each calendar year, submit a report to the Authority on the status of prospecting. Such reports shall be submitted by the Secretary-General to the Legal and Technical Commission. Each such report shall contain:

    (a) A general description of the status of prospecting and of the results obtained;

    (b) Information on compliance with the undertakings referred to in regulation 3, paragraph 4 (d); and

    (c) Information on adherence to the relevant guidelines in this regard.

2. If the prospector intends to claim expenditures for prospecting as part of the development costs incurred prior to the commencement of commercial production, the prospector shall submit an annual statement, in conformity with internationally accepted accounting principles and certified by a duly qualified firm of public accountants, of the actual and direct expenditures incurred by the prospector in carrying out prospecting.

Regulation 7
Confidentiality of data and information from prospecting contained in the annual report

1. The Secretary-General shall ensure the confidentiality of all data and information contained in the reports submitted under regulation 6 applying mutatis mutandis the provisions of regulations 38 and 39, provided that data and information relating to the protection and preservation of the marine environment, in particular those from environmental monitoring programmes, shall not be considered confidential. The prospector may request that such data not be disclosed for up to three years following the date of their submission.

2. The Secretary-General may, at any time, with the consent of the prospector concerned, release data and information relating to prospecting in an area in respect of which a notification has been submitted. If, after having made reasonable efforts for at least two years, the Secretary-General determines that the prospector no longer exists or cannot be located, the Secretary-General may release such data and information.

Regulation 8
Objects of an archaeological or historical nature

A prospector shall immediately notify the Secretary-General in writing of any finding in the Area of an object of actual or potential archaeological or historical nature and its location. The Secretary-General shall transmit such information to the Director-General of the United Nations Educational, Scientific and Cultural Organization.

Part III
Applications for approval of plans of work for exploration in the form of contracts

Section 1
General provisions

Regulation 9
General

Subject to the provisions of the Convention, the following may apply to the Authority for approval of plans of work for exploration:

(a) The Enterprise, on its own behalf or in a joint arrangement;

(b) States Parties, State enterprises or natural or juridical persons which possess the nationality of States or are effectively controlled by them or their nationals, when sponsored by such States, or any group of the foregoing which meets the requirements of these Regulations.

Section 2
Content of applications

Regulation 10
Form of applications

1. Each application for approval of a plan of work for exploration shall be in the form prescribed in annex 2 to these Regulations, shall be addressed to the Secretary-General, and shall conform to the requirements of these Regulations.

2. Each application shall be submitted:

(a) In the case of a State, by the authority designated for that purpose by it;

(b) In the case of an entity, by its designated representative or the authority designated for that purpose by the sponsoring State or States; and

(c) In the case of the Enterprise, by its competent authority.

3. Each application by a State enterprise or one of the entities referred to in subparagraph (b) of regulation 9 shall also contain:

(a) Sufficient information to determine the nationality of the applicant or the identity of the State or States by which, or by whose nationals, the applicant is effectively controlled; and

(b) The principal place of business or domicile and, if applicable, place of registration of the applicant.

4. Each application submitted by a partnership or consortium of entities shall contain the required information in respect of each member of the partnership or consortium.

Regulation 11
Certificate of sponsorship

1. Each application by a State enterprise or one of the entities referred to in subparagraph (b) of regulation 9 shall be accompanied by a certificate of sponsorship issued by the State of which it is a national or by which or by whose nationals it is effectively controlled. If the applicant has more than one nationality, as in the case of a partnership or consortium of entities from more than one State, each State involved shall issue a certificate of sponsorship.

2. Where the applicant has the nationality of one State but is effectively controlled by another State or its nationals, each State involved shall issue a certificate of sponsorship.

3. Each certificate of sponsorship shall be duly signed on behalf of the State by which it is submitted, and shall contain:

(a) The name of the applicant;

(b) The name of the sponsoring State;

(c) A statement that the applicant is:

(i) A national of the sponsoring State; or

(ii) Subject to the effective control of the sponsoring State or its nationals;

(d) A statement by the sponsoring State that it sponsors the applicant;

(e) The date of deposit by the sponsoring State of its instrument of ratification of, or accession or succession to, the Convention;

(f) A declaration that the sponsoring State assumes responsibility in accordance with article 139, article 153, paragraph 4, and annex III, article 4, paragraph 4, of the Convention.

4. States or entities in a joint arrangement with the Enterprise shall also comply with this regulation.

Regulation 12
Total area covered by the application

1. For the purposes of these Regulations, a "polymetallic sulphide block" means a cell of a grid as provided by the Authority, which shall be approximately 10 kilometres by 10 kilometres and no greater than 100 square kilometres.

2. The area covered by each application for approval of a plan of work for exploration for polymetallic sulphides shall be comprised of not more than 100 polymetallic sulphide blocks which shall be arranged by the applicant in at least five clusters, as set out in paragraph 3 below.

3. Each cluster of polymetallic sulphide blocks shall contain at least five contiguous blocks. Two such blocks that touch at any point shall be considered to be contiguous. Clusters of polymetallic sulphide blocks need not be contiguous but shall be proximate and confined within a rectangular area not exceeding 300,000 square kilometres in size and where the longest side does not exceed 1,000 kilometres in length.

4. Notwithstanding the provisions in paragraph 2 above, where an applicant has elected to contribute a reserved area to carry out activities pursuant to article 9 of annex III to the Convention, in accordance with regulation 17, the total area covered by an application shall not exceed 200 polymetallic sulphide blocks. Such blocks shall be arranged in two groups of equal estimated commercial value and each such group of polymetallic sulphide blocks shall be arranged by the applicant in clusters, as set out in paragraph 3 above.

Regulation 13
Financial and technical capabilities

1. Each application for approval of a plan of work for exploration shall contain specific and sufficient information to enable the Council to determine whether the applicant is financially and technically capable of carrying out the proposed plan of work for exploration and of fulfilling its financial obligations to the Authority.

2. An application for approval of a plan of work for exploration by the Enterprise shall include a statement by its competent authority certifying that the Enterprise has the necessary financial resources to meet the estimated costs of the proposed plan of work for exploration.

3. An application for approval of a plan of work for exploration by a State or a State enterprise shall include a statement by the State or the sponsoring State certifying that the applicant has the necessary financial resources to meet the estimated costs of the proposed plan of work for exploration.

4. An application for approval of a plan of work for exploration by an entity shall include copies of its audited financial statements, including balance sheets and profit-and-loss statements, for the most recent three years, in conformity with internationally accepted accounting principles and certified by a duly qualified firm of public accountants; and

 (a) If the applicant is a newly organized entity and a certified balance sheet is not available, a pro forma balance sheet certified by an appropriate official of the applicant;

 (b) If the applicant is a subsidiary of another entity, copies of such financial statements of that entity and a statement from that entity, in conformity with internationally accepted accounting principles and certified by a duly qualified firm of public accountants, that the applicant will have the financial resources to carry out the plan of work for exploration;

 (c) If the applicant is controlled by a State or a State enterprise, a statement from the State or State enterprise certifying that the applicant will have the financial resources to carry out the plan of work for exploration.

5. Where an applicant referred to in paragraph 4 intends to finance the proposed plan of work for exploration by borrowings, its application shall include the amount of such borrowings, the repayment period and the interest rate.

6. Each application shall include:

 (a) A general description of the applicant's previous experience, knowledge, skills, technical qualifications and expertise relevant to the proposed plan of work for exploration;

(b) A general description of the equipment and methods expected to be used in carrying out the proposed plan of work for exploration and other relevant non-proprietary information about the characteristics of such technology;

(c) A general description of the applicant's financial and technical capability to respond to any incident or activity which causes serious harm to the marine environment.

7. Where the applicant is a partnership or consortium of entities in a joint arrangement, each member of the partnership or consortium shall provide the information required by this regulation.

Regulation 14
Previous contracts with the Authority

Where the applicant or, in the case of an application by a partnership or consortium of entities in a joint arrangement, any member of the partnership or consortium, has previously been awarded any contract with the Authority, the application shall include:

(a) The date of the previous contract or contracts;

(b) The date, reference number and title of each report submitted to the Authority in connection with the contract or contracts; and

(c) The date of termination of the contract or contracts, if applicable.

Regulation 15
Undertakings

Each applicant, including the Enterprise, shall, as part of its application for approval of a plan of work for exploration, provide a written undertaking to the Authority that it will:

(a) Accept as enforceable and comply with the applicable obligations created by the provisions of the Convention and the rules, regulations and procedures of the Authority, the decisions of the organs of the Authority and the terms of its contracts with the Authority;

(b) Accept control by the Authority of activities in the Area, as authorized by the Convention; and

(c) Provide the Authority with a written assurance that its obligations under the contract will be fulfilled in good faith.

Regulation 16
Applicant's election of a reserved area contribution or equity interest in a joint venture arrangement

Each applicant shall, in the application, elect either to:

(a) Contribute a reserved area to carry out activities pursuant to Annex III, article 9, of the Convention, in accordance with regulation 17; or

(b) Offer an equity interest in a joint venture arrangement in accordance with regulation 19.

Regulation 17
Data and information to be submitted before the designation of a reserved area

1. Where the applicant elects to contribute a reserved area to carry out activities pursuant to article 9 of annex III to the Convention, the area covered by the application shall be sufficiently large and of sufficient estimated commercial value to allow two mining operations and shall be configured by the applicant in accordance with regulation 12, paragraph 4.

2. Each such application shall contain sufficient data and information, as prescribed in section II of annex 2 to these Regulations, with respect to the area under application to enable the Council, on the recommendation of the Legal and Technical Commission, to designate a reserved area based on the estimated commercial value of each part. Such data and information shall consist of data available to the applicant with respect to both parts of the area under application, including the data used to determine their commercial value.

3. The Council, on the basis of the data and information submitted by the applicant pursuant to section II of annex 2 to these Regulations, if found satisfactory, and taking into account the recommendation of the Legal and Technical Commission, shall designate the part of the area under application which is to be a reserved area. The area so designated shall become a reserved area as soon as the plan of work for exploration for the non-reserved area is approved and the contract is signed. If the Council determines that additional information, consistent with these Regulations and annex 2, is needed to designate the reserved area, it shall refer the matter back to the Commission for further consideration, specifying the additional information required.

4. Once the plan of work for exploration is approved and a contract has been issued, the data and information transferred to the Authority by the applicant in respect of the reserved area may be disclosed by the Authority in accordance with article 14, paragraph 3, of annex III to the Convention.

Regulation 18
Applications for approval of plans of work with respect to a reserved area

1. Any State which is a developing State or any natural or juridical person sponsored by it and effectively controlled by it or by any other developing State, or any group of the foregoing, may notify the Authority that it wishes to submit a plan of work for exploration with respect to a reserved area. The Secretary-General shall forward such notification to the Enterprise, which shall inform the Secretary-General in writing within six months whether or not it intends to carry out activities in that area. If the Enterprise intends to carry out activities in that area, it shall, pursuant to paragraph 4, also inform in writing the contractor whose application for approval of a plan of work for exploration originally included that area.

2. An application for approval of a plan of work for exploration in respect of a reserved area may be submitted at any time after such an area becomes available following a decision by the Enterprise that it does not intend to carry out activities in that area or where the Enterprise has not, within six months of the notification by the Secretary-General, either taken a decision on whether it intends to carry out activities in that area or notified the Secretary-General in writing that it is engaged in discussions regarding a potential joint venture. In the latter instance, the

Enterprise shall have one year from the date of such notification in which to decide whether to conduct activities in that area.

3. If the Enterprise or a developing State or one of the entities referred to in paragraph 1 does not submit an application for approval of a plan of work for exploration for activities in a reserved area within 15 years of the commencement by the Enterprise of its functions independent of the Secretariat of the Authority or within 15 years of the date on which that area is reserved for the Authority, whichever is the later, the contractor whose application for approval of a plan of work for exploration originally included that area shall be entitled to apply for a plan of work for exploration for that area provided it offers in good faith to include the Enterprise as a joint-venture partner.

4. A contractor has the right of first refusal to enter into a joint venture arrangement with the Enterprise for exploration of the area which was included in its application for approval of a plan of work for exploration and which was designated by the Council as a reserved area.

Regulation 19
Equity interest in a joint venture arrangement

1. Where the applicant elects to offer an equity interest in a joint venture arrangement, it shall submit data and information in accordance with regulation 20. The area to be allocated to the applicant shall be subject to the provisions of regulation 27.

2. The joint venture arrangement, which shall take effect at the time the applicant enters into a contract for exploitation, shall include the following:

(a) The Enterprise shall obtain a minimum of 20 per cent of the equity participation in the joint venture arrangement on the following basis:

(i) Half of such equity participation shall be obtained without payment, directly or indirectly, to the applicant and shall be treated *pari passu* for all purposes with the equity participation of the applicant;

(ii) The remainder of such equity participation shall be treated *pari passu* for all purposes with the equity participation of the applicant except that the Enterprise shall not receive any profit distribution with respect to such participation until the applicant has recovered its total equity participation in the joint venture arrangement;

(b) Notwithstanding subparagraph (a), the applicant shall nevertheless offer the Enterprise the opportunity to purchase a further thirty per cent of the equity in the joint venture arrangement, or such lesser percentage as the Enterprise may elect to purchase, on the basis of *pari passu* treatment with the applicant for all purposes;[2]

(c) Except as specifically provided in the agreement between the applicant and the Enterprise, the Enterprise shall not by reason of its equity participation be otherwise obligated to provide funds or credits or issue guarantees or otherwise accept any financial liability whatsoever for or on behalf of the joint venture

---

[2] The terms and conditions upon which such equity participation may be obtained would need to be further elaborated.

arrangement, nor shall the Enterprise be required to subscribe for additional equity participation so as to maintain its proportionate participation in the joint venture arrangement.

Regulation 20
Data and information to be submitted for approval of the plan of work for exploration

1. Each applicant shall submit, with a view to receiving approval of the plan of work for exploration in the form of a contract, the following information:

(a) A general description and a schedule of the proposed exploration programme, including the programme of activities for the immediate five-year period, such as studies to be undertaken in respect of the environmental, technical, economic and other appropriate factors that must be taken into account in exploration;

(b) A description of the programme for oceanographic and environmental baseline studies in accordance with these Regulations and any environmental rules, regulations and procedures established by the Authority that would enable an assessment of the potential environmental impact including, but not restricted to, the impact on biodiversity, of the proposed exploration activities, taking into account any recommendations issued by the Legal and Technical Commission;

(c) A preliminary assessment of the possible impact of the proposed exploration activities on the marine environment;

(d) A description of proposed measures for the prevention, reduction and control of pollution and other hazards, as well as possible impacts, to the marine environment;

(e) Data necessary for the Council to make the determination it is required to make in accordance with regulation 13, paragraph 1; and

(f) A schedule of anticipated yearly expenditures in respect of the programme of activities for the immediate five-year period.

2. Where the applicant elects to contribute a reserved area, the data and information relating to such area shall be transferred to the Authority by the applicant after the Council has designated the reserved area in accordance with regulation 17, paragraph 3.

3. Where the applicant elects to offer an equity interest in a joint venture arrangement, the data and information relating to such area shall be transferred to the Authority by the applicant at the time of the election.

Section 3
Fees

Regulation 21
Fee for applications

1. The fee for processing an application for approval of a plan of work for exploration of polymetallic sulphides shall be a fixed amount of 500,000 United

States dollars or its equivalent in a freely convertible currency, to be paid in full at the time of the submission of an application.

2. If the administrative costs incurred by the Authority in processing an application are less than the fixed amount indicated in paragraph 1 above, the Authority shall refund the difference to the applicant. If the administrative costs incurred by the Authority in processing an application are more than the fixed amount indicated in paragraph 1 above, the applicant shall pay the difference to the Authority, provided that any additional amount to be paid by the applicant shall not exceed 10 per cent of the fixed fee referred to in paragraph 1.

3. Taking into account any criteria established for this purpose by the Finance Committee, the Secretary-General shall determine the amount of such differences as indicated in paragraph 2 above and notify the applicant of the amount. The notification shall include a statement of the expenditure incurred by the Authority. The amount due shall be paid by the applicant or reimbursed by the Authority within three months of the signing of the contract referred to in regulation 25 below.

4. The fixed amount referred to in paragraph 1 above shall be reviewed on a regular basis by the Council in order to ensure that it covers the expected administrative costs of processing applications and to avoid the need for applicants to pay additional amounts in accordance with paragraph 2 above.[3]

Section 4
Processing of applications

Regulation 22
Receipt, acknowledgement and safe custody of applications

The Secretary-General shall:

(a) Acknowledge in writing within 30 days receipt of every application for approval of a plan of work for exploration submitted under this Part, specifying the date of receipt;

(b) Place the application together with the attachments and annexes thereto in safe custody and ensure the confidentiality of all confidential data and information contained in the application; and

(c) Notify the members of the Authority of the receipt of such application and circulate to them information of a general nature which is not confidential regarding the application.

---

[3] ISBA/20/A/10, dated 24 July 2014, Amendments.

Regulation 23
Consideration by the Legal and Technical Commission

1. Upon receipt of an application for approval of a plan of work for exploration, the Secretary-General shall notify the members of the Legal and Technical Commission and place consideration of the application as an item on the agenda for the next meeting of the Commission. The Commission shall only consider applications in respect of which notification and information has been circulated by the Secretary-General in accordance with regulation 22 (c) at least 30 days prior to the commencement of the meeting of the Commission at which they are to be considered.

2. The Commission shall examine applications in the order in which they are received.

3. The Commission shall determine if the applicant:

   (a) Has complied with the provisions of these Regulations;

   (b) Has given the undertakings and assurances specified in regulation 15;

   (c) Possesses the financial and technical capability to carry out the proposed plan of work for exploration and has provided details as to its ability to comply promptly with emergency orders; and

   (d) Has satisfactorily discharged its obligations in relation to any previous contract with the Authority.

4. The Commission shall, in accordance with the requirements set forth in these Regulations and its procedures, determine whether the proposed plan of work for exploration will:

   (a) Provide for effective protection of human health and safety;

   (b) Provide for effective protection and preservation of the marine environment including, but not restricted to, the impact on biodiversity;

   (c) Ensure that installations are not established where interference may be caused to the use of recognized sea lanes essential to international navigation or in areas of intense fishing activity.

5. If the Commission makes the determinations specified in paragraph 3 and determines that the proposed plan of work for exploration meets the requirements of paragraph 4, the Commission shall recommend approval of the plan of work for exploration to the Council.

6. The Commission shall not recommend approval of the plan of work for exploration if part or all of the area covered by the proposed plan of work for exploration is included in:

   (a) A plan of work for exploration approved by the Council for polymetallic sulphides; or

   (b) A plan of work approved by the Council for exploration for or exploitation of other resources if the proposed plan of work for exploration for polymetallic sulphides might cause undue interference with activities under such approved plan of work for other resources; or

(c) An area disapproved for exploitation by the Council in cases where substantial evidence indicates the risk of serious harm to the marine environment.

7. The Legal and Technical Commission may recommend approval of a plan of work if it determines that such approval would not permit a State Party or entities sponsored by it to monopolize the conduct of activities in the Area with regard to polymetallic sulphides or to preclude other States Parties from activities in the Area with regard to polymetallic sulphides.

8. Except in the case of applications by the Enterprise, on its own behalf or in a joint venture, and applications under regulation 18, the Commission shall not recommend approval of the plan of work for exploration if part or all of the area covered by the proposed plan of work for exploration is included in a reserved area or an area designated by the Council to be a reserved area.

9. If the Commission finds that an application does not comply with these Regulations, it shall notify the applicant in writing, through the Secretary-General, indicating the reasons. The applicant may, within 45 days of such notification, amend its application. If the Commission after further consideration is of the view that it should not recommend approval of the plan of work for exploration, it shall so inform the applicant and provide the applicant with a further opportunity to make representations within 30 days of such information. The Commission shall consider any such representations made by the applicant in preparing its report and recommendation to the Council.

10. In considering a proposed plan of work for exploration, the Commission shall have regard to the principles, policies and objectives relating to activities in the Area as provided for in part XI and annex III of the Convention and the Agreement.

11. The Commission shall consider applications expeditiously and shall submit its report and recommendations to the Council on the designation of the areas and on the plan of work for exploration at the first possible opportunity, taking into account the schedule of meetings of the Authority.

12. In discharging its duties, the Commission shall apply these Regulations and the rules, regulations and procedures of the Authority in a uniform and non-discriminatory manner.

Regulation 24
Consideration and approval of plans of work for exploration by the Council

The Council shall consider the reports and recommendations of the Commission relating to approval of plans of work for exploration in accordance with paragraphs 11 and 12 of section 3 of the annex to the Agreement.

Part IV
Contracts for exploration

Regulation 25
The contract

1. After a plan of work for exploration has been approved by the Council, it shall be prepared in the form of a contract between the Authority and the applicant as prescribed in annex 3 to these Regulations. Each contract shall incorporate the

standard clauses set out in annex 4 in effect at the date of entry into force of the contract.

2. The contract shall be signed by the Secretary-General on behalf of the Authority and by the applicant. The Secretary-General shall notify all members of the Authority in writing of the conclusion of each contract.

Regulation 26
Rights of the contractor

1. The contractor shall have the exclusive right to explore an area covered by a plan of work for exploration in respect of polymetallic sulphides. The Authority shall ensure that no other entity operates in the same area for other resources in a manner that might interfere with the operations of the contractor.

2. A contractor who has an approved plan of work for exploration only shall have a preference and a priority among applicants submitting plans of work for exploitation of the same area and resources. Such preference or priority may be withdrawn by the Council if the contractor has failed to comply with the requirements of its approved plan of work for exploration within the time period specified in a written notice or notices from the Council to the contractor indicating which requirements have not been complied with by the contractor. The time period specified in any such notice shall not be unreasonable. The contractor shall be accorded a reasonable opportunity to be heard before the withdrawal of such preference or priority becomes final. The Council shall provide the reasons for its proposed withdrawal of preference or priority and shall consider any contractor's response. The decision of the Council shall take account of that response and shall be based on substantial evidence.

3. A withdrawal of preference or priority shall not become effective until the contractor has been accorded a reasonable opportunity to exhaust the judicial remedies available to it pursuant to part XI, section 5, of the Convention.

Regulation 27
Size of area and relinquishment

1. The contractor shall relinquish the area allocated to it in accordance with paragraph 2 of this regulation. Areas to be relinquished need not be contiguous and shall be defined by the contractor in the form of sub-blocks comprising one or more cells of a grid as provided by the Authority.

2. The total area allocated to the contractor under the contract shall not exceed 10,000 square kilometres. The contractor shall relinquish parts of the area allocated to it in accordance with the following schedule:

    (a) By the end of the eighth year from the date of the contract, the contractor shall have relinquished at least 50 per cent of the original area allocated to it;

    (b) By the end of the tenth year from the date of the contract, the contractor shall have relinquished at least 75 per cent of the original area allocated to it; or

3. The contractor may at any time relinquish parts of the area allocated to it in advance of the schedule set out in paragraph 2, provided that a contractor shall not be required to relinquish any additional part of such area when the remaining area allocated to it after relinquishment does not exceed 2,500 square kilometres.

4. Relinquished areas shall revert to the Area.

5. At the end of the fifteenth year from the date of the contract, or when the contractor applies for exploitation rights, whichever is the earlier, the contractor shall nominate an area from the remaining area allocated to it to be retained for exploitation.

6. The Council may, at the request of the contractor, and on the recommendation of the Commission, in exceptional circumstances, defer the schedule of relinquishment. Such exceptional circumstances shall be determined by the Council and shall include, inter alia, consideration of prevailing economic circumstances or other unforeseen exceptional circumstances arising in connection with the operational activities of the contractor.

Regulation 28
Duration of contracts

1. A plan of work for exploration shall be approved for a period of 15 years. Upon expiration of a plan of work for exploration, the contractor shall apply for a plan of work for exploitation unless the contractor has already done so, has obtained an extension for the plan of work for exploration or decides to renounce its rights in the area covered by the plan of work for exploration.

2. Not later than six months before the expiration of a plan of work for exploration, a contractor may apply for extensions for the plan of work for exploration for periods of not more than five years each. Such extensions shall be approved by the Council, on the recommendation of the Commission, if the contractor has made efforts in good faith to comply with the requirements of the plan of work but for reasons beyond the contractor's control has been unable to complete the necessary preparatory work for proceeding to the exploitation stage or if the prevailing economic circumstances do not justify proceeding to the exploitation stage.

Regulation 29
Training

Pursuant to article 15 of annex III to the Convention, each contract shall include as a schedule a practical programme for the training of personnel of the Authority and developing States and drawn up by the contractor in cooperation with the Authority and the sponsoring State or States. Training programmes shall focus on training in the conduct of exploration, and shall provide for full participation by such personnel in all activities covered by the contract. Such training programmes may be revised and developed from time to time as necessary by mutual agreement.

Regulation 30
Periodic review of the implementation of the plan of work for exploration

1. The contractor and the Secretary-General shall jointly undertake a periodic review of the implementation of the plan of work for exploration at intervals of five years. The Secretary-General may request the contractor to submit such additional data and information as may be necessary for the purposes of the review.

2. In the light of the review, the contractor shall indicate its programme of activities for the following five-year period, making such adjustments to its previous programme of activities as are necessary.

3. The Secretary-General shall report on the review to the Commission and to the Council. The Secretary-General shall indicate in the report whether any observations transmitted to him by States Parties to the Convention concerning the manner in which the contractor has discharged its obligations under these Regulations relating to the protection and preservation of the marine environment were taken into account in the review.

Regulation 31
Termination of sponsorship

1. Each contractor shall have the required sponsorship throughout the period of the contract.

2. If a State terminates its sponsorship it shall promptly notify the Secretary-General in writing. The sponsoring State should also inform the Secretary-General of the reasons for terminating its sponsorship. Termination of sponsorship shall take effect six months after the date of receipt of the notification by the Secretary-General, unless the notification specifies a later date.

3. In the event of termination of sponsorship the contractor shall, within the period referred to in paragraph 2, obtain another sponsor. Such sponsor shall submit a certificate of sponsorship in accordance with regulation 11. Failure to obtain a sponsor within the required period shall result in the termination of the contract.

4. A sponsoring State shall not be discharged by reason of the termination of its sponsorship from any obligations accrued while it was a sponsoring State, nor shall such termination affect any legal rights and obligations created during such sponsorship.

5. The Secretary-General shall notify the members of the Authority of the termination or change of sponsorship.

Regulation 32
Responsibility and liability

Responsibility and liability of the contractor and of the Authority shall be in accordance with the Convention. The contractor shall continue to have responsibility for any damage arising out of wrongful acts in the conduct of its operations, in particular damage to the marine environment, after the completion of the exploration phase.

Part V
Protection and preservation of the marine environment

Regulation 33
Protection and preservation of the marine environment

1. The Authority shall, in accordance with the Convention and the Agreement, establish and keep under periodic review environmental rules, regulations and

procedures to ensure effective protection for the marine environment from harmful effects which may arise from activities in the Area.

2. In order to ensure effective protection for the marine environment from harmful effects which may arise from activities in the Area, the Authority and sponsoring States shall apply a precautionary approach, as reflected in principle 15 of the Rio Declaration, and best environmental practices.

3. The Legal and Technical Commission shall make recommendations to the Council on the implementation of paragraphs 1 and 2 above.

4. The Commission shall develop and implement procedures for determining, on the basis of the best available scientific and technical information, including information provided pursuant to regulation 20, whether proposed exploration activities in the Area would have serious harmful effects on vulnerable marine ecosystems, in particular hydrothermal vents, and ensure that, if it is determined that certain proposed exploration activities would have serious harmful effects on vulnerable marine ecosystems, those activities are managed to prevent such effects or not authorized to proceed.

5. Pursuant to article 145 of the Convention and paragraph 2 of this regulation, each contractor shall take necessary measures to prevent, reduce and control pollution and other hazards to the marine environment arising from its activities in the Area as far as reasonably possible, applying a precautionary approach and best environmental practices.

6. Contractors, sponsoring States and other interested States or entities shall cooperate with the Authority in the establishment and implementation of programmes for monitoring and evaluating the impacts of deep seabed mining on the marine environment. When required by the Council, such programmes shall include proposals for areas to be set aside and used exclusively as impact reference zones and preservation reference zones. "Impact reference zones" means areas to be used for assessing the effect of activities in the Area on the marine environment and which are representative of the environmental characteristics of the Area. "Preservation reference zones" means areas in which no mining shall occur to ensure representative and stable biota of the seabed in order to assess any changes in the biodiversity of the marine environment.

Regulation 34
Environmental baselines and monitoring

1. Each contract shall require the contractor to gather environmental baseline data and to establish environmental baselines, taking into account any recommendations issued by the Legal and Technical Commission pursuant to regulation 41, against which to assess the likely effects of its programme of activities under the plan of work for exploration on the marine environment and a programme to monitor and report on such effects. The recommendations issued by the Commission may, inter alia, list those exploration activities which may be considered to have no potential for causing harmful effects on the marine environment. The contractor shall cooperate with the Authority and the sponsoring State or States in the establishment and implementation of such monitoring programme.

2. The contractor shall report annually in writing to the Secretary-General on the implementation and results of the monitoring programme referred to in paragraph 1 and shall submit data and information, taking into account any recommendations issued by the Commission pursuant to regulation 41. The Secretary-General shall transmit such reports to the Commission for its consideration pursuant to article 165 of the Convention.

Regulation 35
Emergency orders

1. A contractor shall promptly report to the Secretary-General in writing, using the most effective means, any incident arising from activities which have caused, are causing, or pose a threat of, serious harm to the marine environment.

2. When the Secretary-General has been notified by a contractor or otherwise becomes aware of an incident resulting from or caused by a contractor's activities in the Area that has caused, is causing or poses a threat of, serious harm to the marine environment, the Secretary-General shall cause a general notification of the incident to be issued, shall notify in writing the contractor and the sponsoring State or States, and shall report immediately to the Legal and Technical Commission, to the Council and to all other members of the Authority. A copy of the report shall be circulated to competent international organizations and to concerned subregional, regional and global organizations and bodies. The Secretary-General shall monitor developments with respect to all such incidents and shall report on them as appropriate to the Commission, the Council and all other members of the Authority.

3. Pending any action by the Council, the Secretary-General shall take such immediate measures of a temporary nature as are practical and reasonable in the circumstances to prevent, contain and minimize serious harm or the threat of serious harm to the marine environment. Such temporary measures shall remain in effect for no longer than 90 days, or until the Council decides at its next regular session or a special session, what measures, if any, to take pursuant to paragraph 6 of this regulation.

4. After having received the report of the Secretary-General, the Commission shall determine, based on the evidence provided to it and taking into account the measures already taken by the contractor, which measures are necessary to respond effectively to the incident in order to prevent, contain and minimize serious harm or the threat of serious harm to the marine environment, and shall make its recommendations to the Council.

5. The Council shall consider the recommendations of the Commission.

6. The Council, taking into account the recommendations of the Commission, the report of the Secretary-General, any information provided by the Contractor and any other relevant information, may issue emergency orders, which may include orders for the suspension or adjustment of operations, as may be reasonably necessary to prevent, contain and minimize serious harm or the threat of serious harm to the marine environment arising out of activities in the Area.

7. If a contractor does not promptly comply with an emergency order to prevent, contain and minimize serious harm or the threat of serious harm to the marine environment arising out of its activities in the Area, the Council shall take by itself or through arrangements with others on its behalf, such practical measures as are

necessary to prevent, contain and minimize any such serious harm or threat of serious harm to the marine environment.

8. In order to enable the Council, when necessary, to take immediately the practical measures to prevent, contain and minimize the serious harm or threat of serious harm to the marine environment referred to in paragraph 7, the contractor, prior to the commencement of testing of collecting systems and processing operations, will provide the Council with a guarantee of its financial and technical capability to comply promptly with emergency orders or to assure that the Council can take such emergency measures. If the contractor does not provide the Council with such a guarantee, the sponsoring State or States shall, in response to a request by the Secretary-General and pursuant to articles 139 and 235 of the Convention, take necessary measures to ensure that the contractor provides such a guarantee or shall take measures to ensure that assistance is provided to the Authority in the discharge of its responsibilities under paragraph 7.

Regulation 36
Rights of coastal States

1. Nothing in these Regulations shall affect the rights of coastal States in accordance with article 142 and other relevant provisions of the Convention.

2. Any coastal State which has grounds for believing that any activity in the Area by a contractor is likely to cause serious harm or a threat of serious harm to the marine environment under its jurisdiction or sovereignty may notify the Secretary-General in writing of the grounds upon which such belief is based. The Secretary-General shall provide the Contractor and its sponsoring State or States with a reasonable opportunity to examine the evidence, if any, provided by the coastal State as the basis for its belief. The contractor and its sponsoring State or States may submit their observations thereon to the Secretary-General within a reasonable time.

3. If there are clear grounds for believing that serious harm to the marine environment is likely to occur, the Secretary-General shall act in accordance with regulation 35 and, if necessary, shall take immediate measures of a temporary nature as provided for in paragraph 3 of regulation 35.

4. Contractors shall take all measures necessary to ensure that their activities are conducted so as not to cause serious harm to the marine environment, including, but not restricted to, pollution, under the jurisdiction or sovereignty of coastal States, and that such serious harm or pollution arising from incidents or activities in its exploration area does not spread beyond such area.

Regulation 37
Human remains and objects and sites of an archaeological or historical nature

The contractor shall immediately notify the Secretary-General in writing of any finding in the exploration area of any human remains of an archaeological or historical nature, or any object or site of a similar nature and its location, including the preservation and protection measures taken. The Secretary-General shall transmit such information to the Director-General of the United Nations Educational, Scientific and Cultural Organization and any other competent international organization. Following the finding of any such human remains, object or site in the exploration area, and in order to avoid disturbing such human remains, object or site, no further prospecting or exploration shall take place, within a reasonable radius, until such time as the Council decides otherwise after taking account of the views of the Director-General of the United Nations Educational, Scientific and Cultural Organization or any other competent international organization.

Part VI
Confidentiality

Regulation 38
Confidentiality of data and information

1. Data and information submitted or transferred to the Authority or to any person participating in any activity or programme of the Authority pursuant to these Regulations or a contract issued under these Regulations, and designated by the contractor, in consultation with the Secretary-General, as being of a confidential nature, shall be considered confidential unless it is data and information which:

    (a) Is generally known or publicly available from other sources;

    (b) Has been previously made available by the owner to others without an obligation concerning its confidentiality; or

    (c) Is already in the possession of the Authority with no obligation concerning its confidentiality.

Data and information that is necessary for the formulation by the Authority of rules, regulations and procedures concerning protection and preservation of the marine environment and safety, other than proprietary equipment design data, shall not be deemed confidential.

2. Confidential data and information may only be used by the Secretary-General and staff of the Secretariat, as authorized by the Secretary-General, and by the members of the Legal and Technical Commission as necessary for and relevant to the effective exercise of their powers and functions. The Secretary-General shall authorize access to such data and information only for limited use in connection with the functions and duties of the staff of the Secretariat and the functions and duties of the Legal and Technical Commission.

3. Ten years after the date of submission of confidential data and information to the Authority or the expiration of the contract for exploration, whichever is the later, and every five years thereafter, the Secretary-General and the contractor shall review such data and information to determine whether they should remain confidential. Such data and information shall remain confidential if the contractor establishes that there would be a substantial risk of serious and unfair economic prejudice if the data and information were to be released. No such data and information shall be released until the contractor has been accorded a reasonable opportunity to exhaust the judicial remedies available to it pursuant to Part XI, section 5, of the Convention.

4. If, at any time following the expiration of the contract for exploration, the contractor enters into a contract for exploitation in respect of any part of the exploration area, confidential data and information relating to that part of the area shall remain confidential in accordance with the contract for exploitation.

5. The contractor may at any time waive confidentiality of data and information.

Regulation 39
Procedures to ensure confidentiality

1. The Secretary-General shall be responsible for maintaining the confidentiality of all confidential data and information and shall not, except with the prior written consent of the contractor, release such data and information to any person external to the Authority. To ensure the confidentiality of such data and information, the Secretary-General shall establish procedures, consistent with the provisions of the Convention, governing the handling of confidential information by members of the Secretariat, members of the Legal and Technical Commission and any other person participating in any activity or programme of the Authority. Such procedures shall include:

(a) Maintenance of confidential data and information in secure facilities and development of security procedures to prevent unauthorized access to or removal of such data and information;

(b) Development and maintenance of a classification, log and inventory system of all written data and information received, including its type and source and routing from the time of receipt until final disposition.

2. A person who is authorized pursuant to these Regulations to have access to confidential data and information shall not disclose such data and information except as permitted under the Convention and these Regulations. The Secretary-General shall require any person who is authorized to have access to confidential data and information to make a written declaration witnessed by the Secretary-General or his or her authorized representative to the effect that the person so authorized:

(a) Acknowledges his or her legal obligation under the Convention and these Regulations with respect to the non-disclosure of confidential data and information;

(b) Agrees to comply with the applicable regulations and procedures established to ensure the confidentiality of such data and information.

3. The Legal and Technical Commission shall protect the confidentiality of confidential data and information submitted to it pursuant to these Regulations or a contract issued under these Regulations. In accordance with the provisions of article 163, paragraph 8, of the Convention, members of the Commission shall not disclose, even after the termination of their functions, any industrial secret, proprietary data which are transferred to the Authority in accordance with Annex III, article 14, of the Convention, or any other confidential information coming to their knowledge by reason of their duties for the Authority.

4. The Secretary-General and staff of the Authority shall not disclose, even after the termination of their functions with the Authority, any industrial secret, proprietary data which are transferred to the Authority in accordance with Annex III, article 14, of the Convention, or any other confidential information coming to their knowledge by reason of their employment with the Authority.

5. Taking into account the responsibility and liability of the Authority pursuant to Annex III, article 22, of the Convention, the Authority may take such action as may be appropriate against any person who, by reason of his or her duties for the

Authority, has access to any confidential data and information and who is in breach of the obligations relating to confidentiality contained in the Convention and these Regulations.

Part VII
General procedures

Regulation 40
Notice and general procedures

1. Any application, request, notice, report, consent, approval, waiver, direction or instruction hereunder shall be made by the Secretary-General or by the designated representative of the prospector, applicant or contractor, as the case may be, in writing. Service shall be by hand, or by telex, facsimile, registered airmail or electronic mail containing an authorized electronic signature to the Secretary-General at the headquarters of the Authority or to the designated representative.

2. Delivery by hand shall be effective when made. Delivery by telex shall be deemed to be effective on the business day following the day when the "answer back" appears on the sender's telex machine. Delivery by facsimile shall be effective when the "transmit confirmation report" confirming the transmission to the recipient's published facsimile number is received by the transmitter. Delivery by registered airmail shall be deemed to be effective 21 days after posting. An electronic document is presumed to be received by the addressee when it enters an information system designated or used by the addressee for the purpose of receiving documents of the type sent and is capable of being retrieved and processed by the addressee.

3. Notice to the designated representative of the prospector, applicant or contractor shall constitute effective notice to the prospector, applicant or contractor for all purposes under these Regulations, and the designated representative shall be the agent of the prospector, applicant or contractor for the service of process or notification in any proceeding of any court or tribunal having jurisdiction.

4. Notice to the Secretary-General shall constitute effective notice to the Authority for all purposes under these Regulations, and the Secretary-General shall be the Authority's agent for the service of process or notification in any proceeding of any court or tribunal having jurisdiction.

Regulation 41
Recommendations for the guidance of contractors

1. The Legal and Technical Commission may from time to time issue recommendations of a technical or administrative nature for the guidance of contractors to assist them in the implementation of the rules, regulations and procedures of the Authority.

2. The full text of such recommendations shall be reported to the Council. Should the Council find that a recommendation is inconsistent with the intent and purpose of these Regulations, it may request that the recommendation be modified or withdrawn.

Part VIII
Settlement of disputes

Regulation 42
Disputes

1. Disputes concerning the interpretation or application of these Regulations shall be settled in accordance with Part XI, section 5, of the Convention.

2. Any final decision rendered by a court or tribunal having jurisdiction under the Convention relating to the rights and obligations of the Authority and of the Contractor shall be enforceable in the territory of each State Party to the Convention.

Part IX
Resources other than polymetallic sulphides

Regulation 43
Resources other than polymetallic sulphides

If a prospector or contractor finds resources in the Area other than polymetallic sulphides, the prospecting and exploration for and exploitation of such resources shall be subject to the rules, regulations and procedures of the Authority relating to such resources in accordance with the Convention and the Agreement. The prospector or contractor shall notify the Authority of its find.

Part X
Review

Regulation 44
Review

1. Five years following the approval of these Regulations by the Assembly, or at any time thereafter, the Council shall undertake a review of the manner in which the Regulations have operated in practice.

2. If, in the light of improved knowledge or technology, it becomes apparent that the Regulations are not adequate, any State Party, the Legal and Technical Commission, or any contractor through its sponsoring State may at any time request the Council to consider, at its next ordinary session, revisions to these Regulations.

3. In the light of the review, the Council may adopt and apply provisionally, pending approval by the Assembly, amendments to the provisions of these Regulations, taking into account the recommendations of the Legal and Technical Commission or other subordinate organs concerned. Any such amendments shall be without prejudice to the rights conferred on any Contractor with the Authority under the provisions of a contract entered into pursuant to these Regulations in force at the time of any such amendment.

4. In the event that any provisions of these Regulations are amended, the Contractor and the Authority may revise the contract in accordance with section 24 of annex 4.

Annex 1

Notification of intention to engage in prospecting

1. Name of prospector:

2. Street address of prospector:

3. Postal address (if different from above):

4. Telephone number:

5. Facsimile number:

6. Electronic mail address:

7. Nationality of prospector:

8. If prospector is a juridical person, identify prospector's

    (a) Place of registration; and

    (b) Principal place of business/domicile.

and attach a copy of the prospector's certificate of registration.

9. Name of prospector's designated representative:

10. Street address of prospector's designated representative (if different from above):

11. Postal address (if different from above):

12. Telephone number:

13. Facsimile number:

14. Electronic mail address:

15. Attach the coordinates of the broad area or areas in which prospecting is to be conducted (in accordance with the World Geodetic System WGS 84).

16. Attach a general description of the prospecting programme, including the date of commencement and the approximate duration of the programme.

17. Attach a written undertaking that the prospector will:

    (a) Comply with the Convention and the relevant rules, regulations and procedures of the Authority concerning:

    (i) Cooperation in the training programmes in connection with marine scientific research and transfer of technology referred to in articles 143 and 144 of the Convention; and

    (ii) Protection and preservation of the marine environment; and

    (b) Accept verification by the Authority of compliance therewith.

18. List hereunder all the attachments and annexes to this notification (all data and information should be submitted in hard copy and in a digital format specified by the Authority):

Date:_____   _____
                              Signature of prospector's designated representative

ATTESTATION:

_____
Signature of person attesting

_____
Name of person attesting

_____
Title of person attesting

Annex 2

Application for approval of a plan of work for exploration to obtain a contract

Section I
Information concerning the applicant

1. Name of applicant:

2. Street address of applicant:

3. Postal address (if different from above):

4. Telephone number:

5. Facsimile number:

6. Electronic mail address:

7. Name of applicant's designated representative:

8. Street address of applicant's designated representative (if different from above):

9. Postal address (if different from above):

10. Telephone number:

11. Facsimile number:

12. Electronic mail address:

13. If the applicant is a juridical person, identify applicant's

    (a) Place of registration; and

    (b) Principal place of business/domicile.

and attach a copy of the applicant's certificate of registration.

14. Identify the sponsoring State or States.

15. In respect of each sponsoring State, provide the date of deposit of its instrument of ratification of, or accession or succession to, the 1982 United Nations Convention on the Law of the Sea and the date of its consent to be bound by the Agreement relating to the Implementation of Part XI of the United Nations Convention on the Law of the Sea of 10 December 1982.

16. A certificate of sponsorship issued by the sponsoring State must be attached with this application. If the applicant has more than one nationality, as in the case of a partnership or consortium of entities from more than one State, certificates of sponsorship issued by each of the States involved must be attached.

Section II
Information relating to the area under application

17. Define the boundaries of the blocks under application by attaching a chart (on a scale and projection specified by the Authority) and a list of geographical coordinates (in accordance with the World Geodetic System WGS 84).

18. Indicate whether the applicant elects to contribute a reserved area in accordance with regulation 17 or offer an equity interest in a joint venture arrangement in accordance with regulation 19.

19. If the applicant elects to contribute a reserved area:

(a) Attach a chart (on a scale and projection specified by the Authority) and a list of the coordinates dividing the total area into two parts of equal estimated commercial value; and

(b) Include in an attachment sufficient information to enable the Council to designate a reserved area based on the estimated commercial value of each part of the area under application. Such attachment must include the data available to the applicant with respect to both parts of the area under application, including:

(i) Data on the location, survey and evaluation of the polymetallic sulphides in the areas, including:

a. A description of the technology related to the recovery and processing of polymetallic sulphides that is necessary for making the designation of a reserved area;

b. A map of the physical and geological characteristics, such as seabed topography, bathymetry and bottom currents and information on the reliability of such data;

c. A map showing the remotely sensed data (such as electromagnetic surveys) and other survey data used to determine the lateral extent of each polymetallic sulphide bodies;

d. Drill core and other data used to determine the third dimension of the deposits and therefore used to determine the grade and tonnage of the polymetallic sulphide bodies;

e. Data showing the distribution of active and inactive polymetallic sulphide sites and the age that activity ceased in inactive sites and was initiated at active sites;

f. Data showing the average tonnage (in metric tonnes) of each polymetallic sulphide body that will comprise the mine site and an associated tonnage map showing the location of sampling sites;

g. Data showing the average elemental content of metals of economic interest (grade) based on chemical assays in (dry) weight per cent and an associated grade map for data among and within the polymetallic sulphide bodies;

h. Combined maps of tonnage and grade of polymetallic sulphides;

i. A calculation based on standard procedures, including statistical analysis, using the data submitted and assumptions made in the calculations that the two areas could be expected to contain polymetallic sulphides of equal estimated commercial value expressed as recoverable metals in mineable areas;

j. A description of the techniques used by the applicant;

(ii) Information concerning environmental parameters (seasonal and during test period) including, inter alia, wind speed and direction, water salinity, temperature and biological communities.

20. If the area under application includes any part of a reserved area, attach a list of coordinates of the area which forms part of the reserved area and indicate the applicant's qualifications in accordance with regulation 18 of the Regulations.

Section III
Financial and technical information

21. Attach sufficient information to enable the Council to determine whether the applicant is financially capable of carrying out the proposed plan of work for exploration and of fulfilling its financial obligations to the Authority:

(a) If the application is made by the Enterprise, attach certification by its competent authority that the Enterprise has the necessary financial resources to meet the estimated costs of the proposed plan of work for exploration;

(b) If the application is made by a State or a State enterprise, attach a statement by the State or the sponsoring State certifying that the applicant has the necessary financial resources to meet the estimated costs of the proposed plan of work for exploration;

(c) If the application is made by an entity, attach copies of the applicant's audited financial statements, including balance sheets and profit-and-loss statements, for the most recent three years in conformity with internationally accepted accounting principles and certified by a duly qualified firm of public accountants; and

(i) If the applicant is a newly organized entity and a certified balance sheet is not available, a pro forma balance sheet certified by an appropriate official of the applicant;

(ii) If the applicant is a subsidiary of another entity, copies of such financial statements of that entity and a statement from that entity in conformity with internationally accepted accounting practices and certified by a duly qualified firm of public accountants that the applicant will have the financial resources to carry out the plan of work for exploration;

(iii) If the applicant is controlled by a State or a State enterprise, a statement from the State or State enterprise certifying that the applicant will have the financial resources to carry out the plan of work for exploration.

22. If it is intended to finance the proposed plan of work for exploration by borrowings, attach a statement of the amount of such borrowings, the repayment period and the interest rate.

23. Attach sufficient information to enable the Council to determine whether the applicant is technically capable of carrying out the proposed plan of work for exploration, including:

(a) A general description of the applicant's previous experience, knowledge, skills, technical qualifications and expertise relevant to the proposed plan of work for exploration;

(b) A general description of the equipment and methods expected to be used in carrying out the proposed plan of work for exploration and other relevant non-proprietary information about the characteristics of such technology;

(c) A general description of the applicant's financial and technical capability to respond to any incident or activity which causes serious harm to the marine environment.

Section IV
The plan of work for exploration

24. Attach the following information relating to the plan of work for exploration:

(a) A general description and a schedule of the proposed exploration programme, including the programme of activities for the immediate five-year period, such as studies to be undertaken in respect of the environmental, technical, economic and other appropriate factors which must be taken into account in exploration;

(b) A description of a programme for oceanographic and environmental baseline studies in accordance with the Regulations and any environmental rules, regulations and procedures established by the Authority that would enable an assessment of the potential environmental impact including, but not restricted to, the impact on biodiversity, of the proposed exploration activities, taking into account any recommendations issued by the Legal and Technical Commission;

(c) A preliminary assessment of the possible impact of the proposed exploration activities on the marine environment;

(d) A description of proposed measures for the prevention, reduction and control of pollution and other hazards, as well as possible impacts, to the marine environment;

(e) A schedule of anticipated yearly expenditures in respect of the programme of activities for the immediate five-year period.

Section V
Undertakings

25. Attach a written undertaking that the applicant will:

(a) Accept as enforceable and comply with the applicable obligations created by the provisions of the Convention and the rules, regulations and procedures of the Authority, the decisions of the relevant organs of the Authority and the terms of its contracts with the Authority;

(b) Accept control by the Authority of activities in the Area as authorized by the Convention;

(c) Provide the Authority with a written assurance that its obligations under the contract will be fulfilled in good faith.

Section VI
Previous contracts

26. Has the applicant or, in the case of an application by a partnership or consortium of entities in a joint arrangement, any member of the partnership or consortium previously been awarded any contract with the Authority?

27. If the answer to 26 is "yes", the application must include:

   (a) The date of the previous contract or contracts;

   (b) The date, reference number and title of each report submitted to the Authority in connection with the contact or contracts; and

   (c) The date of termination of the contract or contracts, if applicable.

Section VII
Attachments

28. List all the attachments and annexes to this application (all data and information should be submitted in hard copy and in a digital format specified by the Authority):

Date:_____   _____

Signature of applicant's designated representative

ATTESTATION:

_____

Signature of person attesting

_____

Name of person attesting

_____

Title of person attesting

Annex 3

Contract for exploration

THIS CONTRACT made the day of between the INTERNATIONAL SEABED AUTHORITY represented by its SECRETARY-GENERAL (hereinafter referred to as "the Authority") and represented by (hereinafter referred to as "the Contractor") WITNESSETH as follows:

Incorporation of clauses

A. The standard clauses set out in annex 4 to the Regulations on Prospecting and Exploration for Polymetallic Sulphides in the Area shall be incorporated herein and shall have effect as if herein set out at length.

Exploration area

B. For the purposes of this contract, the "exploration area" means that part of the Area allocated to the Contractor for exploration, defined by the coordinates listed in schedule 1 hereto, as reduced from time to time in accordance with the standard clauses and the Regulations.

Grant of rights

C. In consideration of:

(1) Their mutual interest in the conduct of exploration activities in the exploration area pursuant to the Convention and the Agreement;

(2) The responsibility of the Authority to organize and control activities in the Area, particularly with a view to administering the resources of the Area, in accordance with the legal regime established in Part XI of the Convention and the Agreement and Part XII of the Convention respectively; and

(3) The interest and financial commitment of the Contractor in conducting activities in the exploration area and the mutual covenants made herein, the Authority hereby grants to the Contractor the exclusive right to explore for polymetallic sulphides in the exploration area in accordance with the terms and conditions of this contract.

Entry into force and contract term

D. This contract shall enter into force on signature by both parties and, subject to the standard clauses, shall remain in force for a period of fifteen years thereafter unless:

(1) The Contractor obtains a contract for exploitation in the exploration area which enters into force before the expiration of such period of fifteen years; or

(2) The contract is sooner terminated provided that the term of the contract may be extended in accordance with standard clauses 3.2 and 17.2.

Schedules

E. The schedules referred to in the standard clauses, namely section 4 and section 8, are for the purposes of this contract schedules 2 and 3 respectively.

Entire agreement

F. This contract expresses the entire agreement between the parties, and no oral understanding or prior writing shall modify the terms hereof.

IN WITNESS WHEREOF the undersigned, being duly authorized thereto by the respective parties, have signed this contract at …, this … day of …

Schedule 1

[Coordinates and illustrative chart of the exploration area]

Schedule 2

[The current five-year programme of activities as revised from time to time]

Schedule 3

[The training programme shall become a schedule to the contract when approved by the Authority in accordance with section 8 of the standard clauses.]

Annex 4

Standard clauses for exploration contract

Section 1
Definitions

1.1 In the following clauses:

(a) "exploration area" means that part of the Area allocated to the Contractor for exploration, described in schedule 1 hereto, as the same may be reduced from time to time in accordance with this contract and the Regulations;

(b) "programme of activities" means the programme of activities which is set out in schedule 2 hereto as the same may be adjusted from time to time in accordance with sections 4.3 and 4.4 hereof;

(c) "regulations" means the Regulations on Prospecting and Exploration for Polymetallic Sulphides in the Area, adopted by the Authority.

1.2 Terms and phrases defined in the Regulations shall have the same meaning in these standard clauses.

1.3 In accordance with the Agreement relating to the Implementation of Part XI of the United Nations Convention on the Law of the Sea of 10 December 1982, its provisions and Part XI of the Convention are to be interpreted and applied together as a single instrument; this contract and references in this contract to the Convention are to be interpreted and applied accordingly.

1.4 This contract includes the schedules to this contract, which shall be an integral part hereof.

Section 2
Security of tenure

2.1 The Contractor shall have security of tenure and this contract shall not be suspended, terminated or revised except in accordance with sections 20, 21 and 24 hereof.

2.2 The Contractor shall have the exclusive right to explore for polymetallic sulphides in the exploration area in accordance with the terms and conditions of this contract. The Authority shall ensure that no other entity operates in the exploration area for a different category of resources in a manner that might unreasonably interfere with the operations of the Contractor.

2.3 The Contractor, by notice to the Authority, shall have the right at any time to renounce without penalty the whole or part of its rights in the exploration area, provided that the Contractor shall remain liable for all obligations accrued prior to the date of such renunciation in respect of the area renounced.

2.4 Nothing in this contract shall be deemed to confer any right on the Contractor other than those rights expressly granted herein. The Authority reserves the right to enter into contracts with respect to resources other than polymetallic sulphides with third parties in the area covered by this contract.

Section 3
Contract term

3.1 This contract shall enter into force on signature by both parties and shall remain in force for a period of fifteen years thereafter unless:

(a) The Contractor obtains a contract for exploitation in the exploration area which enters into force before the expiration of such period of fifteen years; or

(b) The contract is sooner terminated,

provided that the term of the contract may be extended in accordance with sections 3.2 and 17.2 hereof.

3.2 Upon application by the Contractor, not later than six months before the expiration of this contract, this contract may be extended for periods of not more than five years each on such terms and conditions as the Authority and the Contractor may then agree in accordance with the Regulations. Such extensions shall be approved if the Contractor has made efforts in good faith to comply with the requirements of this contract but for reasons beyond the Contractor's control has been unable to complete the necessary preparatory work for proceeding to the exploitation stage or if the prevailing economic circumstances do not justify proceeding to the exploitation stage.

3.3 Notwithstanding the expiration of this contract in accordance with section 3.1 hereof, if the Contractor has, at least 90 days prior to the date of expiration, applied for a contract for exploitation, the Contractor's rights and obligations under this contract shall continue until such time as the application has been considered and a contract for exploitation has been issued or refused.

Section 4
Exploration

4.1 The Contractor shall commence exploration in accordance with the time schedule stipulated in the programme of activities set out in schedule 2 hereto and shall adhere to such time periods or any modification thereto as provided for by this contract.

4.2 The Contractor shall carry out the programme of activities set out in schedule 2 hereto. In carrying out such activities the Contractor shall spend in each contract year not less than the amount specified in such programme, or any agreed review thereof, in actual and direct exploration expenditures.

4.3 The Contractor, with the consent of the Authority, which consent shall not be unreasonably withheld, may from time to time make such changes in the programme of activities and the expenditures specified therein as may be necessary and prudent in accordance with good mining industry practice, and taking into account the market conditions for the metals contained in polymetallic sulphides and other relevant global economic conditions.

4.4 Not later than 90 days prior to the expiration of each five-year period from the date on which this contract enters into force in accordance with section 3 hereof, the Contractor and the Secretary-General shall jointly undertake a review of the implementation of the plan of work for exploration under this contract. The Secretary-General may require the Contractor to submit such additional data and information as may be necessary for the purposes of the review. In the light of the review, the Contractor shall make such adjustments to its plan of work as are necessary and shall indicate its programme of activities for the following five-year period, including a revised schedule of anticipated yearly expenditures. Schedule 2 hereto shall be adjusted accordingly.

Section 5
Environmental monitoring

5.1 The Contractor shall take necessary measures to prevent, reduce and control pollution and other hazards to the marine environment arising from its activities in the Area as far as reasonably possible applying a precautionary approach and best environmental practices.

5.2 Prior to the commencement of exploration activities, the Contractor shall submit to the Authority:

(a) An impact assessment of the potential effects on the marine environment of the proposed activities;

(b) A proposal for a monitoring programme to determine the potential effect on the marine environment of the proposed activities; and

(c) Data that could be used to establish an environmental baseline against which to assess the effect of the proposed activities.

5.3 The Contractor shall, in accordance with the Regulations, gather environmental baseline data as exploration activities progress and develop and shall establish environmental baselines against which to assess the likely effects of the Contractor's activities on the marine environment.

5.4 The Contractor shall, in accordance with the Regulations, establish and carry out a programme to monitor and report on such effects on the marine environment. The Contractor shall cooperate with the Authority in the implementation of such monitoring.

5.5 The Contractor shall, within 90 days of the end of each calendar year, report to the Secretary-General on the implementation and results of the monitoring programme referred to in section 5.4 hereof and shall submit data and information in accordance with the Regulations.

Section 6
Contingency plans and emergencies

6.1 The Contractor shall, prior to the commencement of its programme of activities under this contract, submit to the Secretary-General a contingency plan to respond effectively to incidents that are likely to cause serious harm or a threat of serious harm to the marine environment arising from the Contractor's activities at sea in the exploration area. Such contingency plan shall establish special procedures and provide for adequate and appropriate equipment to deal with such incidents and, in particular, shall include arrangements for:

(a) The immediate raising of a general alarm in the area of the exploration activities;

(b) Immediate notification to the Secretary-General;

(c) The warning of ships which might be about to enter the immediate vicinity;

(d) A continuing flow of full information to the Secretary-General relating to particulars of the contingency measures already taken and further actions required;

(e) The removal, as appropriate, of polluting substances;

(f) The reduction and, so far as reasonably possible, prevention of serious harm to the marine environment, as well as mitigation of such effects;

(g) As appropriate, cooperation with other contractors with the Authority to respond to an emergency; and

(h) Periodic emergency response exercises.

6.2 The Contractor shall promptly report to the Secretary-General any incident arising from its activities that has caused, is causing or poses a threat of serious harm to the marine environment. Each such report shall contain the details of such incident, including, inter alia:

(a) The coordinates of the area affected or which can reasonably be anticipated to be affected;

(b) The description of the action being taken by the Contractor to prevent, contain, minimize and repair the serious harm or threat of serious harm to the marine environment;

(c) A description of the action being taken by the Contractor to monitor the effects of the incident on the marine environment; and

(d) Such supplementary information as may reasonably be required by the Secretary-General.

6.3 The Contractor shall comply with emergency orders issued by the Council and immediate measures of a temporary nature issued by the Secretary-General in accordance with the Regulations, to prevent, contain, minimize or repair serious harm or the threat of serious harm to the marine environment, which may include orders to the Contractor to immediately suspend or adjust any activities in the exploration area.

6.4 If the Contractor does not promptly comply with such emergency orders or immediate measures of a temporary nature, the Council may take such reasonable measures as are necessary to prevent, contain, minimize or repair any such serious harm or the threat of serious harm to the marine environment at the Contractor's expense. The Contractor shall promptly reimburse the Authority the amount of such expenses. Such expenses shall be in addition to any monetary penalties which may be imposed on the Contractor pursuant to the terms of this contract or the Regulations.

Section 7
Human remains and objects and sites of an archaeological or historical nature

The Contractor shall immediately notify the Secretary-General in writing of any finding in the exploration area of any human remains of an archaeological or historical nature, or any object or site of a similar nature and its location, including the preservation and protection measures taken. The Secretary-General shall

transmit such information to the Director-General of the United Nations Educational, Scientific and Cultural Organization and any other competent international organization. Following the finding of any such human remains, object or site in the exploration area, and in order to avoid disturbing such human remains, object or site, no further prospecting or exploration shall take place, within a reasonable radius, until such time as the Council decides otherwise after taking account of the views of the Director-General of the United Nations Educational, Scientific and Cultural Organization or any other competent international organization.

Section 8
Training

8.1 In accordance with the Regulations, the Contractor shall, prior to the commencement of exploration under this contract, submit to the Authority for approval proposed training programmes for the training of personnel of the Authority and developing States, including the participation of such personnel in all of the Contractor's activities under this contract.

8.2 The scope and financing of the training programme shall be subject to negotiation between the Contractor, the Authority and the sponsoring State or States.

8.3 The Contractor shall conduct training programmes in accordance with the specific programme for the training of personnel referred to in section 8.1 hereof approved by the Authority in accordance with the Regulations, which programme, as revised and developed from time to time, shall become a part of this contract as schedule 3.

Section 9
Books and records

The Contractor shall keep a complete and proper set of books, accounts and financial records, consistent with internationally accepted accounting principles. Such books, accounts and financial records shall include information which will fully disclose the actual and direct expenditures for exploration and such other information as will facilitate an effective audit of such expenditures.

Section 10
Annual reports

10.1 The Contractor shall, within 90 days of the end of each calendar year, submit a report to the Secretary-General in such format as may be recommended from time to time by the Legal and Technical Commission covering its programme of activities in the exploration area and containing, as applicable, information in sufficient detail on:

(a) The exploration work carried out during the calendar year, including maps, charts and graphs illustrating the work that has been done and the results obtained;

(b) The equipment used to carry out the exploration work, including the results of tests conducted of proposed mining technologies, but not equipment design data; and

(c) The implementation of training programmes, including any proposed revisions to or developments of such programmes.

10.2 Such reports shall also contain:

(a) The results obtained from environmental monitoring programmes, including observations, measurements, evaluations and analyses of environmental parameters;

(b) A statement of the quantity of polymetallic sulphides recovered as samples or for the purpose of testing;

(c) A statement, in conformity with internationally accepted accounting principles and certified by a duly qualified firm of public accountants, or, where the Contractor is a State or a State enterprise, by the sponsoring State, of the actual and direct exploration expenditures of the Contractor in carrying out the programme of activities during the Contractor's accounting year. Such expenditures may be claimed by the contractor as part of the contractor's development costs incurred prior to the commencement of commercial production; and

(d) Details of any proposed adjustments to the programme of activities and the reasons for such adjustments.

10.3 The Contractor shall also submit such additional information to supplement the reports referred to in section 10.1 and 10.2 hereof as the Secretary-General may from time to time reasonably require in order to carry out the Authority's functions under the Convention, the Regulations and this contract.

10.4 The Contractor shall keep, in good condition, a representative portion of samples and cores of the polymetallic sulphides obtained in the course of exploration until the expiration of this contract. The Authority may request the Contractor in writing to deliver to it for analysis a portion of any such sample and cores obtained during the course of exploration.

10.5 The contractor shall pay at the time of submission of the annual report an annual overhead charge of $47,000 (or such sum as may be fixed in accordance with section 10.6 hereof) to cover the Authority's costs of the administration and supervision of this contract and of reviewing the reports submitted in accordance with section 10.1 hereof.

10.6 The amount of the annual overhead charge may be revised by the Authority to reflect its costs actually and reasonably incurred.[4]

Section 11
Data and information to be submitted on expiration of the contract

11.1 The Contractor shall transfer to the Authority all data and information that are both necessary for and relevant to the effective exercise of the powers and functions of the Authority in respect of the exploration area in accordance with the provisions of this section.

---

[4] ISBA/19/A/12, dated 25 July 2013, Amendments.

11.2 Upon expiration or termination of this contract the Contractor, if it has not already done so, shall submit the following data and information to the Secretary-General:

(a) Copies of geological, environmental, geochemical and geophysical data acquired by the Contractor in the course of carrying out the programme of activities that are necessary for and relevant to the effective exercise of the powers and functions of the Authority in respect of the exploration area;

(b) The estimation of mineable deposits, when such deposits have been identified, which shall include details of the grade and quantity of the proven, probable and possible polymetallic sulphide reserves and the anticipated mining conditions;

(c) Copies of geological, technical, financial and economic reports made by or for the Contractor that are necessary for and relevant to the effective exercise of the powers and functions of the Authority in respect of the exploration area;

(d) Information in sufficient detail on the equipment used to carry out the exploration work, including the results of tests conducted of proposed mining technologies, but not equipment design data;

(e) A statement of the quantity of polymetallic sulphides recovered as samples or for the purpose of testing; and

(f) A statement on how and where samples of cores are archived and their availability to the Authority.

11.3 The data and information referred to in section 11.2 hereof shall also be submitted to the Secretary-General if, prior to the expiration of this contract, the Contractor applies for approval of a plan of work for exploitation or if the Contractor renounces its rights in the exploration area to the extent that such data and information relates to the renounced area.

Section 12
Confidentiality

Data and information transferred to the Authority in accordance with this contract shall be treated as confidential in accordance with the provisions of the Regulations.

Section 13
Undertakings

13.1 The Contractor shall carry out exploration in accordance with the terms and conditions of this contract, the Regulations, Part XI of the Convention, the Agreement and other rules of international law not incompatible with the Convention.

13.2 The Contractor undertakes:

(a) To accept as enforceable and comply with the terms of this contract;

(b) To comply with the applicable obligations created by the provisions of the Convention, the rules, regulations and procedures of the Authority and the decisions of the relevant organs of the Authority;

(c) To accept control by the Authority of activities in the Area as authorized by the Convention;

(d) To fulfil its obligations under this contract in good faith; and

(e) To observe, as far as reasonably practicable, any recommendations which may be issued from time to time by the Legal and Technical Commission.

13.3 The Contractor shall actively carry out the programme of activities:

(a) With due diligence, efficiency and economy;

(b) With due regard to the impact of its activities on the marine environment; and

(c) With reasonable regard for other activities in the marine environment.

13.4 The Authority undertakes to fulfil in good faith its powers and functions under the Convention and the Agreement in accordance with article 157 of the Convention.

Section 14
Inspection

14.1 The Contractor shall permit the Authority to send its inspectors on board vessels and installations used by the Contractor to carry out activities in the exploration area to:

(a) Monitor the Contractor's compliance with the terms and conditions of this contract and the Regulations; and

(b) Monitor the effects of such activities on the marine environment.

14.2 The Secretary-General shall give reasonable notice to the Contractor of the projected time and duration of inspections, the name of the inspectors and any activities the inspectors are to perform that are likely to require the availability of special equipment or special assistance from personnel of the Contractor.

14.3 Such inspectors shall have the authority to inspect any vessel or installation, including its log, equipment, records, facilities, all other recorded data and any relevant documents which are necessary to monitor the Contractor's compliance.

14.4 The Contractor, its agents and employees shall assist the inspectors in the performance of their duties and shall:

(a) Accept and facilitate prompt and safe boarding of vessels and installations by inspectors;

(b) Cooperate with and assist in the inspection of any vessel or installation conducted pursuant to these procedures;

(c) Provide access to all relevant equipment, facilities and personnel on vessels and installations at all reasonable times;

(d) Not obstruct, intimidate or interfere with inspectors in the performance of their duties;

(e) Provide reasonable facilities, including, where appropriate, food and accommodation, to inspectors; and

(f) Facilitate safe disembarkation by inspectors.

14.5 Inspectors shall avoid interference with the safe and normal operations on board vessels and installations used by the Contractor to carry out activities in the area visited and shall act in accordance with the Regulations and the measures adopted to protect confidentiality of data and information.

14.6 The Secretary-General and any duly authorized representatives of the Secretary-General, shall have access, for purposes of audit and examination, to any books, documents, papers and records of the Contractor which are necessary and directly pertinent to verify the expenditures referred to in section 10.2 (c).

14.7 The Secretary-General shall provide relevant information contained in the reports of inspectors to the Contractor and its sponsoring State or States where action is necessary.

14.8 If for any reason the Contractor does not pursue exploration and does not request a contract for exploitation, it shall, before withdrawing from the exploration area, notify the Secretary-General in writing in order to permit the Authority, if it so decides, to carry out an inspection pursuant to this section.

Section 15
Safety, labour and health standards

15.1 The Contractor shall comply with the generally accepted international rules and standards established by competent international organizations or general diplomatic conferences concerning the safety of life at sea, and the prevention of collisions and such rules, regulations and procedures as may be adopted by the Authority relating to safety at sea. Each vessel used for carrying out activities in the Area shall possess current valid certificates required by and issued pursuant to such international rules and standards.

15.2 The Contractor shall, in carrying out exploration under this contract, observe and comply with such rules, regulations and procedures as may be adopted by the Authority relating to protection against discrimination in employment, occupational safety and health, labour relations, social security, employment security and living conditions at the work site. Such rules, regulations and procedures shall take into account conventions and recommendations of the International Labour Organization and other competent international organizations.

Section 16
Responsibility and liability

16.1 The Contractor shall be liable for the actual amount of any damage, including damage to the marine environment, arising out of its wrongful acts or omissions, and those of its employees, subcontractors, agents and all persons engaged in working or acting for them in the conduct of its operations under this contract, including the costs of reasonable measures to prevent or limit damage to the marine environment, account being taken of any contributory acts or omissions by the Authority.

16.2 The Contractor shall indemnify the Authority, its employees, subcontractors and agents against all claims and liabilities of any third party arising out of any wrongful acts or omissions of the Contractor and its employees, agents and subcontractors, and all persons engaged in working or acting for them in the conduct of its operations under this contract.

16.3 The Authority shall be liable for the actual amount of any damage to the Contractor arising out of its wrongful acts in the exercise of its powers and functions, including violations under article 168, paragraph 2, of the Convention, account being taken of contributory acts or omissions by the Contractor, its employees, agents and subcontractors, and all persons engaged in working or acting for them in the conduct of its operations under this contract.

16.4 The Authority shall indemnify the Contractor, its employees, subcontractors, agents and all persons engaged in working or acting for them in the conduct of its operations under this contract, against all claims and liabilities of any third party arising out of any wrongful acts or omissions in the exercise of its powers and functions hereunder, including violations under article 168, paragraph 2, of the Convention.

16.5 The Contractor shall maintain appropriate insurance policies with internationally recognized carriers, in accordance with generally accepted international maritime practice.

Section 17
Force majeure

17.1 The Contractor shall not be liable for an unavoidable delay or failure to perform any of its obligations under this contract due to force majeure. For the purposes of this contract, force majeure shall mean an event or condition that the Contractor could not reasonably be expected to prevent or control; provided that the event or condition was not caused by negligence or by a failure to observe good mining industry practice.

17.2 The Contractor shall, upon request, be granted a time extension equal to the period by which performance was delayed hereunder by force majeure and the term of this contract shall be extended accordingly.

17.3 In the event of force majeure, the Contractor shall take all reasonable measures to remove its inability to perform and comply with the terms and conditions of this contract with a minimum of delay.

17.4 The Contractor shall give notice to the Authority of the occurrence of an event of force majeure as soon as reasonably possible, and similarly give notice to the Authority of the restoration of normal conditions.

Section 18
Disclaimer

Neither the Contractor nor any affiliated company or subcontractor shall in any manner claim or suggest, whether expressly or by implication, that the Authority or any official thereof has, or has expressed, any opinion with respect to polymetallic sulphides in the exploration area and a statement to that effect shall not be included in or endorsed on any prospectus, notice, circular, advertisement, press release or similar document issued by the Contractor, any affiliated company or any subcontractor that refers directly or indirectly to this contract. For the purposes of this section, an "affiliated company" means any person, firm or company or State-owned entity controlling, controlled by, or under common control with, the Contractor.

Section 19
Renunciation of rights

The Contractor, by notice to the Authority, shall have the right to renounce its rights and terminate this contract without penalty, provided that the Contractor shall remain liable for all obligations accrued prior to the date of such renunciation and those obligations required to be fulfilled after termination in accordance with the Regulations.

Section 20
Termination of sponsorship

20.1 If the nationality or control of the Contractor changes or the Contractor's sponsoring State, as defined in the Regulations, terminates its sponsorship, the Contractor shall promptly notify the Authority forthwith.

20.2 In either such event, if the Contractor does not obtain another sponsor meeting the requirements prescribed in the Regulations which submits to the Authority a certificate of sponsorship for the Contractor in the prescribed form within the time specified in the Regulations, this contract shall terminate forthwith.

Section 21
Suspension and termination of contract and penalties

21.1 The Council may suspend or terminate this contract, without prejudice to any other rights that the Authority may have, if any of the following events should occur:

(a) If, in spite of written warnings by the Authority, the Contractor has conducted its activities in such a way as to result in serious persistent and wilful violations of the fundamental terms of this contract, Part XI of the Convention, the Agreement and the rules, regulations and procedures of the Authority; or

(b) If the Contractor has failed to comply with a final binding decision of the dispute settlement body applicable to it; or

(c) If the Contractor becomes insolvent or commits an act of bankruptcy or enters into any agreement for composition with its creditors or goes into liquidation or receivership, whether compulsory or voluntary, or petitions or applies to any tribunal for the appointment of a receiver or a trustee or receiver for itself or commences any proceedings relating to itself under any bankruptcy, insolvency or readjustment of debt law, whether now or hereafter in effect, other than for the purpose of reconstruction.

21.2 The Council may, without prejudice to Section 17, after consultation with the contractor, suspend or terminate this contract, without prejudice to any other rights that the Authority may have, if the Contractor is prevented from performing its obligations under this contract by reason of an event or condition of force majeure, as described in Section 17.1, which has persisted for a continuous period exceeding two years, despite the Contractor having taken all reasonable measures to remove its inability to perform and comply with the terms and conditions of this contract with a minimum of delay.

21.3 Any suspension or termination shall be by notice, through the Secretary-General, which shall include a statement of the reasons for taking such action. The suspension or termination shall be effective 60 days after such notice, unless the Contractor within such period disputes the Authority's right to suspend or terminate this contract in accordance with Part XI, section 5, of the Convention.

21.4 If the Contractor takes such action, this contract shall only be suspended or terminated in accordance with a final binding decision in accordance with Part XI, section 5, of the Convention.

21.5 If the Council has suspended this contract, the Council may by notice require the Contractor to resume its operations and comply with the terms and conditions of this contract, not later than 60 days after such notice.

21.6 In the case of any violation of this contract not covered by section 21.1 (a) hereof, or in lieu of suspension or termination under section 21.1 hereof, the Council may impose upon the Contractor monetary penalties proportionate to the seriousness of the violation.

21.7 The Council may not execute a decision involving monetary penalties until the Contractor has been accorded a reasonable opportunity to exhaust the judicial remedies available to it pursuant to Part XI, section 5, of the Convention.

21.8 In the event of termination or expiration of this contract, the Contractor shall comply with the Regulations and shall remove all installations, plant, equipment and materials in the exploration area and shall make the area safe so as not to constitute a danger to persons, shipping or to the marine environment.

Section 22
Transfer of rights and obligations

22.1 The rights and obligations of the Contractor under this contract may be transferred in whole or in part only with the consent of the Authority and in accordance with the Regulations.

22.2 The Authority shall not unreasonably withhold consent to the transfer if the proposed transferee is in all respects a qualified applicant in accordance with the Regulations and assumes all of the obligations of the Contractor and if the transfer does not confer to the transferee a plan of work, the approval of which would be forbidden by Annex III, article 6, paragraph 3 (c), of the Convention.

22.3 The terms, undertakings and conditions of this contract shall inure to the benefit of and be binding upon the parties hereto and their respective successors and assigns.

Section 23
No waiver

No waiver by either party of any rights pursuant to a breach of the terms and conditions of this contract to be performed by the other party shall be construed as a waiver by the party of any succeeding breach of the same or any other term or condition to be performed by the other party.

Section 24
Revision

24.1 When circumstances have arisen or are likely to arise which, in the opinion of the Authority or the Contractor, would render this contract inequitable or make it impracticable or impossible to achieve the objectives set out in this contract or in Part XI of the Convention or the Agreement, the parties shall enter into negotiations to revise it accordingly.

24.2 This contract may also be revised by agreement between the Contractor and the Authority to facilitate the application of any rules, regulations and procedures adopted by the Authority subsequent to the entry into force of this contract.

24.3 This contract may be revised, amended or otherwise modified only with the consent of the Contractor and the Authority by an appropriate instrument signed by the authorized representatives of the parties.

Section 25
Disputes

25.1 Any dispute between the parties concerning the interpretation or application of this contract shall be settled in accordance with Part XI, section 5, of the Convention.

25.2 In accordance with article 21, paragraph 2, of Annex III to the Convention, any final decision rendered by a court or tribunal having jurisdiction under the Convention relating to the rights and obligations of the Authority and of the Contractor shall be enforceable in the territory of any State Party to the Convention affected thereby.

Section 26
Notice

26.1 Any application, request, notice, report, consent, approval, waiver, direction or instruction hereunder shall be made by the Secretary-General or by the designated representative of the Contractor, as the case may be, in writing. Service shall be by hand, or by telex, facsimile, registered airmail or electronic mail containing an authorized signature to the Secretary-General at the headquarters of the Authority or to the designated representative. The requirement to provide any information in writing under these Regulations is satisfied by the provision of the information in an electronic document containing a digital signature.

26.2 Either party shall be entitled to change any such address to any other address by not less than ten days' notice to the other party.

26.3 Delivery by hand shall be effective when made. Delivery by telex shall be deemed to be effective on the business day following the day when the "answer back" appears on the sender's telex machine. Delivery by facsimile shall be effective when the "transmit confirmation report" confirming the transmission to the recipient's published facsimile number is received by the transmitter. Delivery by registered airmail shall be deemed to be effective 21 days after posting. An electronic document is presumed to have been received by the addressee when it enters an information system designated or used by the addressee for the purpose of receiving documents of the type sent and it is capable of being retrieved and processed by the addressee.

26.4 Notice to the designated representative of the Contractor shall constitute effective notice to the Contractor for all purposes under this contract, and the designated representative shall be the Contractor's agent for the service of process or notification in any proceeding of any court or tribunal having jurisdiction.

26.5 Notice to the Secretary-General shall constitute effective notice to the Authority for all purposes under this contract, and the Secretary-General shall be the Authority's agent for the service of process or notification in any proceeding of any court or tribunal having jurisdiction.

Section 27
Applicable law

27.1 This contract shall be governed by the terms of this contract, the rules, regulations and procedures of the Authority, Part XI of the Convention, the Agreement and other rules of international law not incompatible with the Convention.

27.2 The Contractor, its employees, subcontractors, agents and all persons engaged in working or acting for them in the conduct of its operations under this contract shall observe the applicable law referred to in section 27.1 hereof and shall not engage in any transaction, directly or indirectly, prohibited by the applicable law.

27.3 Nothing contained in this contract shall be deemed an exemption from the necessity of applying for and obtaining any permit or authority that may be required for any activities under this contract.

Section 28
Interpretation

The division of this contract into sections and subsections and the insertion of headings are for convenience of reference only and shall not affect the construction or interpretation hereof.

Section 29
Additional documents

Each party hereto agrees to execute and deliver all such further instruments, and to do and perform all such further acts and things as may be necessary or expedient to give effect to the provisions of this contract.

International Seabed Authority

Assembly

ISBA/18/A/11

Distr.: General
22 October 2012

Original: English

Eighteenth session
Kingston, Jamaica
16-27 July 2012

Decision of the Assembly of the International Seabed Authority relating to the Regulations on Prospecting and Exploration for Cobalt-rich Ferromanganese Crusts in the Area

The Assembly of the International Seabed Authority,

Having considered the Regulations on Prospecting and Exploration for Cobalt-rich Ferromanganese Crusts in the Area, as provisionally adopted by the Council at its 181st meeting, on 26 July 2012,

Approves the Regulations on Prospecting and Exploration for Cobalt-rich Ferromanganese Crusts in the Area as contained in the annex to the present decision.

138th meeting
27 July 2012

Annex

Regulations on Prospecting and Exploration for Cobalt-rich Ferromanganese Crusts in the Area

Preamble

In accordance with the United Nations Convention on the Law of the Sea of 10 December 1982 ("the Convention"), the seabed and ocean floor and the subsoil thereof beyond the limits of national jurisdiction, as well as its resources, are the common heritage of mankind, the exploration and exploitation of which shall be carried out for the benefit of mankind as a whole, on whose behalf the International Seabed Authority acts. The objective of this set of Regulations is to provide for prospecting and exploration for cobalt-rich ferromanganese crusts.

Part I
Introduction

Regulation 1
Use of terms and scope

1. Terms used in the Convention shall have the same meaning in these Regulations.

2. In accordance with the Agreement relating to the Implementation of Part XI of the United Nations Convention on the Law of the Sea of 10 December 1982 ("the Agreement"), the provisions of the Agreement and Part XI of the Convention shall be interpreted and applied together as a single instrument. These Regulations and references in these Regulations to the Convention are to be interpreted and applied accordingly.

3. For the purposes of these Regulations:

    (a) "Cobalt crusts" means cobalt-rich iron/manganese (ferromanganese) hydroxide/oxide deposits formed from direct precipitation of minerals from seawater onto hard substrates containing minor but significant concentrations of cobalt, titanium, nickel, platinum, molybdenum, tellurium, cerium, other metallic and rare earth elements;

    (b) "Exploitation" means the recovery for commercial purposes of cobalt crusts in the Area and the extraction of minerals therefrom, including the construction and operation of mining, processing and transportation systems, for the production and marketing of metals;

    (c) "Exploration" means the searching for deposits of cobalt crusts in the Area with exclusive rights, the analysis of such deposits, the use and testing of recovery systems and equipment, processing facilities and transportation systems and the carrying out of studies of the environmental, technical, economic, commercial and other appropriate factors that must be taken into account in exploitation;

    (d) "Marine environment" includes the physical, chemical, geological and biological components, conditions and factors which interact and determine the productivity, state, condition and quality of the marine ecosystem, the waters of the seas and oceans and the airspace above those waters, as well as the seabed and ocean floor and subsoil thereof;

(e) "Prospecting" means the search for deposits of cobalt crusts in the Area, including estimation of the composition, sizes and distributions of deposits of cobalt crusts and their economic values, without any exclusive rights;

(f) "Serious harm to the marine environment" means any effect from activities in the Area on the marine environment which represents a significant adverse change in the marine environment determined according to the rules, regulations and procedures adopted by the Authority on the basis of internationally recognized standards and practices.

4. These Regulations shall not in any way affect the freedom of scientific research, pursuant to article 87 of the Convention, or the right to conduct marine scientific research in the Area pursuant to articles 143 and 256 of the Convention. Nothing in these Regulations shall be construed in such a way as to restrict the exercise by States of the freedom of the high seas as reflected in article 87 of the Convention.

5. These Regulations may be supplemented by further rules, regulations and procedures, in particular on the protection and preservation of the marine environment. These Regulations shall be subject to the provisions of the Convention and the Agreement and other rules of international law not incompatible with the Convention.

Part II
Prospecting

Regulation 2
Prospecting

1. Prospecting shall be conducted in accordance with the Convention and these Regulations and may commence only after the prospector has been informed by the Secretary-General that its notification has been recorded pursuant to regulation 4 (2).

2. Prospectors and the Authority shall apply a precautionary approach, as reflected in principle 15 of the Rio Declaration on Environment and Development.[1]

3. Prospecting shall not be undertaken if substantial evidence indicates the risk of serious harm to the marine environment.

4. Prospecting shall not be undertaken in an area covered by an approval plan of work for exploration for cobalt crusts or in a reserved area; nor may there be prospecting in an area which the International Seabed Authority Council has disapproved for exploitation because of the risk of serious harm to the marine environment.

---

[1] *Report of the United Nations Conference on Environment and Development, Rio de Janeiro, 3-14 June 1992* (United Nations publication, Sales No. E.93.I.8 and corrigendum), vol. I, *Resolutions adopted by the Conference*, resolution 1, annex I.

5. Prospecting shall not confer on the prospector any rights with respect to resources. A prospector may, however, recover a reasonable quantity of minerals, being the quantity necessary for testing and not for commercial use.

6. There shall be no time limit on prospecting except that prospecting in a particular area shall cease upon written notification to the prospector by the Secretary-General that a plan of work for exploration has been approved with regard to that area.

7. Prospecting may be conducted simultaneously by more than one prospector in the same area or areas.

Regulation 3
Notification of prospecting

1. A proposed prospector shall notify the Authority of its intention to engage in prospecting.

2. Each notification of prospecting shall be in the form prescribed in annex I to these Regulations, shall be addressed to the Secretary-General and shall conform to the requirements of these Regulations.

3. Each notification shall be submitted:

(a) In the case of a State, by the authority designated for that purpose by it;

(b) In the case of an entity, by its designated representative;

(c) In the case of the Enterprise, by its competent authority.

4. Each notification shall be in one of the languages of the Authority and shall contain:

(a) The name, nationality and address of the proposed prospector and its designated representative;

(b) The coordinates of the broad area or areas within which prospecting is to be conducted, in accordance with the most recent generally accepted international standard used by the Authority;

(c) A general description of the prospecting programme, including the proposed date of commencement and its approximate duration;

(d) A satisfactory written undertaking that the proposed prospector will:

(i) Comply with the Convention and the relevant rules, regulations and procedures of the Authority concerning:

a. Cooperation in the training programmes in connection with marine scientific research and transfer of technology referred to in articles 143 and 144 of the Convention; and

b. Protection and preservation of the marine environment;

(ii) Accept verification by the Authority of compliance therewith; and

(iii) Make available to the Authority, as far as practicable, such data as may be relevant to the protection and preservation of the marine environment.

Regulation 4
Consideration of notifications

1. The Secretary-General shall acknowledge in writing receipt of each notification submitted under regulation 3, specifying the date of receipt.

2. The Secretary-General shall review and act on the notification within 45 days of its receipt. If the notification conforms with the requirements of the Convention and these Regulations, the Secretary-General shall record the particulars of the notification in a register maintained for that purpose and shall inform the prospector in writing that the notification has been so recorded.

3. The Secretary-General shall, within 45 days of receipt of the notification, inform the proposed prospector in writing if the notification includes any part of an area included in an approved plan of work for exploration or exploitation of any category of resources, or any part of a reserved area, or any part of an area which has been disapproved by the Council for exploitation because of the risk of serious harm to the marine environment, or if the written undertaking is not satisfactory, and shall provide the proposed prospector with a written statement of reasons. In such cases, the proposed prospector may, within 90 days, submit an amended notification. The Secretary-General shall, within 45 days, review and act upon such amended notification.

4. A prospector shall inform the Secretary-General in writing of any change in the information contained in the notification.

5. The Secretary-General shall not release any particulars contained in the notification except with the written consent of the prospector. The Secretary-General shall, however, from time to time inform all members of the Authority of the identity of prospectors and the general areas in which prospecting is being conducted.

Regulation 5
Protection and preservation of the marine environment during prospecting

1. Each prospector shall take necessary measures to prevent, reduce and control pollution and other hazards to the marine environment arising from prospecting as far as reasonably possible, applying a precautionary approach and best environmental practices. In particular, each prospector shall minimize or eliminate:

   (a) Adverse environmental impacts from prospecting; and

   (b) Actual or potential conflicts or interference with existing or planned marine scientific research activities, in accordance with the relevant future guidelines in this regard.

2. Prospectors shall cooperate with the Authority in the establishment and implementation of programmes for monitoring and evaluating the potential impacts of the exploration for and exploitation of cobalt crusts on the marine environment.

3. A prospector shall immediately notify the Secretary-General in writing, using the most effective means, of any incident arising from prospecting which has caused, is causing or poses a threat of serious harm to the marine environment. Upon receipt of such notification the Secretary-General shall act in a manner consistent with regulation 35.

Regulation 6
Annual report

1. A prospector shall, within 90 days of the end of each calendar year, submit a report to the Authority on the status of prospecting. Such reports shall be submitted by the Secretary-General to the Legal and Technical Commission. Each such report shall contain:

    (a) A general description of the status of prospecting and of the results obtained;

    (b) Information on compliance with the undertakings referred to in regulation 3 (4) (d); and

    (c) Information on adherence to the relevant guidelines in this regard.

2. If the prospector intends to claim expenditures for prospecting as part of the development costs incurred prior to the commencement of commercial production, the prospector shall submit an annual statement, in conformity with internationally accepted accounting principles and certified by a duly qualified firm of public accountants, of the actual and direct expenditures incurred by the prospector in carrying out prospecting.

Regulation 7
Confidentiality of data and information from prospecting contained in the annual report

1. The Secretary-General shall ensure the confidentiality of all data and information contained in the reports submitted under regulation 6 applying mutatis mutandis the provisions of regulations 38 and 39, provided that data and information relating to the protection and preservation of the marine environment, in particular those from environmental monitoring programmes, shall not be considered confidential. The prospector may request that such data not be disclosed for up to three years following the date of their submission.

2. The Secretary-General may, at any time, with the consent of the prospector concerned, release data and information relating to prospecting in an area in respect of which a notification has been submitted. If, after having made reasonable efforts for at least two years, the Secretary-General determines that the prospector no longer exists or cannot be located, the Secretary-General may release such data and information.

Regulation 8
Objects of an archaeological or historical nature

A prospector shall immediately notify the Secretary-General in writing of any finding in the Area of an object of actual or potential archaeological or historical nature and its location. The Secretary-General shall transmit such information to the Director-General of the United Nations Educational, Scientific and Cultural Organization.

Part III
Applications for approval of plans of work for exploration in the form of contracts

Section 1
General provisions

Regulation 9
General

Subject to the provisions of the Convention, the following may apply to the Authority for approval of plans of work for exploration:

(a) The Enterprise, on its own behalf or in a joint arrangement;

(b) States parties, State enterprises or natural or juridical persons which possess the nationality of States or are effectively controlled by them or their nationals, when sponsored by such States, or any group of the foregoing which meets the requirements of these Regulations.

Section 2
Content of applications

Regulation 10
Form of applications

1. Each application for approval of a plan of work for exploration shall be in the form prescribed in annex II to these Regulations, shall be addressed to the Secretary-General and shall conform to the requirements of these Regulations.

2. Each application shall be submitted:

   (a) In the case of a State, by the authority designated for that purpose by it;

   (b) In the case of an entity, by its designated representative or the authority designated for that purpose by the sponsoring State or States; and

   (c) In the case of the Enterprise, by its competent authority.

3. Each application by a State enterprise or one of the entities referred to in regulation 9 (b) shall also contain:

   (a) Sufficient information to determine the nationality of the applicant or the identity of the State or States by which, or by whose nationals, the applicant is effectively controlled; and

   (b) The principal place of business or domicile and, if applicable, place of registration of the applicant.

4. Each application submitted by a partnership or consortium of entities shall contain the required information in respect of each member of the partnership or consortium.

Regulation 11
Certificate of sponsorship

1. Each application by a State enterprise or one of the entities referred to in regulation 9 (b) shall be accompanied by a certificate of sponsorship issued by the State of which it is a national or by which or by whose nationals it is effectively controlled. If the applicant has more than one nationality, as in the case of a partnership or consortium of entities from more than one State, each State involved shall issue a certificate of sponsorship.

2. Where the applicant has the nationality of one State but is effectively controlled by another State or its nationals, each State involved shall issue a certificate of sponsorship.

3. Each certificate of sponsorship shall be duly signed on behalf of the State by which it is submitted, and shall contain:

   (a) The name of the applicant;

   (b) The name of the sponsoring State;

   (c) A statement that the applicant is:

   (i) A national of the sponsoring State; or

   (ii) Subject to the effective control of the sponsoring State or its nationals;

   (d) A statement by the sponsoring State that it sponsors the applicant;

   (e) The date of deposit by the sponsoring State of its instrument of ratification of, or accession or succession to, the Convention;

   (f) A declaration that the sponsoring State assumes responsibility in accordance with articles 139 and 153 (4) of the Convention and article 4 (4) of annex III to the Convention.

4. States or entities in a joint arrangement with the Enterprise shall also comply with this regulation.

Regulation 12
Total area covered by the application

1. For the purposes of these Regulations, a "cobalt crust block" is one or more cells of a grid as provided by the Authority, which may be square or rectangular in shape and no greater than 20 square kilometres in size.

2. The area covered by each application for approval of a plan of work for exploration for cobalt crusts shall be comprised of not more than 150 cobalt crust blocks, which shall be arranged by the applicant in clusters, as set out in paragraph 3 below.

3. Five contiguous cobalt crust blocks form a cluster of cobalt crust blocks. Two such blocks that touch at any point shall be considered to be contiguous. Clusters of cobalt crust blocks need not be contiguous but shall be proximate and located entirely within a geographical area measuring not more than 550 kilometres by 550 kilometres.

4. Notwithstanding the provisions in paragraph 2 above, where an applicant has elected to contribute a reserved area to carry out activities pursuant to article 9 of

annex III to the Convention, in accordance with regulation 17, the total area covered by an application shall not exceed 300 cobalt crust blocks. Such blocks shall be arranged in two groups of equal estimated commercial value and each such group of cobalt crust blocks shall be arranged by the applicant in clusters, as set out in paragraph 3 above.

Regulation 13
Financial and technical capabilities

1. Each application for approval of a plan of work for exploration shall contain specific and sufficient information to enable the Council to determine whether the applicant is financially and technically capable of carrying out the proposed plan of work for exploration and of fulfilling its financial obligations to the Authority.

2. An application for approval of a plan of work for exploration by the Enterprise shall include a statement by its competent authority certifying that the Enterprise has the necessary financial resources to meet the estimated costs of the proposed plan of work for exploration.

3. An application for approval of a plan of work for exploration by a State or a State enterprise shall include a statement by the State or the sponsoring State certifying that the applicant has the necessary financial resources to meet the estimated costs of the proposed plan of work for exploration.

4. An application for approval of a plan of work for exploration by an entity shall include copies of its audited financial statements, including balance sheets and profit-and-loss statements, for the most recent three years, in conformity with internationally accepted accounting principles and certified by a duly qualified firm of public accountants.

5. If the applicant is a newly organized entity and a certified balance sheet is not available, the application shall include a pro forma balance sheet certified by an appropriate official of the applicant.

6. If the applicant is a subsidiary of another entity, the application shall include copies of such financial statements of that entity and a statement from that entity, in conformity with internationally accepted accounting principles and certified by a duly qualified firm of public accountants, that the applicant will have the financial resources to carry out the plan of work for exploration.

7. If the applicant is controlled by a State or a State enterprise, the application shall include a statement from the State or State enterprise certifying that the applicant will have the financial resources to carry out the plan of work for exploration.

8. Where an applicant seeking approval of a plan of work for exploration intends to finance the proposed plan of work for exploration by borrowings, its application shall include the amount of such borrowings, the repayment period and the interest rate.

9. Each application shall include:

(a) A general description of the applicant's previous experience, knowledge, skills, technical qualifications and expertise relevant to the proposed plan of work for exploration;

(b) A general description of the equipment and methods expected to be used in carrying out the proposed plan of work for exploration and other relevant non-proprietary information about the characteristics of such technology;

(c) A general description of the applicant's financial and technical capability to respond to any incident or activity which causes serious harm to the marine environment.

10. Where the applicant is a partnership or consortium of entities in a joint arrangement, each member of the partnership or consortium shall provide the information required by this regulation.

Regulation 14
Previous contracts with the Authority

Where the applicant or, in the case of an application by a partnership or consortium of entities in a joint arrangement, any member of the partnership or consortium, has previously been awarded any contract with the Authority, the application shall include:

(a) The date of the previous contract or contracts;

(b) The dates, reference numbers and titles of each report submitted to the Authority in connection with the contract or contracts; and

(c) The date of termination of the contract or contracts, if applicable.

Regulation 15
Undertakings

Each applicant, including the Enterprise, shall, as part of its application for approval of a plan of work for exploration, provide a written undertaking to the Authority that it will:

(a) Accept as enforceable and comply with the applicable obligations created by the provisions of the Convention and the rules, regulations and procedures of the Authority, the decisions of the organs of the Authority and the terms of its contracts with the Authority;

(b) Accept control by the Authority of activities in the Area, as authorized by the Convention; and

(c) Provide the Authority with a written assurance that its obligations under the contract will be fulfilled in good faith.

Regulation 16
Applicant's election of a reserved area contribution or equity interest in a joint venture arrangement

Each applicant shall, in the application, elect either to:

(a) Contribute a reserved area to carry out activities pursuant to article 9 of annex III to the Convention, in accordance with regulation 17; or

(b) Offer an equity interest in a joint venture arrangement in accordance with regulation 19.

Regulation 17
Data and information to be submitted before the designation of a reserved area

1. Where the applicant elects to contribute a reserved area to carry out activities pursuant to article 9 of annex III to the Convention, the area covered by the application shall be sufficiently large and of sufficient estimated commercial value to allow two mining operations and shall be configured by the applicant in accordance with regulation 12 (4).

2. Each such application shall contain sufficient data and information, as prescribed in section II of annex II to these Regulations, with respect to the area under application to enable the Council, on the recommendation of the Legal and Technical Commission, to designate a reserved area based on the estimated commercial value of each part. Such data and information shall consist of data available to the applicant with respect to both parts of the area under application, including the data used to determine their commercial value.

3. The Council, on the basis of the data and information submitted by the applicant pursuant to section II of annex II to these Regulations, if found satisfactory and taking into account the recommendation of the Legal and Technical Commission, shall designate the part of the area under application which is to be a reserved area. The area so designated shall become a reserved area as soon as the plan of work for exploration for the non-reserved area is approved and the contract is signed. If the Council determines that additional information, consistent with these Regulations and annex II, is needed to designate the reserved area, it shall refer the matter back to the Commission for further consideration, specifying the additional information required.

4. Once the plan of work for exploration is approved and a contract has been issued, the data and information transferred to the Authority by the applicant in respect of the reserved area may be disclosed by the Authority in accordance with article 14 (3) of annex III to the Convention.

Regulation 18
Applications for approval of plans of work with respect to a reserved area

1. Any State which is a developing State or any natural or juridical person sponsored by it and effectively controlled by it or by any other developing State, or any group of the foregoing, may notify the Authority that it wishes to submit a plan of work for exploration with respect to a reserved area. The Secretary-General shall forward such notification to the Enterprise, which shall inform the Secretary-General in writing within six months whether or not it intends to carry out activities in that area. If the Enterprise intends to carry out activities in that area, it shall, pursuant to paragraph 4, also inform in writing the contractor whose application for approval of a plan of work for exploration originally included that area.

2. An application for approval of a plan of work for exploration in respect of a reserved area may be submitted at any time after such an area becomes available following a decision by the Enterprise that it does not intend to carry out activities in that area or where the Enterprise has not, within six months of the notification by the Secretary-General, either taken a decision on whether it intends to carry out activities in that area or notified the Secretary-General in writing that it is engaged in discussions regarding a potential joint venture. In the latter instance, the

Enterprise shall have one year from the date of such notification in which to decide whether to conduct activities in that area.

3. If the Enterprise or a developing State or one of the entities referred to in paragraph 1 does not submit an application for approval of a plan of work for exploration for activities in a reserved area within 15 years of the commencement by the Enterprise of its functions independent of the Secretariat of the Authority or within 15 years of the date on which that area is reserved for the Authority, whichever is the later, the contractor whose application for approval of a plan of work for exploration originally included that area shall be entitled to apply for a plan of work for exploration for that area provided it offers in good faith to include the Enterprise as a joint-venture partner.

4. A contractor has the right of first refusal to enter into a joint venture arrangement with the Enterprise for exploration of the area which was included in its application for approval of a plan of work for exploration and which was designated by the Council as a reserved area.

Regulation 19
Equity interest in a joint venture arrangement

1. Where the applicant elects to offer an equity interest in a joint venture arrangement, it shall submit data and information in accordance with regulation 20. The area to be allocated to the applicant shall be subject to the provisions of regulation 27.

2. The joint venture arrangement, which shall take effect at the time the applicant enters into a contract for exploitation, shall include the following:

(a) The Enterprise shall obtain a minimum of 20 per cent of the equity participation in the joint venture arrangement on the following basis:

(i) Half of such equity participation shall be obtained without payment, directly or indirectly, to the applicant and shall be treated pari passu for all purposes with the equity participation of the applicant;

(ii) The remainder of such equity participation shall be treated pari passu for all purposes with the equity participation of the applicant except that the Enterprise shall not receive any profit distribution with respect to such participation until the applicant has recovered its total equity participation in the joint venture arrangement;

(b) Notwithstanding subparagraph (a), the applicant shall nevertheless offer the Enterprise the opportunity to purchase a further 30 per cent of the equity participation in the joint venture arrangement, or such lesser percentage as the Enterprise may elect to purchase, on the basis of pari passu treatment with the applicant for all purposes;[2]

(c) Except as specifically provided in the agreement between the applicant and the Enterprise, the Enterprise shall not by reason of its equity participation be otherwise obligated to provide funds or credits or issue guarantees or otherwise accept any financial liability whatsoever for or on behalf of the joint venture

---

[2] The terms and conditions upon which such equity participation may be obtained would need to be further elaborated.

arrangement, nor shall the Enterprise be required to subscribe for additional equity participation so as to maintain its proportionate participation in the joint venture arrangement.

Regulation 20
Data and information to be submitted for approval of the plan of work for exploration

1. Each applicant shall submit, with a view to receiving approval of the plan of work for exploration in the form of a contract, the following information:

(a) A general description and a schedule of the proposed exploration programme, including the programme of activities for the immediate five-year period, such as studies to be undertaken in respect of the environmental, technical, economic and other appropriate factors that must be taken into account in exploration;

(b) A description of the programme for oceanographic and environmental baseline studies in accordance with these Regulations and any environmental rules, regulations and procedures established by the Authority that would enable an assessment of the potential environmental impact, including, but not restricted to, the impact on biodiversity, of the proposed exploration activities, taking into account any recommendations issued by the Legal and Technical Commission;

(c) A preliminary assessment of the possible impact of the proposed exploration activities on the marine environment;

(d) A description of proposed measures for the prevention, reduction and control of pollution and other hazards, as well as possible impacts, to the marine environment;

(e) Data necessary for the Council to make the determination it is required to make in accordance with regulation 13 (1); and

(f) A schedule of anticipated yearly expenditures in respect of the programme of activities for the immediate five-year period.

2. Where the applicant elects to contribute a reserved area, the data and information relating to such area shall be transferred by the applicant to the Authority after the Council has designated the reserved area in accordance with regulation 17 (3).

3. Where the applicant elects to offer an equity interest in a joint venture arrangement, the data and information relating to such area shall be transferred by the applicant to the Authority at the time of the election.

Section 3
Fees

Regulation 21
Fee for applications

1. The fee for processing an application for approval of a plan for exploration of cobalt crusts shall be a fixed amount of 500,000 United States dollars or its

equivalent in a freely convertible currency, to be paid in full at the time of the submission of an application.

2. If the administrative costs incurred by the Authority in processing an application are less than the fixed amount indicated in paragraph 1 above, the Authority shall refund the difference to the applicant. If the administrative costs incurred by the Authority in processing an application are more than the fixed amount indicated in paragraph 1 above, the applicant shall pay the difference to the Authority, provided that any additional amount to be paid by applicant shall not exceed 10 per cent of the fixed fee referred to in paragraph 1.

3. Taking into account any criteria established for this purpose by the Finance Committee, the Secretary-General shall determine the amount of such differences as indicated in paragraph 2 above, and notify the applicant of its amount. The notification shall include a statement of the expenditure incurred by the Authority. The amount due shall be paid by the applicant or reimbursed by the Authority within three months of the signing of the Contract referred to in Regulation 25 below.

4. The fixed amount referred to in paragraph 1 above shall be reviewed on a regular basis by the Council in order to ensure that it covers the expected administrative costs of processing applications and to avoid the need for applicants to pay additional amounts in accordance with paragraph 2 above.

Section 4
Processing of applications

Regulation 22
Receipt, acknowledgement and safe custody of applications

The Secretary-General shall:

(a) Acknowledge in writing within 30 days receipt of every application for approval of a plan of work for exploration submitted under this Part, specifying the date of receipt;

(b) Place the application together with the attachments and annexes thereto in safe custody and ensure the confidentiality of all confidential data and information contained in the application; and

(c) Notify the members of the Authority of receipt of such application and circulate to them information of a general nature which is not confidential regarding the application.

Regulation 23
Consideration by the Legal and Technical Commission

1. Upon receipt of an application for approval of a plan of work for exploration, the Secretary-General shall notify the members of the Legal and Technical Commission and place consideration of the application as an item on the agenda for the next meeting of the Commission. The Commission shall only consider applications in respect of which notification and information has been circulated by the Secretary-General in accordance with regulation 22 (c) at least 30 days prior to the commencement of the meeting of the Commission at which they are to be considered.

2. The Commission shall examine applications in the order in which they are received.

3. The Commission shall determine if the applicant:

(a) Has complied with the provisions of these Regulations;

(b) Has given the undertakings and assurances specified in regulation 15;

(c) Possesses the financial and technical capability to carry out the proposed plan of work for exploration and has provided details as to its ability to comply promptly with emergency orders; and

(d) Has satisfactorily discharged its obligations in relation to any previous contract with the Authority.

4. The Commission shall, in accordance with the requirements set forth in these Regulations and its procedures, determine whether the proposed plan of work for exploration will:

(a) Provide for effective protection of human health and safety;

(b) Provide for effective protection and preservation of the marine environment, including, but not restricted to, the impact on biodiversity;

(c) Ensure that installations are not established where interference may be caused to the use of recognized sea lanes essential to international navigation or in areas of intense fishing activity.

5. If the Commission makes the determinations specified in paragraph 3 and determines that the proposed plan of work for exploration meets the requirements of paragraph 4, the Commission shall recommend approval of the plan of work for exploration to the Council.

6. The Commission shall not recommend approval of the plan of work for exploration if part or all of the area covered by the proposed plan of work for exploration is included in:

(a) A plan of work for exploration approved by the Council for cobalt crusts; or

(b) A plan of work approved by the Council for exploration for or exploitation of other resources if the proposed plan of work for exploration for cobalt crusts might cause undue interference with activities under such approved plan of work for other resources; or

(c) An area disapproved for exploitation by the Council in cases where substantial evidence indicates the risk of serious harm to the marine environment.

7. The Commission may recommend the approval of a plan of work if it determines that such approval would not permit a State party or entities sponsored by it to monopolize the conduct of activities in the Area with regard to cobalt crusts or to preclude other States parties from activities in the Area with regard to cobalt crusts.

8. Except in the case of applications by the Enterprise, on its own behalf or in a joint venture, and applications under regulation 18, the Commission shall not recommend approval of the plan of work for exploration if part or all of the area

covered by the proposed plan of work for exploration is included in a reserved area or an area designated by the Council to be a reserved area.

9. If the Commission finds that an application does not comply with these Regulations, it shall notify the applicant in writing, through the Secretary-General, indicating the reasons. The applicant may, within 45 days of such notification, amend its application. If the Commission after further consideration is of the view that it should not recommend approval of the plan of work for exploration, it shall so inform the applicant and provide the applicant with a further opportunity to make representations within 30 days of such information. The Commission shall consider any such representations made by the applicant in preparing its report and recommendation to the Council.

10. In considering a proposed plan of work for exploration, the Commission shall have regard to the principles, policies and objectives relating to activities in the Area as provided for in part XI and annex III of the Convention and the Agreement.

11. The Commission shall consider applications expeditiously and shall submit its report and recommendations to the Council on the designation of the areas and on the plan of work for exploration at the first possible opportunity, taking into account the schedule of meetings of the Authority.

12. In discharging its duties, the Commission shall apply these Regulations and the rules, regulations and procedures of the Authority in a uniform and non discriminatory manner.

Regulation 24
Consideration and approval of plans of work for exploration by the Council

The Council shall consider the reports and recommendations of the Legal and Technical Commission relating to approval of plans of work for exploration in accordance with paragraphs 11 and 12 of section 3 of the annex to the Agreement.

Part IV
Contracts for exploration

Regulation 25
The contract

1. After a plan of work for exploration has been approved by the Council, it shall be prepared in the form of a contract between the Authority and the applicant as prescribed in annex III to these Regulations. Each contract shall incorporate the standard clauses set out in annex IV in effect at the date of entry into force of the contract.

2. The contract shall be signed by the Secretary-General on behalf of the Authority and by the applicant. The Secretary-General shall notify all members of the Authority in writing of the conclusion of each contract.

Regulation 26
Rights of the contractor

1.   The contractor shall have the exclusive right to explore an area covered by a plan of work for exploration in respect of cobalt crusts. The Authority shall ensure that no other entity operates in the same area for other resources in a manner that might interfere with the operations of the contractor.

2.   A contractor who has an approved plan of work for exploration only shall have a preference and a priority among applicants submitting plans of work for exploitation of the same area and resources. Such preference or priority may be withdrawn by the Council if the contractor has failed to comply with the requirements of its approved plan of work for exploration within the time period specified in a written notice or notices from the Council to the contractor indicating which requirements have not been complied with by the contractor. The time period specified in any such notice shall not be unreasonable. The contractor shall be accorded a reasonable opportunity to be heard before the withdrawal of such preference or priority becomes final. The Council shall provide the reasons for its proposed withdrawal of preference or priority and shall consider any contractor's response. The decision of the Council shall take account of that response and shall be based on substantial evidence.

3.   A withdrawal of preference or priority shall not become effective until the contractor has been accorded a reasonable opportunity to exhaust the judicial remedies available to it pursuant to part XI, section 5, of the Convention.

Regulation 27
Size of area and relinquishment

1.   The contractor shall relinquish the area allocated to it in accordance with paragraph 1 of this regulation. Areas to be relinquished need not be contiguous and shall be defined by the contractor in the form of sub-blocks comprising one or more cells of a grid as provided by the Authority. By the end of the eighth year from the date of the contract, the contractor shall have relinquished at least one third of the original area allocated to it; by the end of the tenth year from the date of the contract, the contractor shall have relinquished at least two thirds of the original area allocated to it; or, at the end of the fifteenth year from the date of the contract, or when the contractor applies for exploitation rights, whichever is the earlier, the contractor shall nominate an area from the remaining area allocated to it to be retained for exploitation.

2.   Notwithstanding the provisions in paragraph 1, a contractor shall not be required to relinquish any additional part of such area when the remaining area allocated to it after relinquishment does not exceed 1,000 square kilometres.

3.   The contractor may at any time relinquish parts of the area allocated to it in advance of the schedule set out in paragraph 1.

4.   Relinquished areas shall revert to the Area.

5.   The Council may, at the request of the contractor, and on the recommendation of the Commission, in exceptional circumstances, defer the schedule of relinquishment. Such exceptional circumstances shall be determined by the Council and shall include, inter alia, consideration of prevailing economic circumstances or

other unforeseen exceptional circumstances arising in connection with the operational activities of the contractor.

Regulation 28
Duration of contracts

1. A plan of work for exploration shall be approved for a period of 15 years. Upon expiration of a plan of work for exploration, the contractor shall apply for a plan of work for exploitation unless the contractor has already done so, has obtained an extension for the plan of work for exploration or decides to renounce its rights in the area covered by the plan of work for exploration.

2. Not later than six months before the expiration of a plan of work for exploration, a contractor may apply for extensions for the plan of work for exploration for periods of not more than five years each. Such extensions shall be approved by the Council, on the recommendation of the Commission, if the contractor has made efforts in good faith to comply with the requirements of the plan of work but for reasons beyond the contractor's control has been unable to complete the necessary preparatory work for proceeding to the exploitation stage or if the prevailing economic circumstances do not justify proceeding to the exploitation stage.

Regulation 29
Training

Pursuant to article 15 of annex III to the Convention, each contract shall include as a schedule a practical programme for the training of personnel of the Authority and developing States and drawn up by the contractor in cooperation with the Authority and the sponsoring State or States. Training programmes shall focus on training in the conduct of exploration, and shall provide for full participation by such personnel in all activities covered by the contract. Such training programmes may be revised and developed from time to time as necessary by mutual agreement.

Regulation 30
Periodic review of the implementation of the plan of work for exploration

1. The contractor and the Secretary-General shall jointly undertake a periodic review of the implementation of the plan of work for exploration at intervals of five years. The Secretary-General may request the contractor to submit such additional data and information as may be necessary for the purposes of the review.

2. In the light of the review, the contractor shall indicate its programme of activities for the following five-year period, making such adjustments to its previous programme of activities as are necessary.

3. The Secretary-General shall report on the review to the Commission and to the Council. The Secretary-General shall indicate in the report whether any observations transmitted to him by States parties to the Convention concerning the manner in which the contractor has discharged its obligations under these Regulations relating to the protection and preservation of the marine environment were taken into account in the review.

Regulation 31
Termination of sponsorship

1. Each contractor shall have the required sponsorship throughout the period of the contract.

2. If a State terminates its sponsorship it shall promptly notify the Secretary-General in writing. The sponsoring State should also inform the Secretary-General of the reasons for terminating its sponsorship. Termination of sponsorship shall take effect six months after the date of receipt of the notification by the Secretary-General, unless the notification specifies a later date.

3. In the event of termination of sponsorship the contractor shall, within the period referred to in paragraph 2, obtain another sponsor. Such sponsor shall submit a certificate of sponsorship in accordance with regulation 11. Failure to obtain a sponsor within the required period shall result in the termination of the contract.

4. A sponsoring State shall not be discharged by reason of the termination of its sponsorship from any obligations accrued while it was a sponsoring State, nor shall such termination affect any legal rights and obligations created during such sponsorship.

5. The Secretary-General shall notify the members of the Authority of the termination or change of sponsorship.

Regulation 32
Responsibility and liability

Responsibility and liability of the contractor and of the Authority shall be in accordance with the Convention. The contractor shall continue to have responsibility for any damage arising out of wrongful acts in the conduct of its operations, in particular damage to the marine environment, after the completion of the exploration phase.

Part V
Protection and preservation of the marine environment

Regulation 33
Protection and preservation of the marine environment

1. The Authority shall, in accordance with the Convention and the Agreement, establish and keep under periodic review environmental rules, regulations and procedures to ensure effective protection for the marine environment from harmful effects which may arise from activities in the Area.

2. In order to ensure effective protection for the marine environment from harmful effects which may arise from activities in the Area, the Authority and sponsoring States shall apply a precautionary approach, as reflected in principle 15 of the Rio Declaration, and best environmental practices.

3. The Legal and Technical Commission shall make recommendations to the Council on the implementation of paragraphs 1 and 2 above.

4. The Commission shall develop and implement procedures for determining, on the basis of the best available scientific and technical information, including

information provided pursuant to regulation 20, whether proposed exploration activities in the Area would have serious harmful effects on vulnerable marine ecosystems, in particular those associated with seamounts and cold water corals, and ensure that, if it is determined that certain proposed exploration activities would have serious harmful effects on vulnerable marine ecosystems, those activities are managed to prevent such effects or not authorized to proceed.

5. Pursuant to article 145 of the Convention and paragraph 2 of this regulation, each contractor shall take necessary measures to prevent, reduce and control pollution and other hazards to the marine environment arising from its activities in the Area as far as reasonably possible, applying a precautionary approach and best environmental practices.

6. Contractors, sponsoring States and other interested States or entities shall cooperate with the Authority in the establishment and implementation of programmes for monitoring and evaluating the impacts of deep seabed mining on the marine environment. When required by the Council, such programmes shall include proposals for areas to be set aside and used exclusively as impact reference zones and preservation reference zones. "Impact reference zones" means areas to be used for assessing the effect of activities in the Area on the marine environment and which are representative of the environmental characteristics of the Area. "Preservation reference zones" means areas in which no mining shall occur to ensure representative and stable biota of the seabed in order to assess any changes in the biodiversity of the marine environment.

Regulation 34
Environmental baselines and monitoring

1. Each contract shall require the contractor to gather environmental baseline data and to establish environmental baselines, taking into account any recommendations issued by the Legal and Technical Commission pursuant to regulation 41, against which to assess the likely effects of its programme of activities under the plan of work for exploration on the marine environment and a programme to monitor and report on such effects. The recommendations issued by the Commission may, inter alia, list those exploration activities which may be considered to have no potential for causing harmful effects on the marine environment. The contractor shall cooperate with the Authority and the sponsoring State or States in the establishment and implementation of such monitoring programme.

2. The contractor shall report annually in writing to the Secretary-General on the implementation and results of the monitoring programme referred to in paragraph 1 and shall submit data and information, taking into account any recommendations issued by the Commission pursuant to regulation 41. The Secretary-General shall transmit such reports to the Commission for its consideration pursuant to article 165 of the Convention.

Regulation 35
Emergency orders

1. A contractor shall promptly report to the Secretary-General in writing, using the most effective means, any incident arising from activities which have caused, are causing or pose a threat of serious harm to the marine environment.

2. When the Secretary-General has been notified by a contractor or otherwise becomes aware of an incident resulting from or caused by a contractor's activities in the Area that has caused, is causing or poses a threat of serious harm to the marine environment, the Secretary-General shall cause a general notification of the incident to be issued, shall notify in writing the contractor and the sponsoring State or States, and shall report immediately to the Legal and Technical Commission, to the Council and to all other members of the Authority. A copy of the report shall be circulated to competent international organizations and to concerned subregional, regional and global organizations and bodies. The Secretary-General shall monitor developments with respect to all such incidents and shall report on them as appropriate to the Commission, the Council and all other members of the Authority.

3. Pending any action by the Council, the Secretary-General shall take such immediate measures of a temporary nature as are practical and reasonable in the circumstances to prevent, contain and minimize serious harm or the threat of serious harm to the marine environment. Such temporary measures shall remain in effect for no longer than 90 days, or until the Council decides at its next regular session or a special session, what measures, if any, to take pursuant to paragraph 6 of this regulation.

4. After having received the report of the Secretary-General, the Commission shall determine, based on the evidence provided to it and taking into account the measures already taken by the contractor, which measures are necessary to respond effectively to the incident in order to prevent, contain and minimize serious harm or the threat of serious harm to the marine environment, and shall make its recommendations to the Council.

5. The Council shall consider the recommendations of the Commission.

6. The Council, taking into account the recommendations of the Commission, the report of the Secretary-General, any information provided by the contractor and any other relevant information, may issue emergency orders, which may include orders for the suspension or adjustment of operations, as may be reasonably necessary to prevent, contain and minimize serious harm or the threat of serious harm to the marine environment arising out of activities in the Area.

7. If a contractor does not promptly comply with an emergency order to prevent, contain and minimize serious harm or the threat of serious harm to the marine environment arising out of its activities in the Area, the Council shall take by itself or through arrangements with others on its behalf, such practical measures as are necessary to prevent, contain and minimize any such serious harm or threat of serious harm to the marine environment.

8. In order to enable the Council, when necessary, to take immediately the practical measures to prevent, contain and minimize the serious harm or threat of serious harm to the marine environment referred to in paragraph 7, the contractor, prior to the commencement of testing of collecting systems and processing operations, will provide the Council with a guarantee of its financial and technical capability to comply promptly with emergency orders or to assure that the Council can take such emergency measures. If the contractor does not provide the Council with such a guarantee, the sponsoring State or States shall, in response to a request by the Secretary-General and pursuant to articles 139 and 235 of the Convention, take necessary measures to ensure that the contractor provides such a guarantee or

shall take measures to ensure that assistance is provided to the Authority in the discharge of its responsibilities under paragraph 7.

Regulation 36
Rights of coastal States

1. Nothing in these Regulations shall affect the rights of coastal States in accordance with article 142 and other relevant provisions of the Convention.

2. Any coastal State which has grounds for believing that any activity in the Area by a contractor is likely to cause serious harm or a threat of serious harm to the marine environment under its jurisdiction or sovereignty may notify the Secretary-General in writing of the grounds upon which such belief is based. The Secretary-General shall provide the Contractor and its sponsoring State or States with a reasonable opportunity to examine the evidence, if any, provided by the coastal State as the basis for its belief. The contractor and its sponsoring State or States may submit their observations thereon to the Secretary-General within a reasonable time.

3. If there are clear grounds for believing that serious harm to the marine environment is likely to occur, the Secretary-General shall act in accordance with regulation 35 and, if necessary, shall take immediate measures of a temporary nature as provided for in regulation 35 (3).

4. Contractors shall take all measures necessary to ensure that their activities are conducted so as not to cause serious harm to the marine environment, including, but not restricted to, pollution, under the jurisdiction or sovereignty of coastal States, and that such serious harm or pollution arising from incidents or activities in its exploration area does not spread beyond such area.

Regulation 37
Human remains and objects and sites of an archaeological or historical nature

The contractor shall immediately notify the Secretary-General in writing of any finding in the exploration area of any human remains of an archaeological or historical nature, or any object or site of a similar nature and its location, including the preservation and protection measures taken. The Secretary-General shall immediately transmit such information to the Director-General of the United Nations Educational, Scientific and Cultural Organization and any other competent international organization. Following the finding of any such human remains, object or site in the exploration area, and in order to avoid disturbing such human remains, object or site, no further prospecting or exploration shall take place, within a reasonable radius, until such time as the Council decides otherwise after taking account of the views of the Director-General of the United Nations Educational, Scientific and Cultural Organization or any other competent international organization.

Part VI
Confidentiality

Regulation 38
Confidentiality of data and information

1. Data and information submitted or transferred to the Authority or to any person participating in any activity or programme of the Authority pursuant to these Regulations or a contract issued under these Regulations, and designated by the contractor, in consultation with the Secretary-General, as being of a confidential nature, shall be considered confidential unless it is data and information which:

    (a) Is generally known or publicly available from other sources;

    (b) Has been previously made available by the owner to others without an obligation concerning its confidentiality; or

    (c) Is already in the possession of the Authority with no obligation concerning its confidentiality.

2. Data and information that is necessary for the formulation by the Authority of rules, regulations and procedures concerning protection and preservation of the marine environment and safety, other than proprietary equipment design data, shall not be deemed confidential.

3. Confidential data and information may only be used by the Secretary-General and staff of the Secretariat, as authorized by the Secretary-General, and by the members of the Legal and Technical Commission as necessary for and relevant to the effective exercise of their powers and functions. The Secretary-General shall authorize access to such data and information only for limited use in connection with the functions and duties of the staff of the Secretariat and the functions and duties of the Legal and Technical Commission.

4. Ten years after the date of submission of confidential data and information to the Authority or the expiration of the contract for exploration, whichever is the later, and every five years thereafter, the Secretary-General and the contractor shall review such data and information to determine whether they should remain confidential. Such data and information shall remain confidential if the contractor establishes that there would be a substantial risk of serious and unfair economic prejudice if the data and information were to be released. No such data and information shall be released until the contractor has been accorded a reasonable opportunity to exhaust the judicial remedies available to it pursuant to Part XI, section 5, of the Convention.

5. If, at any time following the expiration of the contract for exploration, the contractor enters into a contract for exploitation in respect of any part of the exploration area, confidential data and information relating to that part of the area shall remain confidential in accordance with the contract for exploitation.

6. The contractor may at any time waive confidentiality of data and information.

Regulation 39
Procedures to ensure confidentiality

1. The Secretary-General shall be responsible for maintaining the confidentiality of all confidential data and information and shall not, except with the prior written consent of the contractor, release such data and information to any person external to the Authority. To ensure the confidentiality of such data and information, the Secretary-General shall establish procedures, consistent with the provisions of the Convention, governing the handling of confidential information by members of the Secretariat, members of the Legal and Technical Commission and any other person participating in any activity or programme of the Authority. Such procedures shall include:

(a) Maintenance of confidential data and information in secure facilities and development of security procedures to prevent unauthorized access to or removal of such data and information;

(b) Development and maintenance of a classification, log and inventory system of all written data and information received, including its type and source and routing from the time of receipt until final disposition.

2. A person who is authorized pursuant to these Regulations to have access to confidential data and information shall not disclose such data and information except as permitted under the Convention and these Regulations. The Secretary-General shall require any person who is authorized to have access to confidential data and information to make a written declaration witnessed by the Secretary-General or his or her authorized representative to the effect that the person so authorized:

(a) Acknowledges his or her legal obligation under the Convention and these Regulations with respect to the non-disclosure of confidential data and information;

(b) Agrees to comply with the applicable regulations and procedures established to ensure the confidentiality of such data and information.

3. The Legal and Technical Commission shall protect the confidentiality of confidential data and information submitted to it pursuant to these Regulations or a contract issued under these Regulations. In accordance with the provisions of article 163 (8) of the Convention, members of the Commission shall not disclose, even after the termination of their functions, any industrial secret, proprietary data which are transferred to the Authority in accordance with article 14 of annex III to the Convention, or any other confidential information coming to their knowledge by reason of their duties for the Authority.

4. The Secretary-General and staff of the Authority shall not disclose, even after the termination of their functions with the Authority, any industrial secret, proprietary data which are transferred to the Authority in accordance with article 14 of annex III to the Convention, or any other confidential information coming to their knowledge by reason of their employment with the Authority.

5. Taking into account the responsibility and liability of the Authority pursuant to article 22 of annex III to the Convention, the Authority may take such action as may be appropriate against any person who, by reason of his or her duties for the Authority, has access to any confidential data and information and who is in breach

of the obligations relating to confidentiality contained in the Convention and these Regulations.

Part VII
General procedures

Regulation 40
Notice and general procedures

1. Any application, request, notice, report, consent, approval, waiver, direction or instruction hereunder shall be made by the Secretary-General or by the designated representative of the prospector, applicant or contractor, as the case may be, in writing. Service shall be by hand, or by telex, fax, registered airmail or e-mail containing an authorized electronic signature to the Secretary-General at the headquarters of the Authority or to the designated representative.

2. Delivery by hand shall be effective when made. Delivery by telex shall be deemed to be effective on the business day following the day when the "answer back" appears on the sender's telex machine. Delivery by fax shall be effective when the "transmit confirmation report" confirming the transmission to the recipient's published fax number is received by the transmitter. Delivery by registered airmail shall be deemed to be effective 21 days after posting. An e-mail is presumed to be received by the addressee when it enters an information system designated or used by the addressee for the purpose of receiving documents of the type sent and is capable of being retrieved and processed by the addressee.

3. Notice to the designated representative of the prospector, applicant or contractor shall constitute effective notice to the prospector, applicant or contractor for all purposes under these Regulations, and the designated representative shall be the agent of the prospector, applicant or contractor for the service of process or notification in any proceeding of any court or tribunal having jurisdiction.

4. Notice to the Secretary-General shall constitute effective notice to the Authority for all purposes under these Regulations, and the Secretary-General shall be the Authority's agent for the service of process or notification in any proceeding of any court or tribunal having jurisdiction.

Regulation 41
Recommendations for the guidance of contractors

1. The Legal and Technical Commission may from time to time issue recommendations of a technical or administrative nature for the guidance of contractors to assist them in the implementation of the rules, regulations and procedures of the Authority.

2. The full text of such recommendations shall be reported to the Council. Should the Council find that a recommendation is inconsistent with the intent and purpose of these Regulations, it may request that the recommendation be modified or withdrawn.

Part VIII
Settlement of disputes

Regulation 42
Disputes

1. Disputes concerning the interpretation or application of these Regulations shall be settled in accordance with Part XI, section 5, of the Convention.

2. Any final decision rendered by a court or tribunal having jurisdiction under the Convention relating to the rights and obligations of the Authority and of the Contractor shall be enforceable in the territory of each State party to the Convention.

Part IX
Resources other than cobalt crusts

Regulation 43
Resources other than cobalt crusts

If a prospector or contractor finds resources in the Area other than cobalt crusts, the prospecting and exploration for and exploitation of such resources shall be subject to the rules, regulations and procedures of the Authority relating to such resources in accordance with the Convention and the Agreement. The prospector or contractor shall notify the Authority of its find.

Part X
Review

Regulation 44
Review

1. Five years following the approval of these Regulations by the Assembly, or at any time thereafter, the Council shall undertake a review of the manner in which the Regulations have operated in practice.

2. If, in the light of improved knowledge or technology, it becomes apparent that the Regulations are not adequate, any State party, the Legal and Technical Commission or any contractor through its sponsoring State may at any time request the Council to consider, at its next ordinary session, revisions to these Regulations.

3. In the light of the review, the Council may adopt and apply provisionally, pending approval by the Assembly, amendments to the provisions of these Regulations, taking into account the recommendations of the Legal and Technical Commission or other subordinate organs concerned. Any such amendments shall be without prejudice to the rights conferred on any contractor with the Authority under the provisions of a contract entered into pursuant to these Regulations in force at the time of any such amendment.

4. In the event that any provisions of these Regulations are amended, the contractor and the Authority may revise the contract in accordance with section 24 of annex IV.

Annex I

Notification of intention to engage in prospecting

1. Name of prospector:

2. Street address of prospector:

3. Postal address (if different from above):

4. Telephone number:

5. Fax number:

6. E-mail address:

7. Nationality of prospector:

8. If prospector is a juridical person:

    (a) Identify prospector's place of registration;

    (b) Identify prospector's principal place of business/domicile;

    (c) Attach a copy of prospector's certificate of registration.

9. Name of prospector's designated representative:

10. Street address of prospector's designated representative (if different from above):

11. Postal address (if different from above):

12. Telephone number:

13. Fax number:

14. E-mail address:

15. Attach the coordinates of the broad area or areas in which prospecting is to be conducted (in accordance with the World Geodetic System WGS 84).

16. Attach a general description of the prospecting programme, including the date of commencement and the approximate duration of the programme.

17. Attach a written undertaking that the prospector will:

    (a) Comply with the Convention and the relevant rules, regulations and procedures of the Authority concerning:

    (i) Cooperation in the training programmes in connection with marine scientific research and transfer of technology referred to in articles 143 and 144 of the Convention; and

    (ii) Protection and preservation of the marine environment; and

    (b) Accept verification by the Authority of compliance therewith.

18. List hereunder all the attachments and annexes to this notification (all data and information should be submitted in hard copy and in a digital format specified by the Authority).

_____   _____
Date   Signature of prospector's designated representative

Attestation:

_____
Signature of person attesting

_____
Name of person attesting

_____
Title of person attesting

Annex II

Application for approval of a plan of work for exploration to obtain a contract

Section I
Information concerning the applicant

1. Name of applicant:

2. Street address of applicant:

3. Postal address (if different from above):

4. Telephone number:

5. Fax number:

6. E-mail address:

7. Name of applicant's designated representative:

8. Street address of applicant's designated representative (if different from above):

9. Postal address (if different from above):

10. Telephone number:

11. Fax number:

12. E-mail address:

13. If the applicant is a juridical person:

    (a) Identify applicant's place of registration;

    (b) Identify applicant's principal place of business/domicile;

    (c) Attach a copy of applicant's certificate of registration.

14. Identify the sponsoring State or States.

15. In respect of each sponsoring State, provide the date of deposit of its instrument of ratification of, or accession or succession to, the United Nations Convention on the Law of the Sea of 10 December 1982 and the date of its consent to be bound by the Agreement relating to the Implementation of Part XI of the Convention.

16. A certificate of sponsorship issued by the sponsoring State must be attached with this application. If the applicant has more than one nationality, as in the case of a partnership or consortium of entities from more than one State, certificates of sponsorship issued by each of the States involved must be attached.

Section II
Information relating to the area under application

17. Define the boundaries of the blocks under application by attaching a chart (on a scale and projection specified by the Authority) and a list of geographical coordinates (in accordance with the World Geodetic System WGS 84).

18. Indicate whether the applicant elects to contribute a reserved area in accordance with regulation 17 or offer an equity interest in a joint venture arrangement in accordance with regulation 19.

19. If the applicant elects to contribute a reserved area:

(a) Attach a list of the coordinates designating the two parts of the total area of equal estimated commercial value; and

(b) Include in an attachment sufficient information to enable the Council to designate a reserved area based on the estimated commercial value of each part of the area under application. Such attachment must include the data available to the applicant with respect to both parts of the area under application, including:

(i) Data on the location, survey and evaluation of the cobalt crusts in the areas, including:

a. A description of the technology related to the recovery and processing of cobalt crusts that is necessary for making the designation of a reserved area;

b. A map of the physical and geological characteristics, such as seabed topography, bathymetry and bottom currents and information on the reliability of such data;

c. A map showing the survey data used to determine the parameters of cobalt crusts (thickness etc.) necessary to determine its tonnage within the limits of each block, clusters of blocks of the exploration area and the reserved area;

d. Data showing the average tonnage (in metric tons) of each cluster of cobalt crust blocks that will comprise the mine site and an associated tonnage map showing the location of sampling sites;

e. Combined maps of tonnage and grade of cobalt crusts;

f. A calculation based on standard procedures, including statistical analysis, using the data submitted and assumptions made in the calculations that the two areas could be expected to contain cobalt crusts of equal estimated commercial value expressed as recoverable metals in mineable areas;

g. A description of the techniques used by the applicant;

(ii) Information concerning environmental parameters (seasonal and during test period) including, inter alia, wind speed and direction, water salinity, temperature and biological communities.

20. If the area under application includes any part of a reserved area, attach a list of coordinates of the area which forms part of the reserved area and indicate the applicant's qualifications in accordance with regulation 18 of the Regulations.

Section III
Financial and technical information

21. Attach sufficient information to enable the Council to determine whether the applicant is financially capable of carrying out the proposed plan of work for exploration and of fulfilling its financial obligations to the Authority:

(a) If the application is made by the Enterprise, attach certification by its competent authority that the Enterprise has the necessary financial resources to meet the estimated costs of the proposed plan of work for exploration;

(b) If the application is made by a State or a State enterprise, attach a statement by the State or the sponsoring State certifying that the applicant has the necessary financial resources to meet the estimated costs of the proposed plan of work for exploration;

(c) If the application is made by an entity, attach copies of the applicant's audited financial statements, including balance sheets and profit-and-loss statements, for the most recent three years in conformity with internationally accepted accounting principles and certified by a duly qualified firm of public accountants; and

(i) If the applicant is a newly organized entity and a certified balance sheet is not available, a pro forma balance sheet certified by an appropriate official of the applicant;

(ii) If the applicant is a subsidiary of another entity, copies of such financial statements of that entity and a statement from that entity in conformity with internationally accepted accounting practices and certified by a duly qualified firm of public accountants that the applicant will have the financial resources to carry out the plan of work for exploration;

(iii) If the applicant is controlled by a State or a State enterprise, a statement from the State or State enterprise certifying that the applicant will have the financial resources to carry out the plan of work for exploration.

22. If it is intended to finance the proposed plan of work for exploration by borrowings, attach a statement of the amount of such borrowings, the repayment period and the interest rate.

23. Attach sufficient information to enable the Council to determine whether the applicant is technically capable of carrying out the proposed plan of work for exploration, including:

(a) A general description of the applicant's previous experience, knowledge, skills, technical qualifications and expertise relevant to the proposed plan of work for exploration;

(b) A general description of the equipment and methods expected to be used in carrying out the proposed plan of work for exploration and other relevant non-proprietary information about the characteristics of such technology;

(c) A general description of the applicant's financial and technical capability to respond to any incident or activity which causes serious harm to the marine environment.

Section IV
The plan of work for exploration

24. Attach the following information relating to the plan of work for exploration:

(a) A general description and a schedule of the proposed exploration programme, including the programme of activities for the immediate five-year period, such as studies to be undertaken in respect of the environmental, technical, economic and other appropriate factors which must be taken into account in exploration;

(b) A description of a programme for oceanographic and environmental baseline studies in accordance with the Regulations and any environmental rules, regulations and procedures established by the Authority that would enable an assessment of the potential environmental impact including, but not restricted to, the impact on biodiversity, of the proposed exploration activities, taking into account any recommendations issued by the Legal and Technical Commission;

(c) A preliminary assessment of the possible impact of the proposed exploration activities on the marine environment;

(d) A description of proposed measures for the prevention, reduction and control of pollution of other hazards, as well as possible impacts, to the marine environment;

(e) A schedule of anticipated yearly expenditures in respect of the programme of activities for the immediate five-year period.

Section V
Undertakings

25. Attach a written undertaking that the applicant will:

(a) Accept as enforceable and comply with the applicable obligations created by the provisions of the Convention and the rules, regulations and procedures of the Authority, the decisions of the relevant organs of the Authority and the terms of its contracts with the Authority;

(b) Accept control by the Authority of activities in the Area as authorized by the Convention;

(c) Provide the Authority with a written assurance that its obligations under the contract will be fulfilled in good faith.

Section VI
Previous contracts

26. If the applicant or, in the case of an application by a partnership or consortium of entities in a joint arrangement, any member of the partnership or consortium has previously been awarded any contract with the Authority, the application must include:

(a) The date of the previous contract or contracts;

(b) The dates, reference numbers and titles of each report submitted to the Authority in connection with the contract or contracts; and

(c) The date of termination of the contract or contracts, if applicable.

Section VII
Attachments

27. List all the attachments and annexes to this application (all data and information should be submitted in hard copy and in a digital format specified by the Authority).

_____   _____
Date   Signature of applicant's designated representative

Attestation:

_____
Signature of person attesting

_____
Name of person attesting

_____
Title of person attesting

Annex III

Contract for exploration

THIS CONTRACT made the ... day of ... between the **INTERNATIONAL SEABED AUTHORITY** represented by its **SECRETARY-GENERAL** (hereinafter referred to as "the Authority") and ... represented by ... (hereinafter referred to as "the Contractor") **WITNESSETH** as follows:

Incorporation of clauses

1. The standard clauses set out in annex IV to the Regulations on Prospecting and Exploration for Cobalt-rich Ferromanganese Crusts in the Area shall be incorporated herein and shall have effect as if herein set out at length.

Exploration area

2. For the purposes of this contract, the "exploration area" means that part of the Area allocated to the Contractor for exploration, defined by the coordinates listed in schedule 1 hereto, as reduced from time to time in accordance with the standard clauses and the Regulations.

Grant of rights

3. In consideration of (a) their mutual interest in the conduct of exploration activities in the exploration area pursuant to the United Nations Convention on the Law of the Sea of 10 December 1982 and the Agreement relating to the Implementation of Part XI of the Convention, (b) the responsibility of the Authority to organize and control activities in the Area, particularly with a view to administering the resources of the Area, in accordance with the legal regime established in Part XI of the Convention and the Agreement and Part XII of the Convention, respectively, and (c) the interest and financial commitment of the Contractor in conducting activities in the exploration area and the mutual covenants made herein, the Authority hereby grants to the Contractor the exclusive right to explore for cobalt crusts in the exploration area in accordance with the terms and conditions of this contract.

Entry into force and contract term

4. This contract shall enter into force on signature by both parties and, subject to the standard clauses, shall remain in force for a period of fifteen years thereafter unless:

(a) The Contractor obtains a contract for exploitation in the exploration area which enters into force before the expiration of such period of fifteen years; or

(b) The contract is sooner terminated provided that the term of the contract may be extended in accordance with standard clauses 3.2 and 17.2.

Schedules

5. The schedules referred to in the standard clauses, namely section 4 and section 8, are for the purposes of this contract schedules 2 and 3 respectively.

Entire agreement

6. This contract expresses the entire agreement between the parties, and no oral understanding or prior writing shall modify the terms hereof.

IN WITNESS WHEREOF the undersigned, being duly authorized thereto by the respective parties, have signed this contract at ..., this ... day of ... .

Schedule 1

[Coordinates and illustrative chart of the exploration area]

Schedule 2

[The current five-year programme of activities as revised from time to time]

Schedule 3

[The training programme shall become a schedule to the contract when approved by the Authority in accordance with section 8 of the standard clauses.]

Annex IV

Standard clauses for exploration contract

Section 1
Definitions

1.1 In the following clauses:

(a) "Exploration area" means that part of the Area allocated to the Contractor for exploration, described in schedule 1 hereto, as the same may be reduced from time to time in accordance with this contract and the Regulations;

(b) "Programme of activities" means the programme of activities which is set out in schedule 2 hereto as the same may be adjusted from time to time in accordance with sections 4.3 and 4.4 hereof;

(c) "Regulations" means the Regulations on Prospecting and Exploration for Cobalt-rich Ferromanganese Crusts in the Area, adopted by the Authority.

1.2 Terms and phrases defined in the Regulations shall have the same meaning in these standard clauses.

1.3 In accordance with the Agreement relating to the Implementation of Part XI of the United Nations Convention on the Law of the Sea of 10 December 1982, its provisions and Part XI of the Convention are to be interpreted and applied together as a single instrument; this contract and references in this contract to the Convention are to be interpreted and applied accordingly.

1.4 This contract includes the schedules to this contract, which shall be an integral part hereof.

Section 2
Security of tenure

2.1 The Contractor shall have security of tenure and this contract shall not be suspended, terminated or revised except in accordance with sections 20, 21 and 24 hereof.

2.2 The Contractor shall have the exclusive right to explore for cobalt crusts in the exploration area in accordance with the terms and conditions of this contract. The Authority shall ensure that no other entity operates in the exploration area for a different category of resources in a manner that might unreasonably interfere with the operations of the Contractor.

2.3 The Contractor, by notice to the Authority, shall have the right at any time to renounce without penalty the whole or part of its rights in the exploration area, provided that the Contractor shall remain liable for all obligations accrued prior to the date of such renunciation in respect of the area renounced.

2.4 Nothing in this contract shall be deemed to confer any right on the Contractor other than those rights expressly granted herein. The Authority reserves the right to enter into contracts with respect to resources other than cobalt crusts with third parties in the area covered by this contract.

Section 3
Contract term

3.1 This contract shall enter into force on signature by both parties and shall remain in force for a period of fifteen years thereafter unless:

(a) The Contractor obtains a contract for exploitation in the exploration area which enters into force before the expiration of such period of fifteen years; or

(b) The contract is sooner terminated, provided that the term of the contract may be extended in accordance with sections 3.2 and 17.2 hereof.

3.2 Upon application by the Contractor, not later than six months before the expiration of this contract, this contract may be extended for periods of not more than five years each on such terms and conditions as the Authority and the Contractor may then agree in accordance with the Regulations. Such extensions shall be approved if the Contractor has made efforts in good faith to comply with the requirements of this contract but for reasons beyond the Contractor's control has been unable to complete the necessary preparatory work for proceeding to the exploitation stage or if the prevailing economic circumstances do not justify proceeding to the exploitation stage.

3.3 Notwithstanding the expiration of this contract in accordance with section 3.1 hereof, if the Contractor has, at least 90 days prior to the date of expiration, applied for a contract for exploitation, the Contractor's rights and obligations under this contract shall continue until such time as the application has been considered and a contract for exploitation has been issued or refused.

Section 4
Exploration

4.1 The Contractor shall commence exploration in accordance with the time schedule stipulated in the programme of activities set out in schedule 2 hereto and shall adhere to such time periods or any modification thereto as provided for by this contract.

4.2 The Contractor shall carry out the programme of activities set out in schedule 2 hereto. In carrying out such activities the Contractor shall spend in each contract year not less than the amount specified in such programme, or any agreed review thereof, in actual and direct exploration expenditures.

4.3 The Contractor, with the consent of the Authority, which consent shall not be unreasonably withheld, may from time to time make such changes in the programme of activities and the expenditures specified therein as may be necessary and prudent in accordance with good mining industry practice, and taking into account the market conditions for the metals contained in cobalt crusts and other relevant global economic conditions.

4.4 Not later than 90 days prior to the expiration of each five-year period from the date on which this contract enters into force in accordance with section 3 hereof, the Contractor and the Secretary-General shall jointly undertake a review of the implementation of the plan of work for exploration under this contract. The Secretary-General may require the Contractor to submit such additional data and information as may be necessary for the purposes of the review. In the light of the review, the Contractor shall make such adjustments to its plan of work as are necessary and shall indicate its programme of activities for the following five-year period, including a revised schedule of anticipated yearly expenditures. Schedule 2 hereto shall be adjusted accordingly.

Section 5
Environmental monitoring

5.1 The Contractor shall take necessary measures to prevent, reduce and control pollution and other hazards to the marine environment arising from its activities in the Area as far as reasonably possible applying a precautionary approach and best environmental practices.

5.2 Prior to the commencement of exploration activities, the Contractor shall submit to the Authority:

(a) An impact assessment of the potential effects on the marine environment of the proposed activities;

(b) A proposal for a monitoring programme to determine the potential effect on the marine environment of the proposed activities; and

(c) Data that could be used to establish an environmental baseline against which to assess the effect of the proposed activities.

5.3 The Contractor shall, in accordance with the Regulations, gather environmental baseline data as exploration activities progress and develop and shall establish environmental baselines against which to assess the likely effects of the Contractor's activities on the marine environment.

5.4 The Contractor shall, in accordance with the Regulations, establish and carry out a programme to monitor and report on such effects on the marine environment. The Contractor shall cooperate with the Authority in the implementation of such monitoring.

5.5 The Contractor shall, within 90 days of the end of each calendar year, report to the Secretary-General on the implementation and results of the monitoring programme referred to in section 5.4 hereof and shall submit data and information in accordance with the Regulations.

Section 6
Contingency plans and emergencies

6.1 The Contractor shall, prior to the commencement of its programme of activities under this contract, submit to the Secretary-General a contingency plan to respond effectively to incidents that are likely to cause serious harm or a threat of serious harm to the marine environment arising from the Contractor's activities at sea in the exploration area. Such contingency plan shall establish special procedures and provide for adequate and appropriate equipment to deal with such incidents and, in particular, shall include arrangements for:

(a) The immediate raising of a general alarm in the area of the exploration activities;

(b) Immediate notification to the Secretary-General;

(c) The warning of ships which might be about to enter the immediate vicinity;

(d) A continuing flow of full information to the Secretary-General relating to particulars of the contingency measures already taken and further actions required;

(e) The removal, as appropriate, of polluting substances;

(f) The reduction and, so far as reasonably possible, prevention of serious harm to the marine environment, as well as mitigation of such effects;

(g) As appropriate, cooperation with other contractors with the Authority to respond to an emergency; and

(h) Periodic emergency response exercises.

6.2 The Contractor shall promptly report to the Secretary-General any incident arising from its activities that has caused, is causing or poses a threat of serious harm to the marine environment. Each such report shall contain the details of such incident, including, inter alia:

(a) The coordinates of the area affected or which can reasonably be anticipated to be affected;

(b) The description of the action being taken by the Contractor to prevent, contain, minimize and repair the serious harm or threat of serious harm to the marine environment;

(c) A description of the action being taken by the Contractor to monitor the effects of the incident on the marine environment; and

(d) Such supplementary information as may reasonably be required by the Secretary-General.

6.3 The Contractor shall comply with emergency orders issued by the Council and immediate measures of a temporary nature issued by the Secretary-General in accordance with the Regulations, to prevent, contain, minimize or repair serious harm or the threat of serious harm to the marine environment, which may include orders to the Contractor to immediately suspend or adjust any activities in the exploration area.

6.4 If the Contractor does not promptly comply with such emergency orders or immediate measures of a temporary nature, the Council may take such reasonable measures as are necessary to prevent, contain, minimize or repair any such serious harm or the threat of serious harm to the marine environment at the Contractor's expense. The Contractor shall promptly reimburse the Authority the amount of such expenses. Such expenses shall be in addition to any monetary penalties which may be imposed on the Contractor pursuant to the terms of this contract or the Regulations.

Section 7
Human remains and objects and sites of an archaeological or historical nature

The Contractor shall immediately notify the Secretary-General in writing of any finding in the exploration area of any human remains of an archaeological or historical nature, or any object or site of a similar nature and its location, including the preservation and protection measures taken. The Secretary-General shall

transmit such information to the Director-General of the United Nations Educational, Scientific and Cultural Organization and any other competent international organization. Following the finding of any such human remains, object or site in the exploration area, and in order to avoid disturbing such human remains, object or site, no further prospecting or exploration shall take place, within a reasonable radius, until such time as the Council decides otherwise after taking account of the views of the Director-General of the United Nations Educational, Scientific and Cultural Organization or any other competent international organization.

Section 8
Training

8.1 In accordance with the Regulations, the Contractor shall, prior to the commencement of exploration under this contract, submit to the Authority for approval proposed training programmes for the training of personnel of the Authority and developing States, including the participation of such personnel in all of the Contractor's activities under this contract.

8.2 The scope and financing of the training programme shall be subject to negotiation between the Contractor, the Authority and the sponsoring State or States.

8.3 The Contractor shall conduct training programmes in accordance with the specific programme for the training of personnel referred to in section 8.1 hereof approved by the Authority in accordance with the Regulations, which programme, as revised and developed from time to time, shall become a part of this contract as schedule 3.

Section 9
Books and records

The Contractor shall keep a complete and proper set of books, accounts and financial records, consistent with internationally accepted accounting principles. Such books, accounts and financial records shall include information which will fully disclose the actual and direct expenditures for exploration and such other information as will facilitate an effective audit of such expenditures.

Section 10
Annual reports

10.1 The Contractor shall, within 90 days of the end of each calendar year, submit a report to the Secretary-General in such format as may be recommended from time to time by the Legal and Technical Commission covering its programme of activities in the exploration area and containing, as applicable, information in sufficient detail on:

(a) The exploration work carried out during the calendar year, including maps, charts and graphs illustrating the work that has been done and the results obtained;

(b) The equipment used to carry out the exploration work, including the results of tests conducted of proposed mining technologies, but not equipment design data; and

(c) The implementation of training programmes, including any proposed revisions to or developments of such programmes.

10.2 Such reports shall also contain:

(a) The results obtained from environmental monitoring programmes, including observations, measurements, evaluations and analyses of environmental parameters;

(b) A statement of the quantity of cobalt crusts recovered as samples or for the purpose of testing;

(c) A statement, in conformity with internationally accepted accounting principles and certified by a duly qualified firm of public accountants, or, where the Contractor is a State or a state enterprise, by the sponsoring State, of the actual and direct exploration expenditures of the Contractor in carrying out the programme of activities during the Contractor's accounting year. Such expenditures may be claimed by the contractor as part of the contractor's development costs incurred prior to the commencement of commercial production; and

(d) Details of any proposed adjustments to the programme of activities and the reasons for such adjustments.

10.3 The Contractor shall also submit such additional information to supplement the reports referred to in sections 10.1 and 10.2 hereof as the Secretary-General may from time to time reasonably require in order to carry out the Authority's functions under the Convention, the Regulations and this contract.

10.4 The Contractor shall keep, in good condition, a representative portion of samples and cores of the cobalt crusts obtained in the course of exploration until the expiration of this contract. The Authority may request the Contractor in writing to deliver to it for analysis a portion of any such sample and cores obtained during the course of exploration.

10.5 The contractor shall pay at the time of submission of the annual report an annual overhead charge of $47,000 (or such sum as may be fixed in accordance with section 10.6 hereof) to cover the Authority's costs of the administration and supervision of this contract and of reviewing the reports submitted in accordance with section 10.1 hereof.

10.6 The amount of the annual overhead charge may be revised by the Authority to reflect its costs actually and reasonably incurred.[3]

Section 11
Data and information to be submitted on expiration of the contract

11.1 The Contractor shall transfer to the Authority all data and information that are both necessary for and relevant to the effective exercise of the powers and functions of the Authority in respect of the exploration area in accordance with the provisions of this section.

---

[3] ISBA/19/A/12, dated 25 July 2013, Amendments.

11.2 Upon expiration or termination of this contract the Contractor, if it has not already done so, shall submit the following data and information to the Secretary-General:

(a) Copies of geological, environmental, geochemical and geophysical data acquired by the Contractor in the course of carrying out the programme of activities that are necessary for and relevant to the effective exercise of the powers and functions of the Authority in respect of the exploration area;

(b) The estimation of mineable deposits, when such deposits have been identified, which shall include details of the grade and quantity of the proven, probable and possible cobalt crust reserves and the anticipated mining conditions;

(c) Copies of geological, technical, financial and economic reports made by or for the Contractor that are necessary for and relevant to the effective exercise of the powers and functions of the Authority in respect of the exploration area;

(d) Information in sufficient detail on the equipment used to carry out the exploration work, including the results of tests conducted of proposed mining technologies, but not equipment design data;

(e) A statement of the quantity of cobalt crusts recovered as samples or for the purpose of testing; and

(f) A statement on how and where samples of cores are archived and their availability to the Authority.

11.3 The data and information referred to in section 11.2 hereof shall also be submitted to the Secretary-General if, prior to the expiration of this contract, the Contractor applies for approval of a plan of work for exploitation or if the Contractor renounces its rights in the exploration area to the extent that such data and information relates to the renounced area.

Section 12
Confidentiality

Data and information transferred to the Authority in accordance with this contract shall be treated as confidential in accordance with the provisions of the Regulations.

Section 13
Undertakings

13.1 The Contractor shall carry out exploration in accordance with the terms and conditions of this contract, the Regulations, Part XI of the Convention, the Agreement and other rules of international law not incompatible with the Convention.

13.2 The Contractor undertakes:

(a) To accept as enforceable and comply with the terms of this contract;

(b) To comply with the applicable obligations created by the provisions of the Convention, the rules, regulations and procedures of the Authority and the decisions of the relevant organs of the Authority;

(c) To accept control by the Authority of activities in the Area as authorized by the Convention;

(d) To fulfil its obligations under this contract in good faith; and

(e) To observe, as far as reasonably practicable, any recommendations which may be issued from time to time by the Legal and Technical Commission.

13.3 The Contractor shall actively carry out the programme of activities:

(a) With due diligence, efficiency and economy;

(b) With due regard to the impact of its activities on the marine environment; and

(c) With reasonable regard for other activities in the marine environment.

13.4 The Authority undertakes to fulfil in good faith its powers and functions under the Convention and the Agreement in accordance with article 157 of the Convention.

Section 14
Inspection

14.1 The Contractor shall permit the Authority to send its inspectors on board vessels and installations used by the Contractor to carry out activities in the exploration area to:

(a) Monitor the Contractor's compliance with the terms and conditions of this contract and the Regulations; and

(b) Monitor the effects of such activities on the marine environment.

14.2 The Secretary-General shall give reasonable notice to the Contractor of the projected time and duration of inspections, the name of the inspectors and any activities the inspectors are to perform that are likely to require the availability of special equipment or special assistance from personnel of the Contractor.

14.3 Such inspectors shall have the authority to inspect any vessel or installation, including its log, equipment, records, facilities, all other recorded data and any relevant documents which are necessary to monitor the Contractor's compliance.

14.4 The Contractor, its agents and employees shall assist the inspectors in the performance of their duties and shall:

(a) Accept and facilitate prompt and safe boarding of vessels and installations by inspectors;

(b) Cooperate with and assist in the inspection of any vessel or installation conducted pursuant to these procedures;

(c) Provide access to all relevant equipment, facilities and personnel on vessels and installations at all reasonable times;

(d) Not obstruct, intimidate or interfere with inspectors in the performance of their duties;

(e) Provide reasonable facilities, including, where appropriate, food and accommodation, to inspectors; and

(f) Facilitate safe disembarkation by inspectors.

14.5 Inspectors shall avoid interference with the safe and normal operations on board vessels and installations used by the Contractor to carry out activities in the area visited and shall act in accordance with the Regulations and the measures adopted to protect confidentiality of data and information.

14.6 The Secretary-General and any duly authorized representatives of the Secretary-General, shall have access, for purposes of audit and examination, to any books, documents, papers and records of the Contractor which are necessary and directly pertinent to verify the expenditures referred to in section 10.2 (c).

14.7 The Secretary-General shall provide relevant information contained in the reports of inspectors to the Contractor and its sponsoring State or States where action is necessary.

14.8 If for any reason the Contractor does not pursue exploration and does not request a contract for exploitation, it shall, before withdrawing from the exploration area, notify the Secretary-General in writing in order to permit the Authority, if it so decides, to carry out an inspection pursuant to this section.

Section 15
Safety, labour and health standards

15.1 The Contractor shall comply with the generally accepted international rules and standards established by competent international organizations or general diplomatic conferences concerning the safety of life at sea, and the prevention of collisions and such rules, regulations and procedures as may be adopted by the Authority relating to safety at sea. Each vessel used for carrying out activities in the Area shall possess current valid certificates required by and issued pursuant to such international rules and standards.

15.2 The Contractor shall, in carrying out exploration under this contract, observe and comply with such rules, regulations and procedures as may be adopted by the Authority relating to protection against discrimination in employment, occupational safety and health, labour relations, social security, employment security and living conditions at the work site. Such rules, regulations and procedures shall take into account conventions and recommendations of the International Labour Organization and other competent international organizations.

Section 16
Responsibility and liability

16.1 The Contractor shall be liable for the actual amount of any damage, including damage to the marine environment, arising out of its wrongful acts or omissions, and those of its employees, subcontractors, agents and all persons engaged in working or acting for them in the conduct of its operations under this contract, including the costs of reasonable measures to prevent or limit damage to the marine environment, account being taken of any contributory acts or omissions by the Authority.

16.2 The Contractor shall indemnify the Authority, its employees, subcontractors and agents against all claims and liabilities of any third party arising out of any wrongful acts or omissions of the Contractor and its employees, agents and subcontractors, and all persons engaged in working or acting for them in the conduct of its operations under this contract.

16.3 The Authority shall be liable for the actual amount of any damage to the Contractor arising out of its wrongful acts in the exercise of its powers and functions, including violations under article 168 (2) of the Convention, account being taken of contributory acts or omissions by the Contractor, its employees, agents and subcontractors, and all persons engaged in working or acting for them in the conduct of its operations under this contract.

16.4 The Authority shall indemnify the Contractor, its employees, subcontractors, agents and all persons engaged in working or acting for them in the conduct of its operations under this contract, against all claims and liabilities of any third party arising out of any wrongful acts or omissions in the exercise of its powers and functions hereunder, including violations under article 168 (2) of the Convention.

16.5 The Contractor shall maintain appropriate insurance policies with internationally recognized carriers, in accordance with generally accepted international maritime practice.

Section 17
Force majeure

17.1 The Contractor shall not be liable for an unavoidable delay or failure to perform any of its obligations under this contract due to force majeure. For the purposes of this contract, force majeure shall mean an event or condition that the Contractor could not reasonably be expected to prevent or control; provided that the event or condition was not caused by negligence or by a failure to observe good mining industry practice.

17.2 The Contractor shall, upon request, be granted a time extension equal to the period by which performance was delayed hereunder by force majeure and the term of this contract shall be extended accordingly.

17.3 In the event of force majeure, the Contractor shall take all reasonable measures to remove its inability to perform and comply with the terms and conditions of this contract with a minimum of delay.

17.4 The Contractor shall give notice to the Authority of the occurrence of an event of force majeure as soon as reasonably possible, and similarly give notice to the Authority of the restoration of normal conditions.

Section 18
Disclaimer

Neither the Contractor nor any affiliated company or subcontractor shall in any manner claim or suggest, whether expressly or by implication, that the Authority or any official thereof has, or has expressed, any opinion with respect to cobalt crusts in the exploration area and a statement to that effect shall not be included in or endorsed on any prospectus, notice, circular, advertisement, press release or similar document issued by the Contractor, any affiliated company or any subcontractor that refers directly or indirectly to this contract. For the purposes of this section, an "affiliated company" means any person, firm or company or State-owned entity controlling, controlled by, or under common control with, the Contractor.

Section 19
Renunciation of rights

The Contractor, by notice to the Authority, shall have the right to renounce its rights and terminate this contract without penalty, provided that the Contractor shall remain liable for all obligations accrued prior to the date of such renunciation and those obligations required to be fulfilled after termination in accordance with the Regulations.

Section 20
Termination of sponsorship

20.1 If the nationality or control of the Contractor changes or the Contractor's sponsoring State, as defined in the Regulations, terminates its sponsorship, the Contractor shall promptly notify the Authority forthwith.

20.2 In either such event, if the Contractor does not obtain another sponsor meeting the requirements prescribed in the Regulations which submits to the Authority a certificate of sponsorship for the Contractor in the prescribed form within the time specified in the Regulations, this contract shall terminate forthwith.

Section 21
Suspension and termination of contract and penalties

21.1 The Council may suspend or terminate this contract, without prejudice to any other rights that the Authority may have, if any of the following events should occur:

(a) If, in spite of written warnings by the Authority, the Contractor has conducted its activities in such a way as to result in serious persistent and wilful violations of the fundamental terms of this contract, Part XI of the Convention, the Agreement and the rules, regulations and procedures of the Authority; or

(b) If the Contractor has failed to comply with a final binding decision of the dispute settlement body applicable to it; or

(c) If the Contractor becomes insolvent or commits an act of bankruptcy or enters into any agreement for composition with its creditors or goes into liquidation or receivership, whether compulsory or voluntary, or petitions or applies to any tribunal for the appointment of a receiver or a trustee or receiver for itself or commences any proceedings relating to itself under any bankruptcy, insolvency or readjustment of debt law, whether now or hereafter in effect, other than for the purpose of reconstruction.

21.2 The Council may, without prejudice to section 17, after consultation with the Contractor, suspend or terminate this contract, without prejudice to any other rights that the Authority may have, if the Contractor is prevented from performing its obligations under this contract by reason of an event or condition of force majeure, as described in section 17.1, which has persisted for a continuous period exceeding two years, despite the Contractor having taken all reasonable measures to overcome its inability to perform and comply with the terms and conditions of this contract with minimum delay.

21.3 Any suspension or termination shall be by notice, through the Secretary-General, which shall include a statement of the reasons for taking such action. The suspension or termination shall be effective 60 days after such notice, unless the Contractor within such period disputes the Authority's right to suspend or terminate this contract in accordance with Part XI, section 5, of the Convention.

21.4 If the Contractor takes such action, this contract shall only be suspended or terminated in accordance with a final binding decision in accordance with Part XI, section 5, of the Convention.

21.5 If the Council has suspended this contract, the Council may by notice require the Contractor to resume its operations and comply with the terms and conditions of this contract, not later than 60 days after such notice.

21.6 In the case of any violation of this contract not covered by section 21.1 (a) hereof, or in lieu of suspension or termination under section 21.1 hereof, the Council may impose upon the Contractor monetary penalties proportionate to the seriousness of the violation.

21.7 The Council may not execute a decision involving monetary penalties until the Contractor has been accorded a reasonable opportunity to exhaust the judicial remedies available to it pursuant to Part XI, section 5, of the Convention.

21.8 In the event of termination or expiration of this contract, the Contractor shall comply with the Regulations and shall remove all installations, plant, equipment and materials in the exploration area and shall make the area safe so as not to constitute a danger to persons, shipping or to the marine environment.

Section 22
Transfer of rights and obligations

22.1 The rights and obligations of the Contractor under this contract may be transferred in whole or in part only with the consent of the Authority and in accordance with the Regulations.

22.2 The Authority shall not unreasonably withhold consent to the transfer if the proposed transferee is in all respects a qualified applicant in accordance with the Regulations and assumes all of the obligations of the Contractor.

22.3 The terms, undertakings and conditions of this contract shall inure to the benefit of and be binding upon the parties hereto and their respective successors and assigns.

Section 23
No waiver

No waiver by either party of any rights pursuant to a breach of the terms and conditions of this contract to be performed by the other party shall be construed as a waiver by the party of any succeeding breach of the same or any other term or condition to be performed by the other party.

Section 24
Revision

24.1 When circumstances have arisen or are likely to arise which, in the opinion of the Authority or the Contractor, would render this contract inequitable or make it impracticable or impossible to achieve the objectives set out in this contract or in Part XI of the Convention or the Agreement, the parties shall enter into negotiations to revise it accordingly.

24.2 This contract may also be revised by agreement between the Contractor and the Authority to facilitate the application of any rules, regulations and procedures adopted by the Authority subsequent to the entry into force of this contract.

24.3 This contract may be revised, amended or otherwise modified only with the consent of the Contractor and the Authority by an appropriate instrument signed by the authorized representatives of the parties.

Section 25
Disputes

25.1 Any dispute between the parties concerning the interpretation or application of this contract shall be settled in accordance with Part XI, section 5, of the Convention.

25.2 In accordance with article 21 (2) of annex III to the Convention, any final decision rendered by a court or tribunal having jurisdiction under the Convention relating to the rights and obligations of the Authority and of the Contractor shall be enforceable in the territory of any State party to the Convention affected thereby.

Section 26
Notice

26.1 Any application, request, notice, report, consent, approval, waiver, direction or instruction hereunder shall be made by the Secretary-General or by the designated representative of the Contractor, as the case may be, in writing. Service shall be by hand, or by telex, fax, registered airmail or e-mail containing an authorized signature to the Secretary-General at the headquarters of the Authority or to the designated representative. The requirement to provide any information in writing under these Regulations is satisfied by the provision of the information in an electronic document containing a digital signature.

26.2 Either party shall be entitled to change any such address to any other address by not less than ten days' notice to the other party.

26.3 Delivery by hand shall be effective when made. Delivery by telex shall be deemed to be effective on the business day following the day when the "answer back" appears on the sender's telex machine. Delivery by fax shall be effective when the "transmit confirmation report" confirming the transmission to the recipient's published fax number is received by the transmitter. Delivery by registered airmail shall be deemed to be effective 21 days after posting. An e-mail is presumed to have been received by the addressee when it enters an information system designated or used by the addressee for the purpose of receiving documents of the type sent and it is capable of being retrieved and processed by the addressee.

26.4 Notice to the designated representative of the Contractor shall constitute effective notice to the Contractor for all purposes under this contract, and the designated representative shall be the Contractor's agent for the service of process or notification in any proceeding of any court or tribunal having jurisdiction.

26.5 Notice to the Secretary-General shall constitute effective notice to the Authority for all purposes under this contract, and the Secretary-General shall be the Authority's agent for the service of process or notification in any proceeding of any court or tribunal having jurisdiction.

Section 27
Applicable law

27.1 This contract shall be governed by the terms of this contract, the rules, regulations and procedures of the Authority, Part XI of the Convention, the Agreement and other rules of international law not incompatible with the Convention.

27.2 The Contractor, its employees, subcontractors, agents and all persons engaged in working or acting for them in the conduct of its operations under this contract shall observe the applicable law referred to in section 27.1 hereof and shall not engage in any transaction, directly or indirectly, prohibited by the applicable law.

27.3 Nothing contained in this contract shall be deemed an exemption from the necessity of applying for and obtaining any permit or authority that may be required for any activities under this contract.

Section 28
Interpretation

The division of this contract into sections and subsections and the insertion of headings are for convenience of reference only and shall not affect the construction or interpretation hereof.

Section 29
Additional documents

Each party hereto agrees to execute and deliver all such further instruments, and to do and perform all such further acts and things as may be necessary or expedient to give effect to the provisions of this contract.

II. RECOMMENDATIONS & PROCEDURES

International Seabed Authority

Legal and Technical Commission

ISBA/19/LTC/8

Distr.: General
1 March 2013

Original: English

Nineteenth session
Kingston, Jamaica
15-26 July 2013

Recommendations for the guidance of contractors for the assessment of the possible environmental impacts arising from exploration for marine minerals in the Area

Issued by the Legal and Technical Commission

I. Introduction

1. During prospecting and exploration for marine minerals, the International Seabed Authority is required to, among other things, establish and keep under periodic review environmental rules, regulations and procedures to ensure effective protection for the marine environment from harmful effects which may arise from activities in the Area and, together with sponsoring States, apply a precautionary approach to such activities on the basis of recommendations by the Legal and Technical Commission. In addition, contracts for mineral exploration in the Area require the contractor to gather oceanographic and environmental baseline data and to establish baselines against which to assess the likely effects of its programme of activities under the plan of work for exploration on the marine environment and a programme to monitor and report on such effects. The contractor shall cooperate with the Authority and the sponsoring State or States in the establishment and implementation of such monitoring programmes. The contractor shall report annually on the results of its environmental monitoring programmes. Furthermore, when applying for approval of a plan of work for exploration, each applicant is required to provide, inter alia, a description of a programme for oceanographic and environmental baseline studies in accordance with the relevant Regulations and any environmental rules, regulations and procedures established by the Authority that would enable an assessment of the potential environmental impact of the proposed exploration activities, taking into account any recommendations issued by the Legal and Technical Commission, as well as a preliminary assessment of the possible impact of the proposed exploration activities on the marine environment.

2. The Legal and Technical Commission may from time to time issue recommendations of a technical or administrative nature for the guidance of contractors to assist them in the implementation of the rules, regulations and

procedures of the Authority. Under article 165, paragraph 2 (e), of the 1982 United Nations Convention on the Law of the Sea, the Commission shall also make recommendations to the Council on the protection of the marine environment, taking into account the views of recognized experts in that field.

3. It is recalled that in June 1998 the Authority convened a workshop on the development of environmental guidelines for exploration for polymetallic nodule deposits. The outcome of the workshop was a set of draft guidelines for the assessment of possible environmental impacts from exploration for polymetallic nodule deposits in the Area. The workshop participants noted the need for clear and common methods of environmental characterization based on established scientific principles and taking into account oceanographic constraints. One year after the approval of the Regulations on Prospecting and Exploration for Polymetallic Nodules in the Area (ISBA/6/A/18), the Legal and Technical Commission issued guidelines in 2001 as document ISBA/7/LTC/1/Rev.1 and later revised them in 2010 in the light of increased understanding (see ISBA/16/LTC/7). In the light of the approval of the Regulations on Prospecting and Exploration for Polymetallic Sulphides in the Area (ISBA/16/A/12/Rev.1) in 2010 and of the Regulations on Prospecting and Exploration for Cobalt-rich Ferromanganese Crusts in the Area (ISBA/18/A/11) in 2012, it was decided that there was a need to create a combined set of environmental guidelines that included guidance with regard to exploration for polymetallic sulphides and cobalt-rich ferromanganese crusts.

4. A workshop entitled "Polymetallic sulphides and cobalt crusts: their environment and considerations for the establishment of environmental baselines and an associated monitoring programme for exploration" was held in Kingston from 6 to 10 September 2004 in response to the need for environmental guidance during exploration for those two resources. The recommendations of the workshop were based on the current scientific knowledge of the marine environment and the technology to be used.

5. Unless otherwise noted, the recommendations herein relating to exploration and test mining apply to all types of deposits. At some sites it may not be reasonably feasible to implement some of the specific recommendations. In that situation, the contractor should provide arguments to that effect to the Authority, which can then exempt the contractor from the specific requirement, if appropriate.

6. The Commission was of the opinion that, given the technical nature of the recommendations and the limited understanding of the impact of exploration activities on the marine environment, it was vital to provide, as annex I to the recommendations, an explanatory commentary. The explanatory commentary is supplemented by a glossary of technical terms.

7. The nature of the environmental considerations associated with test mining depends on the type of mining technology used to extract the minerals and on the scale of the operation (i.e. the number of tons extracted per annum per region). Mechanical removal without initial processing at the seabed was deemed the most likely technology to be used and is the method of mineral extraction assumed herein. It is likely that future mining operations will employ techniques not considered here. Given that the recommendations contained herein are based on the current scientific knowledge of the marine environment and the technology to be used at the time at which they were prepared, they may require revision at a later date, taking into account the progress of science and technology. In accordance with

each set of Regulations, the Commission may from time to time review the present recommendations, taking into account the current state of scientific knowledge and information. It is recommended that such a review be carried out periodically and at intervals of no more than five years. To facilitate the review, it is recommended that the Authority convene workshops, at appropriate intervals, in which the members of the Commission, contractors and recognized experts from the scientific community are invited to participate.

8. After approval of the plan of work for exploration in the form of a contract and prior to the commencement of exploration activities, the contractor is required to submit to the Authority:

(a) An impact assessment of the potential effects on the marine environment of all proposed activities, excluding those activities considered by the Legal and Technical Commission to have no potential for causing harmful effects on the marine environment;

(b) A proposal for a monitoring programme to determine the potential effect on the marine environment of proposed activities; and to verify that there is no serious harm to the marine environment arising from the prospecting and exploration for minerals;

(c) Data that could be used to establish an environmental baseline against which to assess the effect of future activities.

II. Scope

A. Purpose

9. These recommendations describe the procedures to be followed in the acquisition of baseline data, and the monitoring to be performed during and after any activities in the exploration area with potential to cause serious harm to the environment. Their specific purposes are:

(a) To define the biological, chemical, geological and physical components to be measured and the procedures to be followed by contractors to ensure effective protection for the marine environment from harmful effects which may arise from the contractors' activities in the Area;

(b) To facilitate reporting by contractors;

(c) To provide guidance to potential contractors in preparing a plan of work for exploration for marine minerals in conformity with the provisions of the Convention, the 1994 Agreement relating to the implementation of Part XI of the United Nations Convention on the Law of the Sea and the relevant Regulations of the Authority.

B. Definitions

10. Except as otherwise specified in this document, terms and phrases defined in each set of the Regulations shall have the same meaning in these recommendations. A glossary of technical terms is contained in annex II to the present document.

C. Environmental studies

11. Every plan of work for exploration for marine minerals shall take into consideration the following phases of environmental studies:

(a) Environmental baseline studies;

(b) Monitoring to ensure that no serious harm is caused to the marine environment from activities during prospecting and exploration;

(c) Monitoring during and after testing of collecting systems and equipment.

12. Contractors shall permit the Authority to send its inspectors on board vessels and installations used by the contractor to carry out exploration activities in the Area to, among other things, monitor the effects of such activities on the marine environment.

III. Environmental baseline studies

13. It is important to obtain sufficient information from the exploration area to document the natural conditions that exist prior to test mining, to gain insight into natural processes such as dispersion and settling of particles and benthic faunal succession, and to gather other data that may make it possible to acquire the capability necessary to make accurate environmental impact predictions. The impact of naturally occurring periodic processes on the marine environment may be significant but is not well quantified. It is therefore important to acquire as long a history as possible of the natural responses of sea-surface, mid-water and seabed communities to natural environmental variability.

Baseline data requirements

14. To set up the environmental baseline in the exploration area as required under the relevant Regulations, the contractor, utilizing the best available technology, including the Geographical Information System, and using robust statistical design in preparing the sampling strategy, shall collect data for the purpose of establishing baseline conditions of physical, chemical, biological and other parameters that characterize the systems likely to be impacted by exploration and possible test-mining activities. Baseline data documenting natural conditions prior to test mining are essential in order to monitor changes resulting from test-mining impacts and to predict impacts of commercial mining activities.

15. Data to be addressed should include:

(a) For physical oceanography:

(i) Collect information on the oceanographic conditions, including the current, temperature and turbidity regimes, along the entire water column and, in particular, near the sea floor;

(ii) Adapt the measurement programme to the geomorphology of the seabed;

(iii) Adapt the measurement programme to the regional hydrodynamic activity at the sea surface, in the upper water column and at the seabed;

(iv) Measure the physical parameters at the depths likely to be impacted by the discharge plumes during the testing of collecting systems and equipment;

(v) Measure particle concentrations and composition to record distribution along the water column;

(b) For geology:

(i) Produce Geographic Information System regional maps with high-resolution bathymetry showing major geological and geomorphological features to reflect the heterogeneity of the environment. These maps should be produced at a scale appropriate to the resource and habitat variability;

(ii) Collect information on heavy metals and trace elements that may be released during test mining and their concentrations;

(c) For chemical oceanography:

(i) Collect information on background water column chemistry, including water overlying the resource, in particular on metals and other elements that may be released during the mining process;

(ii) Collect information on heavy metals and trace elements that may be released during test mining and their concentrations;

(iii) Determine what additional chemicals may be released in the discharge plume following processing of the resource during test mining;

(d) For sediment properties:

(i) Determine the basic properties of the sediment, including measurement of soil mechanics and composition, to adequately characterize the surficial sediment deposits which are the potential source of deep-water plume;

(ii) Sample the sediment taking into account the variability of the seabed;

(e) For biological communities, using high-resolution bathymetric maps to plan the biological sampling strategy, taking into account variability in the environment:

(i) Gather data on biological communities, taking samples of fauna representative of variability of habitats, bottom topography, depth, seabed and sediment characteristics, abundance and mineral resource being targeted;

(ii) Collect data on the sea floor communities specifically relating to megafauna, macrofauna, meiofauna, microfauna, demersal scavengers and fauna associated directly with the resource, both in the exploration area and in areas that may be impacted by operations (e.g. the operational and discharge plumes);

(iii) Assess pelagic communities in the water column and in the benthic boundary layer that may be impacted by operations (e.g. the operational and discharge plumes);

(iv) Record in dominant species baseline levels of metals that may be released during mining;

(v) Record sightings of marine mammals, other near-surface large animals (such as turtles and fish schools) and bird aggregations, identifying the relevant species where possible. Details should be recorded in transit to and from areas of exploration and on passage between stations. Temporal variability should be assessed;

(vi) Establish at least one station within each habitat type or region, as appropriate, to evaluate temporal variations in water column and seabed communities;

(vii) Assess regional distribution of species and genetic connectivity of key species;

(viii) Collections should be photo-documented (and indexed to video imaging) in situ to provide an archive of context/setting information for each sample;

(f) For bioturbation: where appropriate, gather data on the mixing of sediments by organisms;

(g) For sedimentation: gather time series data on the flux and composition of materials from the upper water column into the deep sea.

16. In addition to analyses of the data, raw data should be provided in electronic format with annual reports as agreed with the secretariat. These data will be used for regional environmental management and assessment of cumulative impacts.

IV. Environmental impact assessment

17. The best available technology and methodology for sampling should be used in establishing baseline data for environmental impact assessments.

A. Activities not requiring environmental impact assessment

18. On the basis of available information, a variety of technologies currently used in exploration are considered to have no potential for provoking serious harm to the marine environment and thus do not require environmental impact assessment. These include:

(a) Gravity and magnetometric observations and measurements;

(b) Bottom and subbottom acoustic or electromagnetic profiling of resistivity, self-potential or induced polarization, or imaging without the use of explosives or frequencies known to significantly affect marine life;

(c) Water, biotic, sediment and rock sampling for environmental baseline study, including:

(i) Sampling of small quantities of water, sediment and biota (e.g. from remotely operated vehicles);

(ii) Mineral and rock sampling of a limited nature, such as that using small grab or bucket samplers;

(iii) Sediment sampling by box corer and small diameter corer;

(d) Meteorological observations and measurements, including the setting of instruments (e.g. moorings);

(e) Oceanographic, including hydrographic, observations and measurements, including the setting of instruments (e.g. moorings);

(f) Video/film and still photographic observations and measurements;

(g) Shipboard mineral assaying and analysis;

(h) Positioning systems, including bottom transponders and surface and subsurface buoys filed in notices to mariners;

(i) Towed plume-sensor measurements (chemical analysis, nephelometers, fluorometers, etc.);

(j) In situ faunal metabolic measurements (e.g. sediment oxygen consumption);

(k) DNA screening of biological samples;

(l) Dye release or tracer studies, unless required under national or international laws governing the activities of flagged vessels.

B. Activities requiring environmental impact assessment

19. The following activities require prior environmental impact assessment, as well as an environmental monitoring programme to be carried out during and after the specific activity, in accordance with the recommendations contained in paragraphs 29 and 30. It is important to note that these baseline, monitoring and impact assessment studies are likely to be the primary inputs to the environmental impact assessment for commercial mining:

(a) Sampling for on-land studies for mining and/or processing if the sampling area of any one sampling activity exceeds the limit stipulated in the specific guidance to contractors for specific mineral resources as stated in section IV.F below;

(b) Use of systems to create artificial disturbances on the sea floor;

(c) Testing of collection systems and equipment;

(d) Drilling activities using on-board drilling rigs;

(e) Rock sampling;

(f) Sampling with epibenthic sledge, dredge or trawl, unless permitted for areas less than that stipulated in the specific guidance to contractors for specific mineral resources as stated in section IV.F below.

20. The prior environmental impact assessment and the information set out in the recommendation contained in paragraph 27 and the relevant environmental monitoring programme is to be submitted by the contractor to the Secretary-General at least one year before the activity takes place and at least three months in advance of the annual session of the Authority.

21. Environmental monitoring data are required prior to, during and following test mining at the mining site and at comparable reference sites (to be selected according to their environmental characteristics and faunal composition). Impact assessment

must be based on a properly designed monitoring programme that should be able to detect impacts in time and space and to provide statistically defensible data.

22. The main environmental impacts are expected to be at the sea floor. Additional impacts may occur at the tailings-discharge depth and in the water column. The impact assessment should address impacts on benthic, benthic boundary layer and pelagic environments. The impact assessment should address not only areas directly affected by mining but also the wider region impacted by near-bottom plumes, the discharge plume and material released by transporting the minerals to the ocean surface, depending on the technology used.

23. Mining tests may be conducted by contractors individually or collaboratively. In a mining test, all components of the mining system will be assembled and the entire process of test mining, lifting minerals to the ocean surface and discharge of tailings will be executed. For environmental assessments, this test phase should be monitored intensively, as should tests of any test-mining component. When mining tests have already been carried out, even if by another contractor, the knowledge gained through those tests should be applied, where appropriate, to ensure that unanswered questions are resolved by new investigations.

24. Monitoring of test mining should allow the prediction of impacts to be expected from the development and use of commercial systems.

25. A discharge plume in surface water may interfere with primary productivity by increasing nutrient levels and decreasing light penetration into the ocean. The introduction of cold deep water from depth will also alter sea surface temperature locally and release carbon dioxide into the atmosphere. Before large volumes of deep water are brought to the surface in a test-mining activity, an environmental impact assessment is required, because environmental changes may alter food chains, disturb vertical and other migrations and lead to changes in the geochemistry of an oxygen-minimum zone, if present. Because oxygen-minimum zones vary in size regionally and to some extent seasonally, environmental studies should determine the depth range of the oxygen-minimum layer in each test-mining area.

C. Information to be provided by the contractor

26. The contractor will provide the Authority with a general description and a schedule of the proposed exploration programme, including the programme of work for the immediate five-year period, such as studies to be undertaken in respect of the environmental, technical, economic and other appropriate factors that must be taken into account during test mining. This general description should include:

(a) A programme for oceanographic and environmental baseline studies in accordance with the relevant set of Regulations and any environmental regulations and procedures issued by the Authority that would enable an assessment of the potential environmental impact of the proposed exploration activities, taking into account any guidelines issued by the Authority;

(b) Proposed measures for the prevention, reduction and control of pollution and other hazards to, as well as possible impacts on, the marine environment;

(c) Preliminary assessment of the possible impact of the proposed exploration activities on the marine environment;

(d) Delineation of impact reference areas and preservation reference areas. The impact reference area should be representative of the site to be mined in terms of environmental characteristics and the biota. The preservation reference area should be carefully located and large enough not to be affected by mining activities, including the effects from operational and discharge plumes. The reference site will be important in identifying natural variations in environmental conditions. Its species composition should be comparable to that of the test-mining area.

27. The contractor is to provide the Secretary-General with some or all of the following information, depending on the specific activity to be carried out:

(a) Size, shape, tonnage and grade of the deposit;

(b) Mineral collection technique (passive or active mechanical dredge, hydraulic suction, water jets, etc.);

(c) Depth of penetration into the seabed;

(d) Running gear (skis, wheels, caterpillars, Archimedes screws, bearing plates, water cushion, etc.) which contacts the seabed;

(e) Methods for separation on the sea floor of the mineral resource and the sediment, including washing of the minerals, concentration and composition of sediment mixed with water in the operational plume created at the seabed, height of discharge above the sea floor, modelling of particle size dispersion and settlement, and estimates of depth of sediment smothering with distance from the mining activity;

(f) Processing methods at the seabed;

(g) Mineral crushing methods;

(h) Methods for transporting the material to the surface;

(i) Separation of the mineral resource from the fines and the sediment on the surface vessel;

(j) Methods for dealing with the abraded fines and sediment;

(k) Volume and depth of discharge plume, concentration and composition of particles in the discharged water and chemical and physical characteristics of the discharge;

(l) Mineral resource processing on the surface vessel;

(m) Location of the mining test and boundaries of the test area;

(n) Probable duration of the test;

(o) Test plans (collecting pattern, area to be perturbed, etc.);

(p) Baseline maps (e.g. side-scan sonar, high-resolution bathymetry) of the deposits to be removed;

(q) Status of regional and local environmental baseline data.

28. Each contractor should include in its programme for specific activity a specification of the events that could cause suspension or modification of the activities owing to serious environmental harm, if the effects of the events cannot be adequately mitigated.

D. Observations and measurements to be made while performing a specific activity

29. The contractor is to provide the Secretary-General with some or all of the following information, depending on the specific activity to be carried out:

(a) Width, length and pattern of the collector tracks on the sea floor;

(b) Depth of penetration in the sediment or rock and the lateral disturbance caused by the collector;

(c) Volume and type of material taken by the collector;

(d) Ratio of sediment separated from the mineral source by the collector, volume and size spectra of material rejected by the collector, size and geometry of the operational plume at the seabed, trajectory and spatial extent of the operational plume relative to the particle sizes within it;

(e) Area and thickness of sedimentation from the operational plume and the distance where sedimentation is negligible;

(f) Volume of discharge plume from the surface vessel, concentration and composition of particles in the discharged water, chemical and physical characteristics of the discharge, behaviour of the discharged plume at the surface, in mid-water or at the seabed, as appropriate.

E. Observations and measurements to be made after the performance of a specific activity

30. The contractor is to provide the Secretary-General with some or all of the following information, depending on the specific activity to be carried out:

(a) Thickness of redeposited sediment and rock rubble over the area affected by the operational plume caused by the mining test activity and by the discharge plume;

(b) Abundance and diversity of benthic communities and changes in behaviour of key species subjected to smothering by sedimentation;

(c) Changes in the distribution, abundance and diversity of benthic communities in the mining area, including rates of recolonization;

(d) Possible changes in the benthic communities in adjacent areas not expected to be perturbed by the activity, including the operational and discharge plumes;

(e) Changes in the characteristics of the water at the level of the discharge plume during the mining test, and changes in the behaviour of the fauna at and below the discharge plume;

(f) For mineral deposits, post-test-mining maps of the mined area, highlighting changes in geomorphology;

(g) Levels of metals found in dominant benthic fauna subjected to resettled sediment from the operational and discharge plumes;

(h) Resampling of local environmental baseline data at reference and test zones and evaluation of environmental impacts;

(i) Changes in fluid flux and response of organisms to changes in hydrothermal settings, if relevant;

(j) Changes in water currents and the response of organisms to changes in circulation.

F. Additional requirements specific to individual resource types

Polymetallic nodules

31. In addition to the information provided above, the following information is specific to polymetallic nodules: environmental impact assessment is required if any one sampling activity by epibenthic sled, dredge or trawl, or a similar technique, exceeds 10,000 m^2.

Polymetallic sulphides

32. In addition to the information provided above, the following information is specific to polymetallic sulphides:

(a) Any modification of fluid discharge in hydrothermal settings and associated fauna (using photo documentation, temperature measurements and other metrics, as appropriate) should be recorded;

(b) For active sulphide deposits, temperature-fauna relationships should be analysed (e.g. 5-10 discrete, video-documented temperature measures within each subhabitat);

(c) The presence of key taxa, including specialist localized chemosynthetic communities, should be mapped and their position relative to potential mining locations assessed to a radius of 10 km from the proposed mine site;

(d) Meiofaunal and microbial community structure and biomass associated with the polymetallic sulphide deposits should be examined from rock dredge and rock drill samples, or obtained from remotely operated vehicle/submersible sampling, where possible. A statistically defensible number of samples should be taken from polymetallic sulphides, from which species that live on the rock or in crevices and pits in the deposit should be identified;

(e) Fauna should be collected using precision sampling remotely operated vehicle/submersible technology by subhabitat and placed into discrete sample boxes;

(f) Abundance and coverage of the dominant taxa in each subhabitat should be determined.

Cobalt-rich ferromanganese crusts

33. In addition to the information provided above, the following information is specific to cobalt-rich ferromanganese crusts:

(a) Communities associated with cobalt-rich ferromanganese crusts may have a highly localized distribution. Biological sampling must therefore be stratified by habitat type, which will be defined by topography (e.g. summit, slope and base for seamounts), hydrography, current regime, predominant megafauna (e.g. coral mounds), oxygen content of the water (if the oxygen minimum layer intersects the feature) and, potentially, depth. Replicate biological samples should be obtained using appropriate sampling tools in each subhabitat;

(b) Biological sampling should be carried out, insofar as possible, on a representative subset of all features of potential mining interest within each claim area in order to build a picture of the distribution of the community within that area;

(c) Photographic or video transects should be undertaken to determine habitat type, community structure and associations of megafauna with specific types of substrata. Abundance, percentage cover and diversity of megafauna should be based initially on at least four transects. These transects should extend from the flat sea floor 100 m or more from the base of the seamount, along the slope of the seamount and across its summit. More limited sampling may be required on larger seamount features. Further transects should be carried out in crust areas of potential test-mining interest;

(d) A statistically defensible number of replicate remotely operated vehicle/submersible samples per stratum is recommended for collection of specimens and to assess species richness;

(e) Prior to test mining, demersal fish and other nekton living over the sea floor should be assessed on the basis of towed photographic/video transects, with deployed cameras set up to record at different time periods, or with submersible/remotely operated vehicle observations and photographs. Seamounts can be important ecosystems with a variety of habitats for a number of fish species that form aggregations there for spawning or feeding. Test mining operations could affect fish behaviour;

(f) Meiofaunal and microbial community structure and biomass associated with the cobalt-rich ferromanganese crust should be examined using remotely operated vehicle/submersible sampling. A statistically defensible number of samples should be taken from cobalt-rich ferromanganese crusts, from which species that live on the rock or in crevices and pits in the crust should be identified.

V. Data collection, reporting and archival protocol

A. Data collection and analysis

34. The types of data to be collected, the frequency of collection and the analytical techniques in accordance with the present recommendations should follow the best available methodology and the use of an international quality system and certified operation and laboratories.

B. Data archival and retrieval scheme

35. A cruise report with station list, list of activities and other relevant metadata should be submitted to the secretariat of the Authority within one year of the completion of the cruise.

36. The contractor should provide the Authority with all relevant data, data standards and inventories, including raw environmental data in the format agreed with the Authority. Data and information that are necessary for the formulation by the Authority of rules, regulations and procedures concerning protection and preservation of the marine environment and safety, other than proprietary equipment design data (including hydrographical, chemical and biological data), should be made freely available for scientific analysis no later than four years after the completion of a cruise. An inventory of the data holdings from each contractor should be accessible on the World Wide Web. Metadata that detail the analytical techniques, error analyses, descriptions of failures, techniques and technologies to avoid, comments on sufficiency of data and other relevant descriptors should be included with the actual data.

C. Reporting

37. Assessed and interpreted results of the monitoring shall be periodically reported to the Authority together with the raw data in accordance with the prescribed format.

D. Transmission of data

38. All data relating to the protection and preservation of the marine environment, other than equipment design data, collected pursuant to the recommendations contained in paragraphs 29 and 30 should be transmitted to the Secretary-General to be freely available for scientific analysis and research within four years of the completion of a cruise, subject to confidentiality requirements as contained in the relevant Regulations.

39. The contractor should transmit to the Secretary-General any other non-confidential data in its possession which could be relevant for the purpose of the protection and preservation of the marine environment.

VI. Cooperative research and recommendations to close gaps in knowledge

40. Cooperative research may provide additional data for the protection of the marine environment and may be cost-effective for contractors.

41. Interaction between multiple oceanographic disciplines and multiple institutions can be useful in closing gaps in knowledge resulting from contractors working individually. The Authority can give support in the coordination and dissemination of the results of such research, in accordance with the Convention. The Authority should serve in an advisory capacity to mining contractors in terms of identification of cooperative research opportunities, but contractors should seek their own links to academic and other professional expertise.

42. Cooperative research programmes may prove especially synergistic, bringing together the expertise, research facilities, logistic capability and common interests of mining companies and cooperative institutions and agencies. In this way, contractors may make best use of large-scale research facilities such as vessels,

autonomous underwater vehicles and remotely operated vehicles and expertise in geology, ecology, chemistry and physical oceanography of academic institutions.

43. To answer certain questions on the environmental impacts of mining, specific experiments, observations and measurements must be conducted. All contractors need not execute the same studies. Repeating certain experiments or impact studies would not necessarily add to scientific knowledge or to impact assessments, while needlessly consuming financial, human and technological resources. Contractors are encouraged to explore opportunities to unite their efforts in international cooperative oceanographic studies.

Annex I

Explanatory commentary

1. The aim of these recommendations is to define the biological, chemical, geological and physical oceanographic information required to ensure the effective protection of the marine environment from harmful effects which may arise from activities in the Area. The recommendations also provide guidance to prospective contractors in preparing plans of work for exploration for marine minerals.

2. A plan of work for exploration should include activities that address the following environmental requirements:

    (a) Establish an environmental baseline study against which to compare both natural change and impacts caused by mining activities;

    (b) Provide methods to monitor and evaluate the impacts of deep seabed mining on the marine environment;

    (c) Provide data for an environmental impact assessment required for an exploitation contract for marine minerals in the Area, including the designation of impact reference zones and preservation reference zones;

    (d) Provide data for the regional management of resource exploration and exploitation, the conservation of biodiversity and the recolonization of areas affected by deep seabed mining;

    (e) Establish procedures to demonstrate no serious harm to the environment from exploration for marine minerals.

3. On the basis of current proposed methodologies, the main impacts are expected to occur at the sea floor. Additional impacts may be caused by processing on board the mining vessel and from the discharge plume or as a result of different technologies being used.

4. At the seabed, the mining equipment will disturb and remove the sea floor (rock, nodules and sediment), creating a near-bottom operational plume of particulate material, in some cases potentially releasing harmful chemicals, which will impact marine life. It will be necessary to mitigate the loss of substrate, provide for the natural recolonization of the seabed and develop methods that minimize impacts in space and time from direct disturbance of the sea floor and from material carried in, and deposited from, the operational plume.

5. Processing of mineral slurry at the sea surface on board the mining vessel will bring large quantities of cold, nutrient-rich, carbon-dioxide-replete and particle-laden water to the sea surface, which must be carefully controlled so as not to alter sea surface ecosystems, allow the degassing of climate-active gases and the release of harmful metals and compounds from the mining process, in particular in relation to reduced mineral phases, such as sulphides. Any chemicals added to separate the mineral phases from the waste material and water need to be assessed for potential harmful effects.

6. The discharge plume needs to be controlled to limit harmful environmental effects. Discharge at the sea surface may introduce particle-laden water to oligotrophic particle-sparse waters, limiting light penetration, changing sea temperature and introducing high levels of nutrients to nutrient-poor regions with

significant impacts on the species composition of primary producers and the pelagic ecosystem. Discharge within the deeper waters of the oxygen-minimum zone or zones may trigger the release of harmful bioactive metals, while discharge at even greater depths may introduce particle-rich water to sparse, but generally diverse, pelagic communities. Discharge at the seabed would add to the operational plume with warmer water and finer particles.

7. Baseline data requirements include seven categories: physical oceanography, geology, chemistry/geochemistry, biological communities, sediment properties, bioturbation and sedimentation.

8. Physical oceanographic data are required to estimate the potential influence of the operational and discharge plumes and, together with information on the geomorphology of the sea floor, to predict the potential distribution of species. Information is required on currents, temperature and turbidity at the sea surface, in mid-water and in the benthic boundary layer overlying the sea floor.

9. At the proposed depth of the discharge plume, measurements of the currents and particulate matter are required to predict the behaviour of the discharge plume and to assess natural particle loads in the water.

10. The oceanographic structure of the water column is measured by conductivity-temperature-depth systems. Temporal variation in the physical structure of surface water is required. The conductivity-temperature-depth profiles and sections should be performed from the sea surface to the sea floor so as to characterize the stratification of the entire water column. Current and temperature field structures can be inferred from long-term mooring data and from supplementary acoustic Doppler current profilers. Remote systems such as autonomous underwater vehicles or gliders may be used to provide spatial and temporal information. The number and location of the moorings need to be appropriate for the size of the area to adequately characterize the current regime, in particular in areas of complex geomorphology. The recommended sampling resolution is based on World Ocean Circulation Experiment and Climate Variability and Predictability Research standards, with station spacing not exceeding 50 km. In regions of large lateral gradients (e.g. in boundary currents and near major geomorphologic structures), the horizontal sampling spacing should be decreased in order to allow resolution of the gradients. The number of current meters on a mooring is dependent upon the characteristic scales of topography of the area studied (difference in heights from the bottom). The suggested location of the lowest meter should be as close as possible to the sea floor, normally 1 m to 3 m. The location of the upper current meter should exceed the highest element of the topography by a factor of 1.2 to 2. Along with this, the basic levels of the current meters should be 10 m, 20 m, 50 m, 100 m and 200 m above the seabed.

11. A satellite-data analysis is recommended for understanding synoptic-scale surface activity in the area and for larger-scale events.

12. The water column structure should be defined either by continuous profiling or by water column samples. For samples, measurements of water properties in the vertical plane should be no more than 100 m apart. The resolution should be greater in high-gradient regions (e.g. to locate and quantify the boundaries of oxygen-minimum zones). For parameters without significant horizontal gradients, the determination of base-line ranges (e.g. means and standard deviations) is adequate.

For parameters with significant spatial structure (gradients, extremes), the sampling resolution must allow the physical oceanographic structure of the area to be characterized. Because of the strong influence of topography on the spatial scales of oceanic features, it is expected that this will require a survey plan with station spacing depending on local geomorphological scales (e.g. finer resolution is required in areas with steep slopes).

13. The second baseline data group (chemical oceanography) is a specific requirement targeted at collecting data prior to any discharge in the water column or at the seabed. The data gathered are important for assessing the possible influence of mining, including test mining, on the composition of the water, e.g. concentrations of metals, and on ecosystem processes (biological activity). Samples should be collected at the same locations as the physical oceanography measurements. The water overlying the mineral deposits and the pore water in the sediments should be characterized chemically, where possible, to evaluate processes of chemical exchange between the sediment and the water column. The chemical parameters to be measured and the suggested protocols are listed in chapter 23 of the Authority's report entitled *Standardization of Environmental Data and Information: development of guidelines*. In the same report, table 3 lists the minimum requirements of parameters that should be measured (phosphate, nitrate, nitrite, silicate, carbonate alkalinity, oxygen, zinc, cadmium, lead, copper, mercury and total organic carbon). Once details of the proposed test-mining techniques are known, the parameter lists should be extended to include any potentially hazardous substances that may be released into the water column during test mining. All measurements must be accurate in conformance with accepted scientific standards (e.g. Climate Variability and Predictability Research and GEOTRACES protocols).

14. To allow for later analysis of additional parameters, water samples suitable for analysis of dissolved and particulate matter should be collected and archived in a repository accessible for future study.

15. Vertical profiles and temporal variation also need to be addressed in the field measurement programme.

16. A general scheme for physical and chemical oceanographic baselines includes:

(a) Collection of water column hydrographic and light-transmission data of sufficient resolution to characterize the dominant patterns, taking into account the characteristics of geomorphology and topographic characteristics of the seabed at the exploration site, where appropriate;

(b) Collection of data appropriate for assessing the horizontal and vertical advective and eddy-diffusive dispersal potential of dissolved and particulate matter on environmentally relevant time and space scales;

(c) Set-up and validation of a numerical circulation model that covers the temporal and spatial scales important for dispersal, and the carrying out of experiments, e.g. to investigate the potential impact of accidental spills.

17. Regardless of the mining techniques to be employed, it is expected that some particulate and/or dissolved mining by-products will be released into the water column in the vicinity of the mined deposits, the transport conduits and processing at the sea surface. With the currently proposed exploration and test-mining techniques, the primary anticipated test-mining by-products are particles created by

the mechanical break-up of the mined minerals. While it is expected that mining operators will minimize the loss of economically valuable minerals, it does not seem realistic to assume zero loss. Since the particle size range is not known, it is assumed that the by-products of test mining will include very small particles, which can remain in suspension for months. The possibility of the introduction of toxic substances cannot be excluded. While bound metals are not biologically available, dissolution of metals and consequent metal toxicity may take place under particular environmental conditions (e.g. low pH, including within the guts of marine fauna, oxygen-minimum zones in the water column). Other possible examples include accidental or intended release of chemicals used during exploration and test mining. A primary goal of the physical baseline data collection consists of assessing the dispersal potential both for particles and for dissolved substances. Knowledge of the dispersal potential is also required for monitoring and mitigating the effects of accidental spills relating to the test-mining operations. The dispersal potential near possible mining sites should be assessed even if the design target of the mining technology includes avoidance of the release of any test-mining by-products into the environment.

18. For each test-mining by-product, the timescale over which it causes significant environmental impact must be modelled. If these timescales depend on dilution, determination of vertical and horizontal mixing rates near the target site must be included in the dispersal assessment. Dispersal potential must be assessed over timescales that range from the tidal frequencies to the largest of these environmental-impact timescales. An assessment of the dispersal potential in the deep ocean generally requires long-term monitoring. Even the determination of mean-flow directions and speeds at depth can require several years of current-meter data. Assessing eddy-diffusive dispersal is difficult and generally requires the application of Lagrangian techniques, such as neutrally buoyant floats or dye-release experiments. For these reasons, it is recommended that an assessment of the regional dispersal potential at several levels in the water column begin early during exploration. It may be possible to assess dispersal near the surface and near 1,000 m from available data — surface drifters and Array for Real-time Geostrophic Oceanography floats, respectively. Before test mining is to begin, the dispersal potential must be assessed at all levels where harmful by-products may be released into the water column by test mining and where accidental spills may occur. The required vertical resolution will depend on the regional dynamical regime (vertical shear of the horizontal currents), but it is anticipated that at least three levels will need to be sampled (near-surface, mid-depth and near-bottom). The flow near the seabed in particular must be temporally and spatially resolved, e.g. using bottom-mounted acoustic Doppler current profiler measurements with sufficient sampling to resolve the dominant tidal flows. In regions of geomorphological relief near the test-mining site, horizontal and vertical resolutions should be increased to allow dynamical structures associated with deep-sea geomorphology (e.g. boundary currents, trapped eddies, overflows) to be resolved.

19. Near active hydrothermal vent fields, it is often possible to gain useful first-order dispersal information at the level of neutrally buoyant plumes from hydrographical, chemical and optical observations. Interpreting plume-dispersal observations in terms of dispersal potential for mining by-products is complicated by a variety of factors, including poor knowledge of the temporal and spatial characteristics of hydrothermal sources; that hydrothermal plumes disperse at their

equilibrium level, which depends both on the source and environmental background characteristics; and that the particle composition (and, thus, the settling velocity) of hydrothermal plumes cannot be controlled. Nevertheless, when such plumes occur in the vicinity of a mineral resource, it is expected that hydrothermal-plume dispersal observations will be useful, in particular for designing controlled follow-up dispersal studies. To complete an assessment of the dispersal potential, a three-dimensional hydrodynamic numerical model that covers the temporal and spatial scales important for dispersal must be constructed.

20. The contractor should use a model that is accepted by the ocean modelling community as suitable for dispersal studies near the seabed; simple box models or z-coordinate models with coarse vertical resolution at depth are not expected to be adequate. The details of this model will be dependent on the topographic and oceanographic settings of the target site. Resolution should be in accordance with the scales described above (i.e. gradients should be resolved by several points) and the model needs to be validated by comparison with the observational data. After validation, the numerical model should be used to investigate potential scenarios, such as to estimate the potential impact of accidental spills or for certain extreme cases (e.g. atmospheric storms).

21. Modelling will be important in extrapolating from test mining to commercial-scale mining.

22. The third baseline data group (sediment properties, including pore water chemistry) is targeted at predicting the behaviour of the discharge plume and the effect of test-mining activity on sediment composition. In this context, the following parameters should be measured: specific gravity, bulk density, shear strength and grain size, as well as the sediment depth of change from oxic to suboxic, or suboxic to oxic, conditions. Measurements should include organic and inorganic carbon in the sediment, metals that may be harmful in some forms (iron, manganese, zinc, cadmium, lead, copper and mercury), nutrients (phosphate, nitrate, nitrite and silicate), carbonate (alkalinity) and the redox system in pore waters. The geochemistry of the pore water and sediments should be determined as far down as 20 cm. Recommended protocols are listed in tables 1 and 2 of chapter 23 of the Authority's report entitled *Standardization of Environmental Data and Information: development of guidelines*. Representative pre-test-mining cores and sediment samples should be collected and archived.

23. The fourth baseline data group (biological communities) is targeted to collect data on "natural" communities, including "natural spatial and temporal variability", to evaluate the potential effects of the activities on the benthic and pelagic fauna.

24. The characterization of pelagic and benthic communities should be carried out within all subhabitats that may be impacted by mining operations and to determine the regional distributions for the creation of preservation reference areas and for mitigation strategies to promote the natural recolonization of areas affected by mining activities.

25. Geographic Information System mapping tools are recommended for habitat mapping, recording sampling locations and planning stratified random sampling programmes.

26. Standard practices for the preservation of organisms should be followed, including discrete sampling of subhabitats into separate sample containers

(preferably insulated) with closed lids to prevent washing on recovery; recovery of samples within 12 hours of collection to obtain high-quality material; and immediate processing and preservation of samples on deck or maintenance in cold rooms for durations of no more than six hours before preservation (or less where molecular assays are planned).

27. Multiple preservation methods should be used, including preservation in formalin for taxonomic studies; freezing or preservation in 100 per cent ethanol for molecular studies; drying of whole animals and/or selected tissues for stable isotope analyses; and freezing of whole animals and/or selected tissue for trace metal and biochemical analyses.

28. Colour photographic documentation of organisms should be obtained whenever possible (organisms in situ and/or fresh material on deck to document natural colouration). The photographs should be archived.

29. All samples and sample derivatives (e.g. photographs, preserved material, gene sequences) should be linked to relevant collection information (the minimum requirement is date, time, method of sampling, latitude, longitude, depth).

30. Identification and enumeration of samples at sea and in the laboratory should be complemented by molecular and isotopic analyses, as appropriate. Species-abundance and species-biomass matrices should be standard products wherever practical.

31. Specimens must be archived for comparison with taxonomic identifications from other sites and to understand the details of changes in the composition of species over time. If species composition does change, it might be subtle, and reference back to the original animals (where there might only have been a putative identification) is essential. It is recommended that samples be archived as part of national or international collections.

32. Standardization of methodology and reporting of the results is extremely important. Standardization should include instruments and equipment; quality assurance in general; sample collection; treatment and preservation techniques; determination methods and quality control on board vessels; analytical methods and quality control in laboratories; and data processing and reporting. Method standardization will allow for comparison of results across provinces and lead to selection of critical parameters for monitoring efforts.

33. Spatial variation in the biological community must be evaluated prior to test mining by sampling at least three mineral deposits, if present, in the Area, each separated by a distance greater than the projected deposition of 90 per cent of the particles suspended by the mining operation. Because the populations of fauna of some deposits will be subsets of meta-populations that interact through dispersal and colonization, it is important to know the degree of isolation of populations occupying the mineral deposits that are to be removed and whether a given population serves as a critical brood stock for other populations.

34. Different kinds of sampling equipment can be used depending upon the seabed characteristics and the size of the fauna to be collected. Methods for collecting baseline biological data must therefore be adapted to each specific set of conditions. The use of multiple corers in soft sediments allows the distribution of different sampling tubes from the same station among the specialists that used different

techniques for fauna identification and counting. It should be stressed, however, that the diameter of the tubes must be adjusted to avoid excessive disturbance of the sediment or obstruction by large particles such as nodules and rock fragments and that biological samples must be large enough to generate good sample sizes in terms of abundance and biomass for robust statistical analyses.

35. Hard substrata (such as polymetallic sulphides, cobalt crusts, basalt), especially where the organisms are small, are challenging environments to sample quantitatively. Multiple collection techniques may be required, including slurp sampling and grab samples of larger organisms. Video documentation and photographic transects may be the only means suitable for developing a species-abundance matrix in some cases. Precision sampling using remotely operated vehicles is recommended for all habitats. Autonomous underwater vehicles or hybrid remotely operated-autonomous underwater vehicles may ultimately prove to be useful survey/sampling platforms. Exposed mineral surfaces may be irregular and, potentially, have steep slopes, which make them difficult to image quantitatively without the use of a remotely operated vehicle.

36. The data to be collected and the corresponding methodology for the various classes/sizes of seabed fauna should be as follows:

(a) **Megafauna**. Data on megafauna abundance, biomass, species structure and diversity should be based on video and photographic transects. Photographs need to have a sufficient resolution in order to identify organisms greater than 2 cm in their smallest dimension. The width covered by the photographs should be at least 2 m. As to sampling stations, the pattern of the photographic transects should be defined taking into account the different features of the bottom, such as topography, variability of the sediment characteristics and abundance and type of deposit. Species identification should be confirmed by collection of specimens at the site. Sampling efforts should be used to characterize the less abundant but potentially key megafauna in the system (including fish, crabs and other motile organisms). Representative samples of those organisms should be preserved for taxonomic, molecular and isotopic analyses;

(b) **Macrofauna**. Data on macrofauna (>250 µm) abundance, species structure, biomass and diversity should be obtained through a quantitative analysis of samples. In soft sediments, vertical profiles with a suitable depth distribution (suggested depths: 0-1, 1-5, 5-10 cm) should be obtained from box cores (0.25 m^2) or multiple corers, as appropriate;

(c) **Meiofauna**. Data on meiofauna (<250 µm, >32 µm) abundance, biomass and species structure should be obtained through a quantitative analysis of samples. In soft sediments vertical profiles with a suitable depth distribution (suggested depths: 0-0.5, 0.5-1.0, 1-2, 2-3, 3-4, 4-5 cm) should be obtained from cores. One multicorer tube per station could be devoted for this purpose;

(d) **Microfauna**. Microbial metabolic activity should be determined using adenosine triphosphate or other standard assay. In soft sediment vertical profiles should be obtained with suggested intervals for sampling of 0-0.5, 0.5-1.0, 1-2, 2-3, 3-4, 4-5 cm. One multicorer tube per station could be devoted for this purpose;

(e) **Nodule fauna**. Abundance, biomass and species structure of the fauna attached to the nodules should be determined from selected nodules taken from the top of box corers or sampled by remotely operated vehicle;

(f) **Demersal scavenger**. A time-lapse baited camera should be installed at the study area for at least one year to examine the physical dynamics of surface sediment and to document the activity level of surface megafauna and the frequency of resuspension events. Baited traps may be used to characterize the community species composition. Amphipod necrophage communities should be determined using short-term (24-48 hours) baited traps.

37. If there is potential for surface discharge, the plankton community in the upper 200 m of the water column should be characterized. Depending on plume modelling studies, it may be necessary to study plankton communities, especially gelatinous plankton, over a wide depth range. The pelagic community structure around the depth of the discharge plume, and at depths below, needs to be assessed prior to test mining. In addition, the pelagic community in the benthic boundary layer should be characterized using near-bottom opening/closing pelagic trawls or remotely operated vehicle techniques. Measurements should be made of phytoplankton composition, biomass and production, zooplankton composition, and biomass and bacterial plankton biomass and productivity. Temporal variation of the plankton community in the upper surface waters on seasonal and inter-annual scales should be studied. Remote sensing should be used to augment field programmes. Calibration and validation of remote-sensing data are essential.

38. Trace metals and potential toxic elements should be assessed in muscle and target organs of dominant demersal fish and invertebrate species. This should be replicated over time before test-mining operations begin (to measure natural variability) and thereafter at least annually to monitor possible changes resulting from test-mining activity. A combination of monitoring and shipboard and laboratory experimentation may be necessary to resolve, prior to test mining, potential ecotoxicological impacts, including possible impacts on phytoplankton and zooplankton if the discharge plume occurs at the sea surface or in mid-water.

39. Temporal variation must be evaluated for at least one test-mining site and the preservation reference site prior to the test-mining activity (ideally, with a minimum of annual sampling over at least three years). The temporal study should be reviewed by the Authority prior to the start of test mining. Studies of temporal variation at the seabed should be based on video and/or photographic surveys. For sulphide deposits, associated temperatures and sampling of subhabitats are required. Simple time-lapse photography seabed observatory systems recording the seabed four to five times per day over a period of a year would provide high-resolution temporal data. Where possible, ecosystem studies, such as growth rates, recruitment rates and the trophic status of dominant taxa, should be carried out. Where multiple test-mining sites are identified, the contractor must assess the degree to which temporal studies at one site are applicable to another; this assessment should also be reviewed by the Authority.

40. Taxonomic standardization should be addressed. To facilitate identification, there should be an exchange of identification codes, keys, drawings and sequences at major laboratories and collections that carry out taxonomic studies of marine organisms. Taxonomic expertise is extremely limited, even for major faunal groups (e.g. fish, molluscs, decapod crustaceans, corals, sponges and echinoderms). It will be important for all taxonomic groups to be assessed at each site. This can be accomplished most efficiently through the development of cooperative taxonomic centres or groups of experts. Taxonomy by numbers (e.g. species 1, species 2), if

consistent rules are used and vouchers maintained, is a good basis for baseline studies, but classical and molecular taxonomy must be supported, either directly by the contractor or as part of cooperative research programmes. Molecular methods continue to advance rapidly, making biotic surveys at all levels, especially the level of microorganisms, much more rapid and economically feasible than at present. Molecular sequences should be deposited in Genbank or equivalent internationally recognized sequence databases.

41. Information on faunal succession following test mining is essential to determining recovery rates of benthic populations from the effects of mining. Data should include samples from the immediate test area before and after test mining, from selected distances away from the mined area to determine the effect of the benthic plume, and at repeated intervals after test mining. Such impact experiments may be conducted collaboratively.

42. Additional information on the effects of the discharge plume on pelagic fauna may be gathered by recording unusual natural events, such as fish kills and unusually large concentrations of fish, marine mammals, turtles and birds.

43. The vertical distribution of light directly affects primary productivity in the euphotic zone. If there is surface discharge, vertical light-intensity profiles will show the effect of discharged particles on light attenuation and spectral bands over time, depth and distance from the mining ship. Those values can be used to detect any accumulation of the suspended particles at the pycnocline. In addition, any discharge plume may result in the release of large amounts of nutrients, temperature changes, the release of carbon dioxide and (at sulphide sites) potential changes in pH and ocean acidification.

44. The fifth baseline data group (bioturbation) is targeted at collecting the background "natural" rates of sedimentary processes, including "natural spatial and temporal variability", in order to model and to evaluate the effects of mining activities on such processes. Rates of bioturbation (i.e. the mixing of sediments by organisms) must be measured to analyse the importance of biological activity prior to a mining disturbance and can be evaluated from profiles of excess Pb-210 activity from cores, taking into account the variability in the sediment. Excess Pb-210 activity should be evaluated on at least five levels per core (suggested depths are 0-0.5, 0.5-1.0, 1-1.5, 1.5-2.5 and 2.5-5 cm). Rates and depth of bioturbation are to be evaluated by standard advection or direct diffusion models.

45. The sixth baseline data group (sedimentation) is targeted at collecting data to model and evaluate the effects of the discharge plume. It is recommended that deployment of moorings with sediment traps on a mooring line be undertaken, with one trap below 2,000 m to characterize the particulate flux from the euphotic zone and one trap approximately 500 m above the sea floor to characterize the flux of materials reaching the sea floor. The bottom trap must be high enough above the bottom so as not to be influenced by sediment resuspension. Sediment traps should be installed for a suitable period of time, with samples collected monthly to examine seasonal changes in flux and to evaluate inter-annual variability, in particular between climatic event years (e.g. El Niño, La Niña). The trap installation may share the same mooring as the current meters described above. Given that the flux of materials from the upper water column into the deep sea is ecologically significant in the food cycle of bottom-dwelling organisms, an adequate characterization of the material flux in mid-water and flux to the sea floor is

necessary for a comparison with the effect of the tailings discharge. Knowledge of in situ settling velocities for test-mining discharge particles, both in mid-water and near the sea floor, will help to verify and improve the capacity of mathematical models for predicting the dispersion of the mid-water and benthic plumes. This information is relevant to the concerns expressed regarding the discharge plume and from the operation plume on the benthic biota and benthic boundary layer pelagic organisms. The temporal resolution of the particle-flux measurements must be one month or better and nephelometry time series should be recorded on the sediment traps.

46. The seventh baseline group (geological properties) is targeted at determining the heterogeneity of the environment and assisting the placement of suitable sampling locations.

47. High-resolution, high-quality bathymetric data should be collected over the area where the dispersal of test-mining by-products is expected to significantly affect the environment (i.e. over the entire region covered by the numerical circulation model).

48. As part of the high-resolution baseline survey, a suite of representative pre-mining cores of the sea floor sediment, where appropriate, should be collected and stored in a suitable repository. Sampling devices that collect undisturbed samples of the top few centimetres should be used.

49. For sulphide deposits, hydrothermal vent areas should be classified as either dormant vent sites, which are still under the potential influence of a heat source although there is no current venting of hydrothermal fluids evident at that time, or extinct sites, which are at sites remote from present-day heat sources. From an ecological point of view, these two scenarios can be considered largely equivalent. What is important biologically is whether the proposed mining site has active hydrothermal vents (case 1), inactive vents that may restart owing to mining activity (case 2) or inactive vents that will remain hydrothermally inactive even when disturbed by test mining (case 3). It is important that the baseline assessment determine which of those cases will apply.

50. Part IV of the recommendations deals with environmental impact assessment. Certain activities have no potential for causing serious harm to the marine environment and therefore do not require environmental impact assessment. Such activities are listed. With regard to activities that do require environmental impact assessment, a monitoring programme is needed before, during and after a specific activity to determine the effects of the activity on the biological activities, including the recolonization of the disturbed areas.

51. The environmental studies during exploration will be based on a plan proposed by the contractor and reviewed by the Legal and Technical Commission for completeness, accuracy and statistical reliability. The plan would then be incorporated into the programme of activities under the contract. The environmental studies to be conducted during exploration will include the monitoring of environmental parameters so as to confirm the findings that there is no serious environmental harm from any activities being conducted on the seabed, in mid-water and in the upper water column.

52. Tests of collecting systems are an opportunity to determine the environmental implications of mining. The contractor will submit to the Authority a plan for such

testing, including the details for monitoring the environment, at least one year before testing begins and at least three months in advance of the annual session of the Authority. A plan for testing of collection systems shall include provision for monitoring of those areas impacted by the contractor's activities which have the potential to cause serious environmental harm, even if such areas fall outside the proposed test site. The programme will include, to the maximum extent practicable, specification of those activities or events that could cause suspension or modification of the tests owing to serious environmental harm if the specified activities or events cannot be adequately mitigated. The programme will also authorize refinement of the test plan prior to testing and at other appropriate times, if refinement is necessary. The plan will include strategies to ensure that sampling is based on sound statistical methods, that equipment and methods are scientifically acceptable, that the personnel who are planning, collecting and analysing data are well qualified and that the resultant data are submitted to the Authority in accordance with specified formats.

53. During the mining tests, the notification of proposed impact reference zones and preservation reference zones is recommended. The impact reference zone should be selected based on the area being representative of the environmental characteristics, including the biota, of the site where test mining will take place. The preservation reference zone should be carefully located and be large enough so as not to be affected by the natural variations of local environmental conditions. The zone should have species composition comparable to that of the test area. The preservation reference zone should be outside the test area and areas influenced by the plume.

54. The monitoring programme proposed by the contractor must provide details of how the impacts of the test-mining activities will be assessed.

55. Part V of the recommendations deals with data collection and reporting. It is recommended that collection and analytical techniques follow best practices such as those developed by the Intergovernmental Oceanographic Commission of the United Nations Educational, Scientific and Cultural Organization and available at world data centres, national oceanographic data centres or those recommended by the Authority. An inventory of the data holdings from each contractor should be accessible on the World Wide Web via the Authority.

56. The environmental baseline studies and the monitoring programmes represent a significant source of data and knowledge. A data archival and retrieval scheme could assist all contractors in the search for environmentally significant indicator elements. Syntheses of data and experience can work to the advantage of all contractors. Increased data accessibility increases the likely accuracy of models and will assist in:

(a) Identification of best practices;

(b) Development of a common approach to data management;

(c) Multilateral exchange of views and data leading to international cooperation;

(d) Savings of time, effort and costs in alerting the community to failures;

(e) Savings through reduction of measurement of some parameters.

57. Models can be validated and fine-tuned by such sea-truthing of data and can then partially supplement costly data collection exercises. Some claim areas may lie adjacent to or in the vicinity of other claims, providing further justification for data accessibility and joint efforts in modelling, so that the impact of activities in neighbouring areas can be evaluated without repeating all aspects of environmental assessment.

58. Part VI of the recommendations deals with cooperative research and recommendations to close gaps in knowledge. Recent years have witnessed a revolution in the development of knowledge and technology in deep-sea science. A number of research institutes around the world are carrying out extensive research programmes. Those institutions have considerable biological and scientific expertise and could be willing to join with mining contractors in conducting some of the required environmental research. They could provide sampling equipment and expertise and would probably be eager to join the contractor's vessel and to assist in sampling remote areas.

59. Cooperative research can facilitate the establishment of baselines of natural variability on the basis of geological, biological and other environmental records acquired in selected areas.

60. A partnership between the scientific community and contractors may result in voucher collection repositories, a gene sequence database repository, stable isotope analysis and interpretation and a photographic library of species/specimens. The basic scientific information acquired in partnership should result in the cost-effective acquisition of information that will assist in development planning and decision-making and the timely recognition of any significant environmental effects or issues prior to and during test mining. This information can be used to find solutions with a minimum-conflict approach.

61. The risk of extinction for a significant fraction of a community of fauna within a test-mine site will depend largely on how localized or widespread the species are distributed. Assessment will require syntheses of the biogeography of the fauna. This assessment should be facilitated by collaboration among contractors and with the scientific community.

62. Modelling studies should be undertaken collaboratively and linked closely to the field studies so as to assess extinction risks under various management strategies, including various options for the design of protected areas. Overall conservation strategies need to take into account non-test-mining impacts on faunal communities.

63. The contractors should work together, with the Authority and with national and international scientific research agencies on cooperative research programmes to maximize the assessment of environmental impact and minimize the cost of these assessments.

64. The Convention states that the Authority shall promote and encourage the conduct of marine scientific research in the Area, and shall coordinate and disseminate the results of such research and analysis when available.

Annex II

Glossary of technical terms

Active sulphides	Polymetallic sulphides through which warm water is flowing. Active sulphides (also called hydrothermal vents) deliver reduced compounds (e.g. sulphide) to the sea floor-seawater interface where they can be oxidized or otherwise autotrophically metabolized by free-living or symbiotic microorganisms.
ATP	Adenosine triphosphate, a complex organic compound which serves for short-term energy storage and conversion in all organisms. The amount of ATP present can be used as a measure of total microbial biomass in the sediment, as it corresponds to the number of active cells, most of which are bacteria.
Bathypelagic	Pertaining to open-ocean environments at depths greater than 3,000 m, deeper than the mesopelagic zone.
Benthic	Pertaining to the ocean bottom.
Benthic boundary layer	Pertaining to the layer of water immediately above the ocean bottom water layer/sediment interface.
Benthopelagic	Pertaining to the zone very close to, and to some extent having contact with, the sea floor of deeper portions of the open ocean.
Benthos	The forms of marine life that live on, or in, the ocean bottom.
Chemosynthesis	Process by which microorganisms metabolically transform inorganic carbon to organic carbon (cells), using energy derived from oxidation of reduced compounds. Chemosynthesis is the basis for the food web associated with deep-sea hydrothermal vents. "Chemoautotrophy" is a more descriptive and precise term for the general phenomenon of chemosynthesis; the two words are often used interchangeably.
Cobalt-rich ferromanganese crusts	Ferromanganese crusts with enriched cobalt content typically formed by precipitation and found on hard substrates in the deep sea on features with significant topographic relief, such as seamounts and ridges.
CTD	Pertaining to a system for measuring conductivity (indicator of salinity), temperature and depth (defined from pressure measurements). The first two parameters are essential in oceanographic observations and the depth profile is required to delineate the vertical structure of the ocean. Additional parameters, such as pH and dissolved oxygen concentration, can be measured if optional sensors are installed.

Cumulative impacts	Impacts resulting from incremental changes caused by other past, present or foreseeable actions.
Demersal	Organisms living at, or near the bottom of, a body of water.
Diel	Involving a 24-hour period that usually includes a day and the adjoining night.
Direct impacts	Impacts caused as a direct result of an action, such as loss of habitat and populations owing to removal of sulphides or other materials.
Embolism	The blood and tissues of fish contain dissolved gases. If fish from the deep ocean are brought to the surface, the decrease in pressure allows the dissolved gas to expand in the form of bubbles (embolism), causing disfiguration and protrusion of the internal organs through the mouth and other orifices.
Endemism	The degree to which a species is restricted to a particular geographic region; usually occurs in areas that are isolated in some way. Biologists also use the term "endemic" to refer to an organism that may be geographically widespread, but is restricted to a specific habitat, e.g. hydrothermal vents.
Epifauna	Animals that live on the bottom, either attached to the sea floor or freely moving over it.
Epipelagic	Referring to the upper region of the ocean depths, above the mesopelagic and generally below the oxygen-minimum zone.
Euphotic zone	The upper section of the ocean which receives sufficient light for photosynthesis. In clear oceanic waters, the euphotic zone can extend to a maximum water depth of 150 m.
Fauna	Invertebrates and vertebrates.
Halocline	A layer of water in which there is a steep gradient in salinity.
Hard substrata	Outcrops in the form of carbonate concretions, solid material, crustal rocks or deposits of precipitated materials, metals and minerals discharged from the subsurface by hydrothermal systems.
Hydrodynamic	Referring to any event relevant to the movement of sea water.
Impact zone	Zone where impacts (direct, indirect, cumulative and/or interactive) result from the activity.

Impact reference zones	Areas used to assess the effect of activities in the Area on the marine environment; must be representative of the environmental characteristics (physical, chemical, biological) of the area to be mined.
Inactive (or dormant) sulphides	Polymetallic sulphides through which warm water is no longer flowing into the overlying seawater (i.e. they are "cold"). Disturbance of these sulphides may result in renewal of hydrothermal fluxes into the water column, turning inactive sulphides into active sulphides (hence the concept of "dormant" sulphides).
Indirect impacts	Impacts on the environment that are not a direct result of the activity, often produced away from or as a result of a complex pathway (physical, chemical and biological). Often referred to as secondary (or even tertiary) impacts.
Infauna	Organisms that live within the sediment.
Macrofauna	Animals large enough to be seen by the naked eye, up to 2 cm long.
Megafauna	Animals large enough (larger than 2 cm) to be determined in photographs, proposed as key taxon (see taxonomy) for environmental impact assessment in deep-sea mining.
Meiofauna	Animals of the benthic community that are intermediate in size between macrofauna and microfauna. Operationally defined as >32 μm and <250 μm.
Mesopelagic	Referring to the portion of the oceanic province that is below the epipelagic and above the bathypelagic, usually corresponding to the dimly lit ocean or "twilight zone".
Microfauna	Organisms invisible to the naked eye, smaller than meiofauna. Operationally defined as <32 μm.
Microorganisms	Includes bacteria, Archaea and microscopic Eukarya.
Nekton	Fish, squids, crustaceans and marine mammals that are active swimmers in the open ocean environment.
Nematoda	The class of roundworms; a dominant meiofauna constituent.
Oxygen minimum	A water layer present in all oceans at depths between 400 and 1,000 m, caused by the sinking and degrading by bacteria of organic matter produced in the surface ocean. The oxygen scarcity can cause particulate metals to dissolve.
Pelagic	Pertaining to the open ocean environment.
pH	A measure of acidity or alkalinity.

Photosynthesis	The biological synthesis of organic material using light as energy source. Plants convert carbon dioxide and water, in the presence of chlorophyll and light energy, into carbohydrate food and oxygen.
Phytoplankton	Microscopic plants that are primary producers in the oceans.
Plankton	Passively drifting or weakly swimming organisms. This includes larval stages of benthic and pelagic organisms, phytoplankton (in surface waters), zooplankton, jellies and other drifting or weakly swimming organisms.
Plume	A dispersion of seawater that contains dense sediment particles. Benthic plume is a stream of water containing suspended particles of sea floor sediment, abraded manganese nodules and macerated benthic biota that emanates from the mining collector as a result of collector disturbance of the sea floor and spreads in a zone close to the sea floor. The far-field component of the benthic plume is termed the "rain of fines". Surface plume is a stream of water containing suspended particles of sea floor sediment, abraded manganese nodules and macerated benthic biota resulting from the separation, on board the mining ship, of the nodules from the water carrier and spreads in a zone closer than benthic plume to the ocean surface.
Polymetallic sulphides	Hydrothermally formed deposits of sulphides and accompanying mineral resources in the Area, which contain concentrations of metals including copper, lead, zinc, gold and silver.
Pore water	The water present within the spaces between sediment particles; also called "interstitial water".
Preservation reference zones	Areas representative of the test-mining site, but in which no test mining shall occur; used to assess changes in the biological status of the environment caused by test-mining activities.
Pycnocline	A layer of water in which there is a steep gradient in density with depth. It separates the well-mixed surface waters from the dense waters of the deep ocean. Density of the water is a function of temperature, salinity and, to a lesser extent, pressure.
Rain of fines	Far-field component of the "benthic plume" that consists mainly of fines; sedimentary particles which drift with the bottom current and slowly settle to the sea floor, generally outside the specific mining area.

Redox system	One essential chemical reaction is oxidation (giving electron) and reduction (removing electron). The chemical tendency (environmental strength) of oxidation can be expressed by redox potential (mv) that can be measured by an Eh/Ph meter. Eh is strongly correlated to the dissolved oxygen concentration in the sediment.
Scavenger	An animal that eats waste products and dead remains of other animals and plants that they did not kill themselves.
Seamounts	Isolated topographic features, usually of volcanic origin, of significant height above the sea floor.
Spatial scales	Scales characteristic of dimensions in space, as of oceanic phenomena, for example, the diameter of an eddy or the length of a wave. Also pertains to the geographical arrangement of sampling stations.
Subhabitat	A visually recognizable component of a larger habitat, e.g. tubeworm and mussel beds may be subhabitats of a specific active polymetallic sulphide field; an operational term that facilitates an understanding of the habitat as a whole.
Symbioses (chemosynthetic)	Associations between bacteria (symbionts) and invertebrates or vertebrates (hosts), in which the symbionts are chemosynthetic and provide nourishment to the host. The bacteria may be either endosymbiotic (living within the host tissues, such as tubeworms, clams, mussels) or episymbiotic (living on the outside of the host, such as bresiliid shrimp, alvinellid polychaetes).
Synoptic scales	Scales of hydrodynamic variability or events encompassing temporal scales ranging from one to two weeks to one to two months and spatial scales of one to several hundred kilometres. A typical feature is synoptic eddies 100-200 km in diameter passing through the north-east tropical Pacific from east to west and often penetrating to the sea floor.
Taxonomy	Orderly classification of animals or plants according to their presumed natural relationship.
Test mining	The use and testing of recovery systems and equipment.
Thermocline	A layer of water in which there is a rapid change of temperature with depth.
Transect	The vertical plane (reference for all the measures and sampling taken during the survey), from surface to the sea bottom, of the route of a survey oceanographic vessel, from point A to point B.

Transmissometer	Device used to measure the attenuation of light through a given path, such as of water. Data can be correlated to the amount of particles present.
Zooplankton/Animal plankton	Unlike phytoplankton, these organisms cannot produce organic matter on their own and thus feed on other organisms.

International Seabed Authority

ISBA/19/LTC/14

Legal and Technical Commission

Distr.: Limited
12 July 2013

Original: English

Nineteenth session
Kingston, Jamaica
15-26 July 2013

Recommendations for the guidance of contractors and sponsoring States relating to training programmes under plans of work for exploration

Issued by the Legal and Technical Commission

Introduction

1. The present recommendations are intended to provide guidance to applicants for plans of work for exploration, contractors and sponsoring States on their responsibilities with regard to training programmes under plans of work for exploration.

2. The recommendations cover the following components of the design and implementation of training programmes:

    (a) The process of reviewing and approving the proposed training programmes submitted by applicants for plans of work for exploration;

    (b) The content of the training programmes, including participation by sponsoring States;

    (c) The process of allocating training applicants to training opportunities;

    (d) Procedures for reporting on training activities.

3. The fundamental importance of international technical and scientific cooperation with regard to activities in the Area, including training of personnel of the Enterprise and nationals of developing States, is recognized in articles 144 and 148 of the United Nations Convention on the Law of the Sea as read with section 5 of the annex to the Agreement relating to the implementation of Part XI of the Convention.

I. Legal obligations

4. The legal obligations of contractors with regard to training are contained in article 15 of annex III to the Convention and are elaborated on in the Regulations adopted by the Authority relating to prospecting and exploration. Regulation 27 of the Regulations on prospecting and exploration for polymetallic nodules (the nodules regulations)[1] reads as follows:

> Pursuant to article 15 of annex III to the Convention, each contract shall include as a schedule a practical programme for the training of personnel of the Authority and developing States and drawn up by the contractor in cooperation with the Authority and the sponsoring State or States. Training programmes shall focus on training in the conduct of exploration, and shall provide for full participation by such personnel in all activities covered by the contract. Such training programmes may be revised and developed from time to time as necessary by mutual agreement.

5. Section 8 of the standard clauses for exploration contracts[2] provides:

> 8.1 In accordance with the Regulations, the Contractor shall, prior to the commencement of exploration under this contract, submit to the Authority for approval proposed training programmes for the training of personnel of the Authority and developing States, including the participation of such personnel in all of the Contractor's activities under this contract.
>
> 8.2 The scope and financing of the training programme shall be subject to negotiation between the Contractor, the Authority and the sponsoring State or States.
>
> 8.3 The Contractor shall conduct training programmes in accordance with the specific programme for the training of personnel referred to in section 8.1 hereof approved by the Authority in accordance with the Regulations, which programme, as revised and developed from time to time, shall become a part of this contract as schedule 3.

II. Training programme objectives and goals

6. Training programmes are designed and carried out for the benefit of the trainee, the nominating country and, more broadly, members of the Authority, especially the developing countries. Members of the Authority who may contribute to the development of the Enterprise should also benefit by having access to the same training opportunities.

7. Every attempt must be made to ensure that the planning and formulation of training programmes are carried out in good faith and that best practice is followed at all times. As such, all parties must make every effort to ensure that training contributes to the training and capacity development needs of the participants' country of origin.

---

[1] Regulation 29 of the sulphides and crusts regulations.
[2] In annex 4 of the nodules, sulphides and crusts regulations.

8. The training programme must be given due prominence in the contractor's programme of work and, as such, should be drawn up in pre-contract discussions and negotiations and inserted as schedule 3 to the contract prior to its signature and the commencement of exploration work.

9. Any contractor applying for approval of a plan of work for exploration must act in good faith and understand that the provision of training is no more or no less important than any other activity in its proposed plan of work and, as such, must be afforded the same priority in terms of time, effort and financing.

10. As important as the training is the use and sustainability of the skills and experience acquired by trainees and their nominating countries. All parties, but more particularly the Authority and the developing countries, must undertake to encourage the use of the training received for the benefit of the trainee and the country's involvement in activities related to the Authority and the Area.

11. All parties must commit to free and open channels of communication to ensure optimum delivery of training programmes, timely reporting and improved performance monitoring.

12. Recommendations for guidance pertaining to specific steps in the implementation of training programmes are set out below.

III. Approval of training programmes

13. The regulations require that an application for a plan of work include a component on training programmes. The usefulness of the proposed programme is directly reflected by the practical links the training has to the contractor's plan of work. It is logical that the two should be considered together.

14. The responsibilities of each party are as follows:

   A. The applicant for a plan of work for exploration should:

   1. Include in the application details of the activities it will undertake during its first five-year programme of activities which lend themselves to training;

   2. Based on the above, include in the application a possible schedule of activities under a proposed training programme, including a general description of the training;

   3. Include a summary of the minimum number of training opportunities that will be made available each year during the first five years of the contract and estimates of the number of opportunities that will be available during each of the subsequent five-year periods of the contract;

   4. Submit a training summary sheet in the format contained in the annex to the present document for each type of training opportunity identified in subparagraph 2 above;

   5. Indicate any training programmes that have been developed in collaboration with sponsoring States;

6. Indicate instances in which the contractor intends to support training programmes in addition to the activities covered by its plan of work;

7. Indicate instances in which part or the whole of a training programme has been developed in collaboration with the sponsoring State, national institutes in the sponsoring State, organizations or any other State party;

B. The sponsoring State will indicate whether it is to provide any other specific input or support to the applicant's training programme;

C. When considering an application for a plan of work for exploration, the Legal and Technical Commission will:

1. Review the training opportunities, programme and matching plan of work of the contractor;

2. Review the training applications, fully appreciating the training and capacity development needs of the nominating developing country and the secretariat;

3. Hold discussions with the contractor regarding its proposed training programme when discussing its plan of work;

4. Advise and make appropriate recommendations to the Secretary-General on the format, content and structure of the proposed training programme;

5. Review the proposed training programme against the present recommendations for guidance;

D. The Secretary-General should:

1. Take into account the recommendations of the Legal and Technical Commission when discussing and negotiating training programmes with contractors;

2. Maintain within the secretariat a database of training candidates and training needs of developing countries, while also identifying and including the future needs of the Enterprise.

IV. Content of training programmes

15. When in doubt, contractors must be guided by their legal obligations. As such, they must provide training which is practical. It should be focused on exploration activities and, where practicable, on all activities within the contractor's plan of work. Training programmes should be offered and run for the full term of a contract.

16. The following recommendations are made regarding the content of training programmes:

A. Contractors should:

1. As soon as practicable, discuss opportunities, scheduling, and possible training programmes with the Legal and Technical Commission;

2. Settle on a range of training opportunities following consultations with the Commission and the sponsoring State;

3. Consider the training and capacity-building needs of developing countries and the secretariat (Enterprise) when developing their training programmes, so as to ensure as wide a range of skill development as possible;

4. As a minimum, provide for the training equivalent of at least 10 trainees during each five-year period of the contract;

5. Identify additional training opportunities that may arise during the contract period, along with any proposed changes to the approved training schedules, if so required;

6. Make an ex gratia contribution to the Authority specifically earmarked for training purposes when circumstances dictate that training programmes cannot be implemented;

7. Make every attempt to avoid penalizing potential deserving candidates who take up training opportunities for issues beyond their control, such as language barriers. In such cases, every attempt must be made to seek viable alternatives;

B. The Legal and Technical Commission should:

1. Be as fully aware as possible of the training needs of the developing States that have nominated candidates for training;

2. Be aware of the training and capacity development needs required for the development of the Enterprise;

3. Be aware of practical training opportunities that may arise from a contractor's five-year plan of work;

4. Be aware of performances under past training programmes to guide future planning and programming;

C. The Secretary-General should:

1. Develop capacity and resources within the secretariat to focus exclusively on training and capacity-building. A key area of focus would be to develop an information system initially, and eventually, a database, of training needs of developing countries;

2. In the short term, develop appropriately designed (electronic) application and nomination forms, which allow for optimum identification of candidate and training needs;

3. Identify and store information on other training opportunities, institutions and potential partners;

4. Draw up and maintain a longer-term programme based on needs and priorities of countries for planning purposes, for use by the Commission in its discussions with contractors;

5. Take into account the recommendations of the Commission when discussing and negotiating training programmes with contractors.

V. Allocating training opportunities

17. Identification of training opportunities has to date been a reactive process driven by the making of an offer by a contractor, followed by the canvassing of interest from countries and, finally, the taking of a decision following the short-listing of candidates by the Commission. If training is to be needs-based, then a proactive process is necessary. The Authority must establish the required capacity, processes and a system whereby it can become proactive in steering any training programme, rather than being a mere conduit and a respondent to ad hoc offers.

18. It is recommended that each party acts as follows:

    A. The contractor should:

        1. Provide as much information to the secretariat as possible about its plan of work and the related available opportunities for training, including the number of trainee places, dates and other specific requirements necessary for carrying out the training activity;

        2. Be proactive in keeping the Authority informed with regard to new opportunities and any changes;

        3. Encourage potential applicants and nominating States to apply to the Authority using the appropriate forms;

        4. Once a training programme is approved, maintain liaison with the secretariat regarding the final selection of candidates that will receive training, for example, in respect of issues such as visa requirements and academic qualifications;

    B. The sponsoring State, particularly if it is also a developing country, should:

        1. Inform the secretariat of the full details of its nominated training candidates;

        2. Whenever possible, ensure that its training requirements are based on a bilateral agreement and a requirement of its sponsorship;

        3. Inform the secretariat if it has training needs over and above its bilateral agreement which its contractor may not be able to satisfy;

    C. The secretariat should:

        1. In the short term, advertise as widely and as soon as possible information about training opportunities. This should be through official notifications to member States as well as direct contact with members of the Commission, relevant international organizations, scientific institutions and other interested parties;

        2. Investigate ways in which to encourage greater participation by nationals of developing countries in the training activities of the Authority;

3. Develop a capacity-building programme and develop the required capacity, policies, strategies and programmes:

   a. Receive training applications and prepare a roster of qualified candidates;

   b. Coordinate applications for training, including maintaining a database of country needs and qualified applicants;

   c. Provide a status update at each meeting of the Commission on training and applications received from interested candidates;

   d. Assist in matching suitable candidates from a roster pre-approved by the Commission, or subgroup thereof, to opportunities as they arise, in consultation with contractors;

4. Ensure that the Commission is at all times fully briefed with up-to-date information so that it can perform its duties as efficiently and effectively as possible;

D. At each meeting of the Legal and Technical Commission, the Commission will:

   1. Appoint a subcommittee or subgroup of the Commission to ensure that matters related to training programmes are reviewed and dealt with as thoroughly as possible;

   2. Review all applications for training that have been referred to it;

   3. On the basis of transparent criteria, agree on a list of pre-approved candidates from the information received from the secretariat;

   4. Provide guidance regarding the type and preferred allocation of candidates, based on available opportunities;

   5. Conduct regular reviews to ensure that the goal of equitable geographic sharing of opportunities is being followed.

VI. Reporting procedure

19. A formal process for reporting on training activities is necessary to meet accountability and transparency objectives. The following process would allow for a better analysis of the training carried out and enable future programmes to be planned more effectively to meet the demands and requirements of developing States. The responsibilities of each party are as follows:

    A. The contractor:

       1. Shall include in its annual reports information on training completed in that reporting year;

       2. Shall include in its plans of work information on any changes to training programmes;

       3. Should consider guidance from the Commission when presenting its initial training programme and also in adjusting its training programme in the light of new developments, when necessary;

B. Trainees should be required to:

1. Provide a report at the end of their training on how they have benefited from the opportunity. If possible, they should indicate objectively whether their expectations have been met. The report shall be made available to the Authority, the contractor and the nominating State. Nothing in the trainee's report should impinge on or jeopardize the rights of the contractor as it might relate to matters of commercial sensitivity, intellectual property rights or anything of a confidential nature;

2. Provide a report five years after training has been completed, to allow for assessment of long-term benefits. The nominating State must ensure that this obligation is met;

3. Provide any comments or information that may assist the Commission in providing guidance for future training programmes. The trainee should report any benefits received or passed on as a result of the training;

4. Indicate that, if required, they could make themselves available for the Enterprise or developing country;

C. The secretariat should:

1. Report any developments in training programmes at each meeting of the Commission, including which candidates have been placed into training positions and what new applications for training have been received, in order to enable the members of the Commission to provide guidance;

2. Maintain contact with past trainees to monitor the benefits of the training and future availability;

3. Report on the progress of any capacity-building programme it has initiated, including but not limited to, the status of the Enterprise;

4. Provide an annual report to the Commission on the status of training and capacity development programmes, including outputs of relevant training achieved through the Endowment Fund and through any collaboration with other institutions and United Nations bodies;

D. The Legal and Technical Commission will:

1. Provide additional guidance on training based on the reports received, including the format, content and structure of future training programmes, and provide advice on the selection criteria required of future candidates;

2. Maintain, where possible, a watching brief on all activities within the Area and identify areas of potential scientific or technology opportunities or gaps that could be the target of future training or marine scientific research programmes;

3. Provide regular feedback to the Council as part of its normal reporting process.

VII. Review process

20. It is recommended that the secretariat monitor the performance of training under the present recommendations for guidance and carry out an evaluation on a regular basis.

21. The present recommendations should be reviewed and updated from time to time.

VIII. Disclaimer

22. Nothing in the present recommendations for guidance should be inconsistent with the intent and purpose of the Regulations.

Annex

Training summary template

(To be completed by the contractor) Type of opportunity (indicate total number to be provided)	
If additional institutions are involved (beyond the contractor), these should be listed	
Objectives and goals of the training programme	
Skills that will be taught or developed	
Schedule of training activities	
Years in which training will occur	
Number of trainees that will be accommodated and in which years	
Any specific suggestions with regard to the selection of potential candidates (language requirements, minimum qualifications, etc.)	

International Seabed Authority

ISBA/21/LTC/11

Legal and Technical Commission

Distr.: General
14 April 2015

Original: English

Twenty-first session
Kingston, Jamaica
13-24 July 2015

Recommendations for the guidance of contractors for the reporting of actual and direct exploration expenditure

Issued by the Legal and Technical Commission

The Legal and Technical Commission, acting pursuant to regulation 39 of the Regulations on Prospecting and Exploration for Polymetallic Nodules in the Area, regulation 41 of the Regulations on Prospecting and Exploration for Polymetallic Sulphides in the Area and regulation 41 of the Regulations on Prospecting and Exploration for Cobalt-rich Ferromanganese Crusts in the Area, issues the following recommendations for the guidance of contractors.

I. Introduction

1. In the present recommendations for guidance, references to "the Regulations" are collective references to the Regulations on Prospecting and Exploration for Polymetallic Nodules in the Area, the Regulations on Prospecting and Exploration for Polymetallic Sulphides in the Area and the Regulations on Prospecting and Exploration for Cobalt-rich Ferromanganese Crusts in the Area. References to "the standard clauses" are references to the standard clauses applicable to the particular contract in question.

2. The purpose of the present recommendations is to provide guidance to contractors in relation to the following matters:

   (a) The books, accounts and financial records to be maintained in accordance with section 9 of annex 4 to the Regulations;

   (b) The identification of internationally accepted accounting principles;

   (c) The presentation of financial information in the annual reports to be submitted pursuant to section 10 of annex 4 to the Regulations;

   (d) The definition of the actual and direct costs of exploration, as set out in section 10.2 (c) of annex 4 to the Regulations;

   (e) The form of certification of actual and direct exploration expenditure.

3. Except otherwise stated, words and phrases defined in the Regulations have the same meaning in the present recommendations for guidance.

4. The purpose of requiring detailed financial reports to be submitted is twofold. First, it is a due diligence requirement that is commonly found in exploration and mining contracts and is included as a means for objective quantification of the contractors' compliance with its plan of work. In this regard, as part of the process of application for a plan of work for exploration, contractors are required to provide a five-year programme of activities and a schedule of anticipated annual expenditure in respect of such programme. Under the standard clauses (annex 4, sect. 4.2), contractors are required to spend in each contract year not less than the amount specified in the programme of activities, or any agreed review thereof, in actual and direct exploration expenditure. The annual financial report is thus the only means by which the Authority is able to verify objectively the contractors' compliance with these provisions.

5. The second reason for requiring financial reports is potentially of direct benefit to the contractor. It is a general practice in the mining industry to allow some element of the costs of developing a mine site to be set off against the eventual income from production. As far as seabed mining is concerned, detailed provisions relating to the definition of "development costs" and their recovery in certain circumstances were included in article 13 of annex III to the United Nations Convention on the Law of the Sea. By reason of the Agreement relating to the Implementation of Part XI of the Convention, these provisions no longer apply. Nevertheless, the possibility that the Authority may in due course make provision for the recovery of some element of development costs is foreseen in annex 4, section 10.2 (c), of the Regulations, which provides that such expenditure may be claimed by the contractor as a part of the contractor's development costs incurred prior to the commencement of commercial production. In these circumstances, it is particularly important that there be some means of verifying objectively the amount of such expenditure, its relationship to the programme of activities and whether it is actual and direct exploration expenditure.

II. Books, accounts and financial records

6. Section 9 of annex 4 to the Regulations requires each contractor to keep a "complete and proper set of books, accounts and financial records, consistent with internationally accepted accounting principles". For the purposes of the Regulations, the Commission recommends that contractors adopt and apply the International Financial Reporting Standards adopted by the International Accounting Standards Board, in particular Standard 6, relating to the financial reporting of expenditure associated with the exploration for and evaluation of mineral resources. Furthermore, in order to ensure comparability with the contractor's financial statements of previous years, as well as with the financial statements of other contractors, all financial statements, including the financial statement to be included in the annual report required under section 10 of annex 4 to the Regulations, should be provided in a format consistent with International Accounting Standard 1.

III. Presentation of financial information

7. Section 9 of annex 4 to the Regulations also stipulates that "such books, accounts and financial records shall include information which will fully disclose the actual and direct expenditures for exploration and such other information as will facilitate an effective audit of such expenditures". Accordingly, the information to be disclosed by contractors should make it possible to identify and explain the reported amounts in the financial statements arising from the exploration and evaluation of mineral resources. To this end, it is recommended that contractors indicate their accounting policies for exploration and evaluation expenditure, including the recognition of exploration and evaluation assets. Contractors should also disclose the amounts of assets, liabilities, income and expense, and operating and investing cash flows arising from the exploration for and evaluation of mineral resources.

8. Financial statements should cover the same period as the reporting period and should normally correspond to a calendar year. Where this is not possible, for example because the country in which the contractor is based has a different financial year, the contractor should indicate the accounting year and, as far as possible, should provide a prorated summary of expenditure matching the reporting year.

9. The financial statement should be consistent with the proposed programme of activities, including the proposed schedule of annual expenditure, contained in schedule 2 of the contract over the equivalent period of time. Any deviation from the proposed programme of activities or schedule of annual expenditure should be clearly reported and explained. This should also be in accordance with a formal adjustment to the proposed programme, which would have been agreed on by the parties.

10. When an exploration activity continues beyond an accounting year, the reported costs should relate only to activities that were carried out during the relevant accounting year. Such expenditure should be clearly distinguished from the costs that are associated with past, previous or future exploration activities.

11. Where expenditure is nil, this should also be stated.

IV. Actual and direct exploration expenditure

12. In accordance with the Regulations, reported expenditure should relate only to the actual and direct costs of exploration. Not all expenditure incurred during a reporting period may be considered as an actual and direct cost of exploration. In general, actual and direct exploration costs are considered to be those that were necessary for carrying out exploration activities for the particular resource covered by the contract within the financial period in question and in accordance with the programme of activities set out in the contract for exploration. Such costs should be properly itemized in the breakdown of expenditure.

13. Pursuant to regulation 1.3 (b) of the Regulations, "exploration" means the search for deposits in the Area with exclusive rights, their analysis, the use and testing of recovery systems and equipment, processing facilities and transportation systems, and the carrying out of studies of the environmental, technical, economic,

commercial and other appropriate factors that must be taken into account in exploitation. Consequently, it may be considered that the costs associated with exploration must be those that fall under the list of activities defining the term "exploration". International Financial Reporting Standard 6 also provides a non-exhaustive list of examples of expenditure that might be presented in the initial measurement of exploration and evaluation assets. To be considered as direct, expenditure must have been incurred directly in connection with the exploration work that has been undertaken in accordance with the programme of work in the contract. A recommended format for the statement of actual and direct exploration expenditure is contained in the annex.

14. Reported expenditure also needs to relate to actual costs. This means that the costs have actually been incurred and are not notional, estimated or projected. Actual costs are also associated in time with those that occurred during the reporting year. Therefore, they exclude those that relate to past or future exploration work. Actual costs may be different from projected costs, but grounds for any variation should be provided in the report.

V. Certification of financial statements

15. It is a requirement of the standard clauses for exploration contracts that the financial statements showing the actual and direct exploration expenditure of the contractor in carrying out the programme of activities during the accounting year be certified by a duly qualified firm of public accountants or, where the contractor is a State or a state enterprise, by the sponsoring State.

16. In order to avoid confusion in the application of these requirements, where the contractor is a State or State-owned enterprise, the contractor should indicate in the annual report which entity of the sponsoring State is entitled to certify the financial statements.

17. The date of receipt of the certification should be the same as for other elements of the annual reports, that is, no later than 31 March of each year. Where this is not possible, for example where the certifying authority applies a different financial reporting period, the contractor should indicate the tentative date of submission in the annual report. Once the certificate is available, the contractor should transmit it to the Secretary-General without delay.

Annex

Recommended format for the statement of actual and direct exploration expenditure

1. Expenditure should be reported against the following headings:

   - **Exploration work**
     - Research and analysis, including field investigation
     - Equipment and instruments
   - **Environmental studies**
     - Research and analysis, including field investigation
     - Equipment and instruments
   - **Mining technology development**
     - Research and analysis, including field investigation
     - Equipment and instruments
   - **Metallurgical process development**
     - Research and analysis, including field investigation
     - Equipment and instruments
   - **Training**
   - **Other activities**
     - Preparation of annual report
     - Any other actual and direct exploration expenditure not covered under the above headings, but forming part of the programme of activities under the contract

2. Where an item of expenditure may be attributed to several activities, it should be reported under one heading only, so as to avoid any duplication.

3. Reported expenditure under each heading should, as far as possible, be broken down into: (a) operational expenditure; (b) capital expenditure; (c) staffing and personnel costs; and (d) overhead costs. If a cruise was undertaken, the actual day rate for ship time and the day rate for any large item of equipment used during the cruise should be specified.

4. Capital expenditure on a single item exceeding $200,000 in any one year should be itemized in the report.

International Seabed Authority

ISBA/21/LTC/15

Legal and Technical Commission

Distr.: General
4 August 2015

Original: English

Recommendations for the guidance of contractors on the content, format and structure of annual reports

1. The Legal and Technical Commission of the International Seabed Authority, acting pursuant to regulation 39 of the Regulations on Prospecting and Exploration for Polymetallic Nodules in the Area, regulation 41 of the Regulations on Prospecting and Exploration for Polymetallic Sulphides in the Area and regulation 41 of the Regulations on Prospecting and Exploration for Cobalt-rich Ferromanganese Crusts in the Area, issues the present recommendations for the guidance of contractors.

I. Introduction

2. In the present recommendations, references to the "Regulations" are collective references to the Regulations on Prospecting and Exploration for Polymetallic Nodules in the Area, the Regulations on Prospecting and Exploration for Polymetallic Sulphides in the Area and the Regulations on Prospecting and Exploration for Cobalt-rich Ferromanganese Crusts in the Area. References to the "clauses" are references to the standard clauses applicable to the particular contract in question.

3. The purpose of the present recommendations is to provide guidance to contractors in relation to the content, format and structure of their annual reports. It includes general requirements for their annual reports and specific guidance for reporting on the exploration under contract for polymetallic nodules, polymetallic sulphides and cobalt-rich ferromanganese crusts. The recommendations supersede the guidance provided by the Commission in the annex to document ISBA/8/LTC/2 and should be applied by all contractors with effect from 1 January 2016.

II. General requirements

4. Annual reports shall be submitted to the Secretary-General by the end of March each year on the activities carried out in the previous year and contain the information specified in section 10 of annex IV to the Regulations.

5. Reports should be submitted in hard copy and electronic format and all environmental and geological data should be submitted in a digital and spatially georeferenced format that is compatible with the Authority's requirements, using the

templates published by the Commission and listed in annex IV to the present document.

6. Reports should present the results of the work of the reporting year with reference to the approved plan of work for exploration. The contractor should indicate its short-term (1 year), medium-term (5 years) and long-term (10-15 years) objectives. The reports should also contain information on project management to enable an overview of progress in the implementation of the programme of work and, where applicable, training programmes.

7. Reports should indicate clearly the actual work carried out during the reporting year.

III. Specific guidance

8. The recommended content, format and structure of annual reports on the exploration under contract for polymetallic nodules is provided in annex I.

9. The recommended content, format and structure of annual reports on the exploration under contract for polymetallic sulphides is provided in annex II.

10. The recommended content, format and structure of annual reports on the exploration under contract for cobalt-rich ferromanganese crusts is provided in annex III.

11. A list of the templates to be used for reporting geological and environmental data is provided in annex IV.

12. The Authority's classification standard for reporting mineral exploration results assessments, mineral resources and mineral reserves, as adopted by the Commission, is provided in annex V.

Annex I

Content, format and structure of annual reports for exploration under contract for polymetallic nodules

I. Executive summary

1. The contractor is requested to provide a summary of major achievements and challenges in 20xx [indicate year] (maximum four pages).

II. General

2. The contractor is requested to provide:

   (a) Information on adjustments made to the programme of activities, if any, for 20xx [indicate year];

   (b) A response to the comments of the International Seabed Authority, if any, on the previous annual report.

III. Result of exploration work

3. Intended programme and actual completion

   The contractor is requested to report on the annual work programme that has been carried out and to provide information on any deviation from the intended programme.

4. Methods and equipment

   The contractor is requested to list and describe the methods applied and equipment used for mapping, sampling or the conduct of any other activities for the exploration of the seabed and its subsoil during its survey cruises.

   (a) Mapping

   The contractor is requested to give a general description of the methods, acquisition equipment and procedures (calibration, installation details, etc.) used for surveying the exploration area. The Authority is aware that these methods include, but are not restricted to, the following:

   (i) Single beam and multibeam echo sounding (hull-mounted and/or from remotely operated vehicles or autonomous underwater vehicles);

   (ii) Side-scan sonar profiling (towed from the vessel, from remotely operated vehicles, autonomous underwater vehicles or other);

   (iii) Subbottom profiling;

   (iv) Photography and video recording done by TV grab, sledge, remotely operated vehicles, autonomous underwater vehicles, submersibles or other;

(b) Sampling

The contractor is requested to give a general description of the sampling programme that has been completed, including the sampling equipment and the procedures for the use thereof, namely corers, grabs, dredges or other methods and equipment. This description should be formulated with a view to supporting the reporting of geological and environmental data on polymetallic nodules in the appropriate templates (see annex IV);

(c) Other activities

The contractor is requested to give a general description of any other activities conducted to obtain relevant seabed or subsurface information and data.

5. Data obtained

The contractor is requested to report the data collected during mapping, sampling or the conduct of any other activities for the exploration of the seabed and its subsoil during its survey cruises.

(a) Navigation data

Full information on the navigation by geographical coordinates should be reported as part of all data sets. However, for easy reference, the contractors are asked to also provide separate electronic files with the coordinates of each of the following items:

(i) Station locations;

(ii) Multibeam, sonar and seismic track lines;

(iii) Ship track.

(b) Bathymetry

The Authority expects the contractor to deliver the collected and processed bathymetric data as digital xyz files in the American standard code for information interchange (ASCII) format or a common geographic information system (GIS) format. The processing sequence must be fully described.

(c) Side-scan sonar and seismic data

The Authority expects the contractor to deliver the collected data as digital files (SEG-Y or XTF) and/or as high-resolution images (JPG, PDF, TIFF, etc.).

(d) Photographs and videos

The Authority expects the contractor to deliver the photographs and videos as high-resolution representative images (JPG, PDF, TIFF, etc.).

(e) Nodule characteristics

The nodules are characterized by their abundance, morphology, mineral composition, chemistry and physical properties. The contractor is requested to give a general description of those characteristics and of the analytical methods applied. The specific results of the analyses of the nodules and substrate at each sampling station should be reported in a table in the format of the template for geological data on polymetallic nodules (see annex IV).

6. Interpretations and assessments

The contractor is requested to report the results of the interpretations of the geology of the mineral deposit and the resource assessments made on the basis of the data that have been collected.

(a) Interpretations of the mineral deposit

The interpretations made by the contractor regarding the different aspects of the mineral deposit may be reported as a set of commented maps, for instance on bathymetry, seabed morphology, geology or lithology, nodule abundance, metal distribution, resource distribution, etc. (as shapefiles and digital images).

(b) Mineral resource estimates

If the contractor has reached the stage of making resource estimates of the mineral deposits, the following items should be reported on in detail:

(i) The estimation method;

(ii) The resource/reserve classification, reported in accordance with the Authority's reporting standard (see annex V).

(c) The report should also contain a statement of the quantity of nodules recovered as samples or for the purpose of testing (even if the quantity is null).

7. Future strategy for exploration work

The contractor is requested to report on any development in its future strategy for exploration work.

IV. Environmental baseline studies (monitoring and assessment)

8. For guidance on environmental baseline studies, the contractor should refer to the recommendations for the guidance of contractors for the assessment of the possible environmental impacts arising from exploration for marine minerals in the Area (ISBA/19/LTC/8, sect. III).

A. Environmental monitoring

9. The contractor is also requested to provide:

(a) A description of the objectives during the reporting period (intended, ongoing and completed);

(b) Information on the technical equipment and methodologies used at depth, on board and in the laboratory (including analysis software);

(c) The results produced (also summarized as graphic representations of data on which the results are based);

(d) An interpretation of the findings, including comparisons with published data from other studies;

(e) Information on physical oceanography (characteristics of water column and near-bed currents, including current speed and direction, temperatures, turbidity at different water depths, as well as any hydrodynamic modelling). Data should be linked to long-term mooring-based observations;

(f) Information on chemical oceanography (characteristics of sea water, including pH value, dissolved oxygen, total alkalinity, nutrient concentrations, dissolved and particulate organic carbon, estimation of mass flux, heavy metals, trace elements and chlorophyll a);

(g) Information on biological communities and biodiversity studies (including megafauna, macrofauna, meiofauna, microflora, nodule fauna, demersal scavengers and pelagic communities);

(h) Information on ecosystem functioning (such as measures of bioturbation, stable isotopes and sediment community oxygen consumption).

B. Environmental assessment

10. The contractor is requested to provide:

(a) Information on the environmental impact of exploration activities including information on a monitoring programme before, during and after specific activities with the potential for causing serious harm;

(b) A statement that activities undertaken in the contract area in the year covered by the annual report have not caused serious harm and the evidence of how this has been determined;

(c) Information on the environmental impact of test-mining activities as measured in the impact reference zones;

(d) An assessment of statistical robustness/power, taking into account sample sizes, sample number and, for biological communities, the abundance of individual species (with evidence for statistical significance);

(e) A gap analysis and future strategy to achieve the goals of the five-year programme of activities and the requirements contained in ISBA/19/LTC/8;

(f) An examination of the recovery over time of seabed communities following disturbance experiments conducted on the sea floor;

(g) An evaluation of the advantages and disadvantages of different sampling and analysis methods, including quality control;

(h) A comparison of environmental results in similar areas to understand species ranges and dispersal on the scale of ocean basins.

11. All data used in the report (figures, graphs and pictures) should be reported using the Excel template for environmental data on polymetallic nodules (see annex IV).

V. Mining tests and proposed mining technologies

12. The contractor is requested to provide:

(a) Data and information on the nature of the mining equipment designed and tested, where applicable, as well as data on the use of equipment not designed by the contractor;

(b) A description of the equipment, the operations and the results of the mining tests;

(c) A description of the nature and results of the experiments (where applicable);

(d) With regard to mining technologies, information on the technological progress made by the contractor with its mining system (e.g. collectors, riser, production vessel or other) development programme;

(e) With regard to processing technologies:

   (i) Information on the mineral processing and metallurgical testing and processing routes, for instance whether three metals, five metals, rare earth elements or other;

   (ii) Information on other methods.

VI. Training programme

13. The contractor is requested to provide detailed information on the implementation of the training programme, in accordance with schedule 3 of the contract, bearing in mind the requirements contained in the recommendations for the guidance of contractors and sponsoring States to training programmes under plans of work for exploration (ISBA/19/LTC/14).

VII. International cooperation

14. The contractor is requested to provide information on:

(a) Participation in cooperative programmes sponsored by the Authority;

(b) Cooperation with other contractors;

(c) Other international cooperation.

VIII. Certified financial statement of actual and direct exploration expenditure

15. The contractor is requested to provide a detailed financial statement that complies with the recommendations for the guidance of contractors for the reporting of actual and direct exploration expenditure (ISBA/21/LTC/11), as required under annex IV, section 10, of the Regulations.

IX. Programme of activities for the following year

16. The contractor is requested:

    (a) To briefly indicate the work proposed to be carried out in the following year;

    (b) To describe the proposed adjustments to the original programme of activities for the following year under the contract;

    (c) To explain the reasons for such adjustments.

X. Additional information provided by the contractor

17. The contractor is requested to provide:

    (a) A list of relevant publications in peer-reviewed journals published during the reporting year;

    (b) Complete references to all relevant documents, press releases and scientific publications cited in the report.

Annex II

Content, format and structure of annual reports for exploration under contract for polymetallic sulphides

I. Executive summary

1. The contractor is requested to provide a summary of major achievements and challenges in 20xx [indicate year] (maximum four pages).

II. General

2. The contractor is requested to provide:

    (a) Information on adjustments made to the programme of activities, if any, for 20xx [indicate year];

    (b) A response to the comments of the International Seabed Authority, if any, on the previous annual report.

III. Result of exploration work

3. Intended programme and actual completion

    The contractor is requested to report on the annual work programme that has been carried out and to provide information on any deviation from the intended programme.

4. Methods and equipment

    The contractor is requested to list and describe the methods applied and equipment used for mapping, sampling or the conduct of any other activities for the exploration of the seabed and its subsoil during its survey cruises.

    (a) Mapping

    The contractor is requested to give a general description of the methods, acquisition equipment and procedures (calibration, installation details, etc.) used for surveying the exploration area (seabed or near bottom waters). The Authority is aware that these methods include, but are not restricted to, the following:

    (i) Single beam and multibeam echo sounding (hull-mounted and/or from remotely operated vehicles, autonomous underwater vehicles);

    (ii) Measurement of the conductivity, temperature and depth (CTD), either hydro-casts or tow-yo;

    (iii) Side-scan sonar profiling (towed from the vessel, from remotely operated vehicles, autonomous underwater vehicles or other);

    (iv) Subbottom profiling;

    (v) Electromagnetic profiling;

(vi) Photography and video recording done by TV grab, sledge, remotely operated vehicles, autonomous underwater vehicles, submersibles or other;

(vii) Other methods.

(b) Sampling

The contractor is requested to give a general description of the sampling programme that has been completed, including the sampling equipment and the procedures for the use thereof, namely corers, grabs, dredges, remotely operated vehicles, submersibles or other methods and equipment. This description should be formulated with a view to supporting the reporting of geological and environmental data on polymetallic sulphides in the appropriate templates (see annex IV).

(c) Other activities

The contractor is requested to give a general description of any other activities conducted to obtain relevant seabed or subsurface information and data.

5. Data obtained

The contractor is requested to report the data collected during mapping, sampling or the conduct of any other activities for the exploration of the seabed and its subsoil during its survey cruises.

(a) Navigation data

Full information on the navigation by geographical coordinates should be reported as part of all data sets. However, for easy reference, the contractors are asked to also provide separate electronic files with the coordinates of each of the following items:

(i) Station locations;

(ii) Multibeam, sonar and seismic track lines;

(iii) Ship track.

(b) Bathymetry

The Authority expects the contractor to deliver the collected and processed bathymetric data as digital xyz files in the American standard code for information interchange (ASCII) format or a common geographic information system (GIS) format. The processing sequence must be fully described.

(c) Side-scan sonar and seismic data

The Authority expects the contractor to deliver the collected data as digital files (SEG-Y or XTF) and/or as high-resolution images (JPG, PDF, TIFF, etc.).

(d) (Electro)Magnetic data

The Authority expects the contractor to deliver the collected (electro)magnetic data as digital grids in a common GIS format.

(e) Electric self-potential data

The Authority expects the contractor to deliver the collected self-potential data as digital grids in a common GIS format.

(f) Near-bottom water parameters

The Authority expects the contractor to deliver the collected near-bottom water data (temperature, salinity, turbidity or transparency, Eh, pH, etc.) as tables (Excel, txt, etc.) and graphs in digital format.

(g) Photographs and videos

The Authority expects the contractor to deliver the photographs and videos as high-resolution representative images (JPEG, PDF, TIFF, etc.).

(h) Polymetallic sulphide characteristics

The polymetallic sulphide deposits are characterized by their mineral composition, chemistry and physical properties. The contractor is requested to give a general description of those characteristics and of the analytical methods applied to the mineral deposit itself and associated metalliferous sediments. The specific results of the analyses of the polymetallic sulphides, low temperature mineralization and substrate at each sampling station should be reported in a table in the format of the template for geological data on polymetallic sulphides (see annex IV).

6. Interpretations and assessments

The contractor is requested to report the results of the interpretations of the geology of the mineral deposit and the resource assessments made on the basis of the data that have been collected.

(a) Interpretations of the mineral deposit

The interpretations made by the contractor regarding the different aspects of the mineral deposit may be reported as a set of commented maps, for instance on bathymetry, seabed morphology, geology (including deposit delineation), lithology, mineralogy, etc. (as shapefiles and digital images).

(b) Hydrothermal activity associated with deposits

Of special interest in the case of polymetallic sulphide deposits is information on the associated hydrothermal activity. The contractor is requested to report such information with regard to active and inactive fields as follows:

(i) Method of hydrothermal activity detection:

– Direct observation (visualization), with representative photographs

– Indirect observation (anomalies in the water column), with hydro-casts and/or tow-yo

(c) Mineral resource estimates

If the contractor has reached the stage of making resource estimates of the mineral deposits, the following items should be reported on in detail:

(i) The estimation method;

(ii) The resource/reserve classification, reported in accordance with the Authority's reporting standard (see annex V).

(d) The report should also contain a statement of the quantity of polymetallic sulphides recovered as samples or for the purpose of testing (even if the quantity is null).

7. Future strategy for exploration work

The contractor is requested to report on any development in its future strategy for exploration work.

IV. Environmental baseline studies (monitoring and assessment)

8. For guidance on environmental baseline studies, the contractor should refer to the recommendations for the guidance of contractors for the assessment of the possible environmental impacts arising from exploration for marine minerals in the Area (ISBA/19/LTC/8, sect. III).

A. Environmental monitoring

9. The contractor is requested to provide:

(a) A description of the objectives during the reporting period (intended, ongoing and completed);

(b) Information on the technical equipment and methodologies used at depth, on board and in the laboratory (including analysis software);

(c) The results produced (also summarized as graphic representations of data on which the results are based);

(d) An interpretation of the findings, including comparisons with published data from other studies;

(e) Information on physical oceanography (characteristics of sea water and bottom currents, including current speed and direction, temperatures, turbidity at different water depths, downslope transport as well as any hydrodynamic modelling). Data should also be linked to any long-term moorings for the exploration work;

(f) Information on chemical oceanography (characteristics of sea water, including pH value, dissolved oxygen, total alkalinity, nutrient concentrations, dissolved and particulate organic carbon, estimation of mass flux, heavy metals, trace elements and chlorophyll a);

(g) Information on biological communities and biodiversity studies (including habitat diversity, megafauna, macrofauna, meiofauna, bacterial mats, demersal scavengers and pelagic communities);

(h) Information on ecosystem functioning (including food webs, stable isotopes, fatty acids and methane and hydrogen sulphide metabolism).

B. Environmental assessment

10. The contractor is requested to provide:

(a) Information on the environmental impact of exploration activities, including information on a monitoring programme before, during and after specific activities with the potential for causing serious harm;

(b) A statement that activities undertaken in the contract area in the year covered by the annual report have not caused serious harm and the evidence of how this has been determined;

(c) Information on the environmental impact of test-mining activities as measured in the impact reference zones;

(d) An assessment of statistical robustness/power, taking into account sample sizes, sample number and, for biological communities, the abundance of individual species (with evidence for statistical significance);

(e) A gap analysis and future strategy to achieve the goals of the five-year programme of activities and the requirements contained in ISBA/19/LTC/8;

(f) An examination of ecosystem change and recovery from natural and anthropogenic disturbances, including drilling activities;

(g) An evaluation of the advantages and disadvantages of different sampling and analysis methods, including quality control;

(h) A comparison of environmental results in similar areas to understand species ranges and dispersal on the scale of ocean basins.

11. All data used in the report (figures, graphs and pictures) should be reported using the Excel template for environmental data on polymetallic sulphides (see annex IV).

V. Mining tests and proposed mining technologies

12. The contractor is requested to provide:

(a) Data and information on the nature of the mining equipment designed and tested, where applicable, as well as data on the use of equipment not designed by the contractor;

(b) A description of the equipment, the operations and the results of the tests;

(c) A description of the nature and results of the experiments (where applicable);

(d) With regard to mining technologies, information on the technological progress made by the contractor with its mining system (e.g. collectors, riser, production vessel or other) development programme;

(e) With regard to processing technologies:

  (i) Information on mineral processing and metallurgical testing and processing routes;

  (ii) Information on other methods.

VI. Training programme

13. The contractor is requested to provide detailed information on the implementation of the training programme, in accordance with schedule 3 of the contract, bearing in mind the requirements contained in the recommendations for the guidance of contractors and sponsoring States to training programmes under plans of work for exploration (ISBA/19/LTC/14).

VII. International cooperation

14. The contractor is requested to provide information on:

    (a) Its participation in cooperative programmes sponsored by the Authority;

    (b) Cooperation with other contractors;

    (c) Other international cooperation.

VIII. Certified financial statement of actual and direct exploration expenditure

15. The contractor is requested to provide a detailed financial statement that complies with the recommendations for the guidance of contractors for the reporting of actual and direct exploration expenditure (ISBA/21/LTC/11), as required under annex 4, section 10, of the Regulations.

IX. Programme of activities for the following year

16. The contractor is requested:

    (a) To briefly indicate the work proposed to be carried out in the following year;

    (b) To describe the proposed adjustments to the original programme of activities for the following year under the contract;

    (c) To explain the reasons for such adjustments.

X. Additional information provided by the contractor

17. The contractor is requested to provide:

    (a) A list of relevant publications in peer-reviewed journals published during the reporting year;

    (b) Complete references to all relevant documents, press releases and scientific publications cited in the report.

Annex III

Content, format and structure of annual reports for exploration under contract for cobalt-rich ferromanganese crusts

I. Executive summary

1. The contractor is requested to provide a summary of major achievements and challenges in 20xx [indicate year] (maximum four pages).

II. General

2. The contractor is requested to provide:

    (a) Information on adjustments made to the programme of activities, if any, for 20xx [indicate year];

    (b) A response to the comments of the International Seabed Authority, if any, on the previous annual report.

III. Result of exploration work

3. Intended programme and its actual completion

    The contractor is requested to report on the annual work programme that has been carried out and to provide information on any deviation from the intended programme.

4. Methods and equipment

    The contractor is requested to list and describe the methods applied and equipment used for mapping, sampling or the conduct of any other activities for the exploration of the seabed and its subsoil during its survey cruises.

    (a) Mapping

    The contractor is requested to give a general description of the methods, acquisition equipment and procedures (calibration, installation details, etc.) used for surveying the exploration area. The Authority is aware that these methods include, but are not restricted to, the following:

    (i) Single beam and multibeam echo sounding (hull-mounted and/or from remotely operated vehicles or autonomous underwater vehicles);

    (ii) Side-scan sonar profiling (towed from the vessel, from remotely operated vehicles, autonomous underwater vehicles or other);

    (iii) Subbottom profiling (done by hull-mounted or remotely operated vehicles and autonomous underwater vehicles);

(iv) Photography and video recording done by TV grab, sledge, remotely operated vehicles, autonomous underwater vehicles, submersibles or other;

(v) Other methods (e.g. gamma-ray detection).

(b) Sampling

The contractor is requested to give a general description of the sampling programme that has been completed, including the sampling equipment and the procedures for the use thereof, namely drill coring, dredges, remotely operated vehicles, submersibles or other methods and equipment. This description should be formulated with a view to supporting the reporting of geological and environmental data on cobalt-rich ferromanganese crusts in the appropriate templates (see annex IV).

(c) Other activities

The contractor is requested to give a general description of any other activities conducted to obtain relevant seabed or subsurface information and data.

5. Data obtained

The contractor is requested to report the data collected during mapping, sampling or the conduct of any other activities for the exploration of the seabed and its subsoil during its survey cruises.

(a) Navigation data

Full information on the navigation by geographical coordinates should be reported as part of all data sets. However, for easy reference, the contractors are asked to also provide separate electronic files with the coordinates of each of the following items:

(i) Station locations;

(ii) Multibeam, sonar and seismic track lines;

(iii) Ship track.

(b) Bathymetry

The Authority expects the contractor to deliver the collected bathymetric data as digital xyz files in the American standard code for information interchange (ASCII) format or a common geographic information system (GIS) format.

(c) Side-scan sonar and seismic data

The Authority expects the contractor to deliver the collected data as digital files (SEG-Y or XTF) and/or as high-resolution images (JPG, PDF, TIFF, etc.).

(d) Photographs and videos

The Authority expects the contractor to deliver the photographs and videos as high-resolution representative images (JPG, PDF, TIFF, etc.).

(e) Cobalt-rich ferromanganese crust characteristics

The cobalt-rich ferromanganese crust deposits are characterized by their thickness, crust coverage, mineral composition, chemistry and physical properties. The contractor is requested to give a general description of those characteristics and of the analytical methods applied. The specific results of the analyses of the cobalt-rich ferromanganese crusts at each sampling station should be reported in a table in the format of the template for geological data on cobalt-rich ferromanganese crusts (see annex IV).

6. Interpretations and assessments

The contractor is requested to report the results of the interpretations of the geology of the mineral deposit and the resource assessments made on the basis of the data that have been collected.

(a) Interpretations of the mineral deposit

The interpretations made by the contractor regarding the different aspects of the mineral deposit may be reported as a set of commented maps, for instance on bathymetry, seabed morphology, geology and lithology, crust coverage, metal distribution, crust thickness and its spatial and regional variation (including variation with depth) as shapefiles and digital images.

(b) Mineral resource estimates

If the contractor has reached the stage of making resource estimates of the mineral deposits, the following items should be reported on in detail:

(i) The estimation method;

(ii) The resource/reserve classification, reported in accordance with the Authority's reporting standard (see annex V).

(c) The report should also contain a statement of the quantity of cobalt-rich ferromanganese crusts recovered as samples or for the purpose of testing (even if the quantity is null).

7. Future strategy for exploration work

The contractor is requested to report on any development in its future strategy for exploration work.

IV. Environmental baseline studies (monitoring and assessment)

8. For guidance on environmental baseline studies, the contractor should refer to the recommendations for the guidance of contractors for the assessment of the possible environmental impacts arising from exploration for marine minerals in the Area (ISBA/19/LTC/8, sect. III).

A. Environmental monitoring

9. The contractor is requested to provide:

(a) A description of the objectives during the reporting period (intended, ongoing and completed);

(b) Information on the technical equipment and methodologies used at depth, on board and in the laboratory (including analysis software);

(c) The results produced (also summarized as graphic representations of data on which the results are based);

(d) An interpretation of the findings, including comparisons with published data from other studies;

(e) Information on physical oceanography (characteristics of sea water and bottom currents, including current speed and direction, temperatures, turbidity at different water depths, downslope transport as well as any hydrodynamic modelling). Data should also be linked to any long-term moorings for the exploration work;

(f) Information on chemical oceanography (characteristics of sea water, including pH value, dissolved oxygen, total alkalinity, nutrient concentrations, dissolved and particulate organic carbon, estimation of mass flux, heavy metals, trace elements and chlorophyll a);

(g) Information on biological communities and biodiversity studies (including habitat diversity, megafauna, macrofauna, meiofauna, bacterial mats, demersal scavengers and pelagic communities);

(h) Information on ecosystem functioning (including food webs, stable isotopes and fatty acids).

B. Environmental assessment

10. The contractor is requested to provide:

(a) Information on the environmental impact of exploration activities, including information on a monitoring programme before, during and after specific activities with the potential for causing serious harm;

(b) A statement that activities undertaken in the contract area in the year covered by the annual report have not caused serious harm and the evidence of how this has been determined;

(c) Information on the environmental impact of test-mining activities as measured in the impact reference zones;

(d) An assessment of statistical robustness/power, taking into account sample sizes, sample number and for biological communities the abundance of individual species (with evidence for statistical significance);

(e) A gap analysis and future strategy to achieve the goals of the five-year programme of activities and the requirements contained in ISBA/19/LTC/8;

(f) An examination of ecosystem recovery from natural and anthropogenic disturbances, where appropriate;

(g) An evaluation of the advantages and disadvantages of different sampling and analysis methods, including quality control;

(h) A comparison of environmental results in similar areas to understand species ranges and dispersal on the scale of ocean basins.

11. All data used in the report (figures, graphs and pictures) should be reported using the Excel template for environmental data on cobalt-rich ferromanganese crusts (see annex IV).

V. Mining tests and proposed mining technologies

12. The contractor is requested to provide:

(a) Data and information on the nature of the mining equipment designed and tested, where applicable, as well as data on the use of equipment not designed by the contractor;

(b) A description of the equipment, the operations and, where relevant, the results of the tests;

(c) A description of the nature and results of the experiments (where applicable);

(d) With regard to mining technologies, information on the technological progress made by the contractor with its mining system (e.g. collectors, riser, production vessel or other) development programme;

(e) With regard to processing technologies:

(i) Information on mineral processing and metallurgical testing and processing routes;

(ii) Information on other methods.

VI. Training programme

13. The contractor is requested to provide detailed information on the implementation of the training programme, in accordance with schedule 3 of the contract, bearing in mind the requirements contained in the recommendations for the guidance of contractors and sponsoring States to training programmes under plans of work for exploration (ISBA/19/LTC/14).

VII. International cooperation

14. The contractor is requested to provide information on:

(a) Its participation in cooperative programmes sponsored by the Authority;

(b) Cooperation with other contractors;

(c) Other international cooperation.

VIII. Certified financial statement of actual and direct exploration expenditure

15. The contractor is requested to provide a detailed financial statement that complies with the recommendations for the guidance of contractors for the reporting

of actual and direct exploration expenditure (ISBA/21/LTC/11), as required under annex IV, section 10, of the Regulations.

IX. Programme of activities for the following year

16. The contractor is requested:

    (a) To briefly indicate the work proposed to be carried out in the following year;

    (b) To describe the proposed adjustments to the original programme of activities for the following year under the contract;

    (c) To explain the reasons for such adjustments.

X. Additional information provided by the contractor

17. The contractor is requested to provide:

    (a) A list of relevant publications in peer-reviewed journals published during the reporting year;

    (b) Complete references to all relevant documents, press releases and scientific publications cited in the report.

Annex IV

List of templates for reporting tabulated geological and environmental data

1. Template for reporting geological data on polymetallic nodules and substrate
2. Template for reporting geological data on polymetallic sulphides and substrate
3. Template for reporting geological data on cobalt-rich ferromanganese crusts
4. Template for reporting environmental data on polymetallic nodules
5. Template for reporting environmental data on polymetallic sulphides
6. Template for reporting environmental data on cobalt-rich ferromanganese crusts

Annex V

Reporting standard of the International Seabed Authority for mineral exploration results assessments, mineral resources and mineral reserves

I. Introduction

1. The present document sets out the standard to be observed in all documents submitted to the International Seabed Authority that include the reporting of estimates of resources in the Area, which that are not intended for public release or for the prime purpose of informing investors or potential investors and their advisers. These estimates should be reported according to the Authority's resource classification system that is based on the three main resource categories:(a) mineral exploration results assessments; (b) mineral resources; and (c) mineral reserves (see figure below). It is based on the November 2013 edition of the international reporting template of the Committee for Mineral Reserves International Reporting Standards (CRIRSCO).[1]

2. In the present document, important terms are defined in paragraphs highlighted in bold. When appearing in the definition of other such terms, those terms are underlined. The template clauses are shown in plain font. Paragraphs in italics that are placed after the respective clauses are intended to provide assistance and guidance to readers for interpreting the application of the clauses in the reporting standard of the Authority. Enclosure 1 contains a list of generic terms, equivalents and definitions provided to avoid duplication or ambiguity.

II. Scope

3. The main principles governing the operation and application of the reporting standard are transparency and materiality:

---

[1] The present annex has been prepared at the request of the International Seabed Authority by a group comprising: C. Antrim, Executive Director at the Rule of Law Committee for Oceans, United States of America; H. Parker, Deputy Chair of the Committee for Mineral Reserves International Reporting Standards (CRIRSCO) and Consulting Mining Geologist and Geostatistician at Amec Foster Wheeler, United States; and P. R. Stephenson, former Co-Chair of CRIRSCO and Director and Principal Geologist at AMC Consultants, Canada; with input from CRIRSCO members. It follows guidelines drawn up by a working group at a workshop convened by the Authority, in collaboration with the Ministry of Earth Sciences of India, on the classification of polymetallic nodule resources, held in Goa, India from 13 to 17 October 2014. The working group members were: Mr. Stephenson; Ms. Antrim; M. Nimmo, Principal Geologist at Golder Associates, Australia; D. MacDonald, Chair of the Expert Group on Resource Classification of the Economic Commission for Europe; P. Kay, Manager at Offshore Minerals, Geoscience Australia; P. Madureira, Deputy Chief of the Task Group for the Extension of the Continental Shelf, Portugal; G. Cherkashov, Deputy Director at All-Russia Research Institute for Geology and Mineral Resources of the World Ocean, Russian Federation; T. Ishiyama, Deep Ocean Resources Development, Japan; T. Abramowski, Director General at the Interoceanmetal Joint Organization, Poland; J. Parionos, Chief Geologist at Tonga Offshore Mining Limited, Tonga; and J. Paynjon, G-TEC Sea Mineral Resources NV.

(a) Transparency requires that the Authority and, particularly, its Legal and Technical Commission be provided with sufficient information, presented in a clear and unambiguous way, so as to understand the report and not to be misled;

(b) Materiality requires that the report contain all the relevant information that the Authority and, particularly, its Legal and Technical Commission may reasonably require and expect to find in the report, for the purpose of making a reasoned and balanced judgement regarding the mineral resources or mineral reserves reported on.

4. **The reporting standard specifies the required minimum standard for all documents submitted to the Authority that include the reporting of mineral exploration results assessments, mineral resources and mineral reserves. It is not intended for release to the general public or for the prime purpose of informing investors or potential investors and their advisers.**[2] Reporting entities are encouraged to provide information that is as comprehensive as possible in their reports.[3]

5. The estimation of mineral resources and mineral reserves is inherently subject to some level of uncertainty and inaccuracy. Considerable skill and experience may be needed to interpret pieces of information, such as geological maps and analytical results based on samples that commonly represent only a small part of a mineral deposit. The uncertainty in the estimates should be discussed in the report and reflected in the appropriate choice of mineral resource and mineral reserve categories.

6. The reporting standard is applicable to all **mineral resources** for which the reporting of **mineral exploration results assessments, mineral resources** and **mineral reserves** is required by the Authority under its rules, regulations and procedures.

7. It is recognized that a further review of the reporting standard will be required from time to time.

---

[2] Where reports are prepared for the prime purpose of release to the general public or for informing investors or potential investors and their advisers, the Authority recommends that they comply with one of the reporting standards that are recognized by CRIRSCO has being consistent with its international reporting template.

[3] While every effort has been made in the reporting standard of the Authority to cover most cases likely to be encountered when reporting on mineral exploration results assessments, mineral resources and mineral reserves, there may be occasions when doubt exists as to the appropriate form of disclosure. On such occasions, users of the reporting standard and those who compile reports to comply with the standard should be guided by its intent, namely, to provide a minimum standard for such reporting and to ensure that such reporting contains all the information that readers may reasonably require and expect for the purpose of making a reasoned and balanced judgement on the mineral exploration results assessments, mineral resources or mineral reserves reported on.

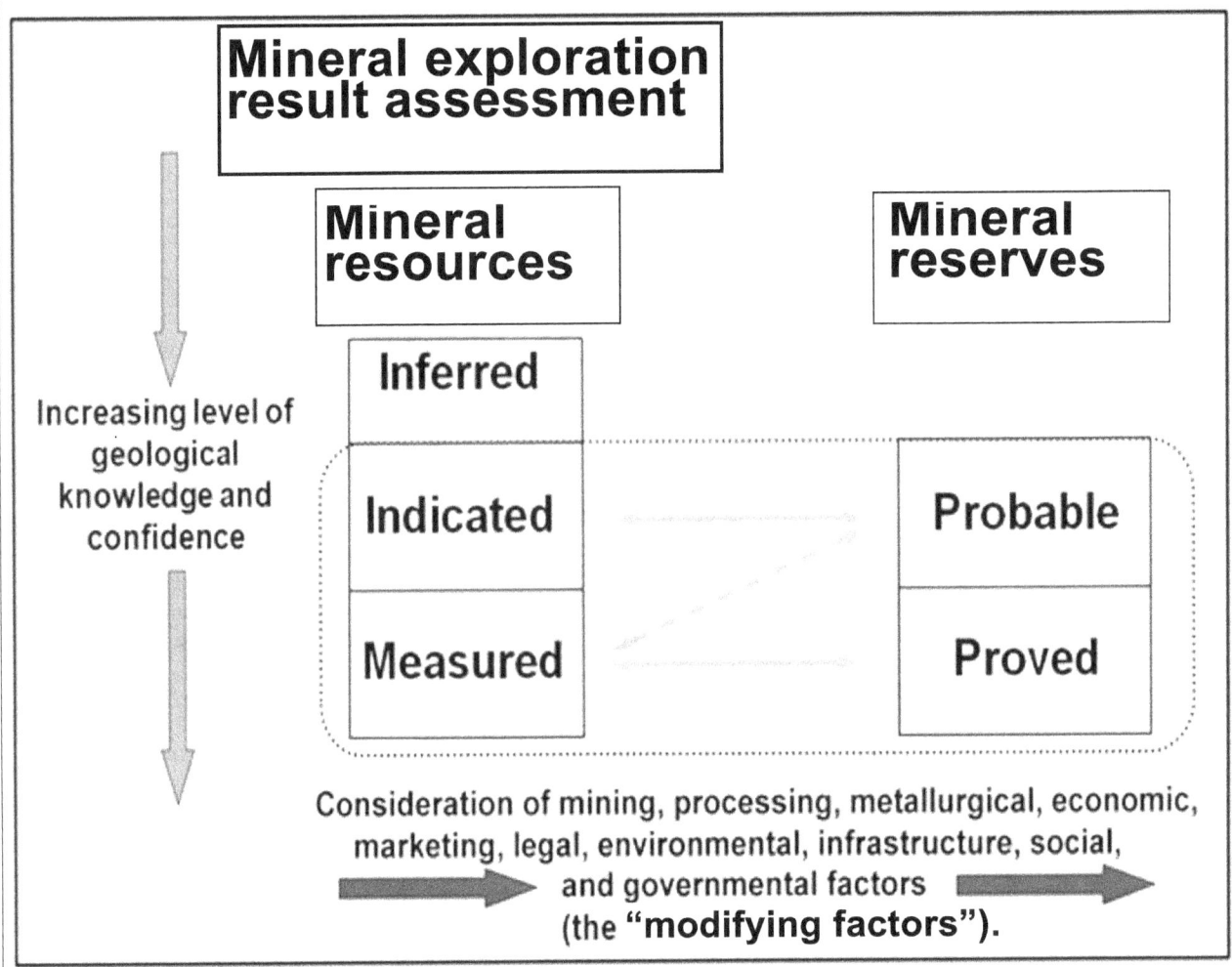

General relationship between mineral exploration results assessments, minerals resources and mineral reserves

III. Reporting terminology

8. Modifying factors are considerations used to convert <u>mineral resources</u> into <u>mineral reserves</u>. These include, but are not restricted to, mining, processing, metallurgical, infrastructure, economic, marketing, legal, environmental, social and governmental factors.

Guidance

9. *The figure in paragraph 7 illustrates the framework for classifying tonnage and grade estimates to reflect different levels of geological confidence and different degrees of technical and economic evaluation. Mineral resources can be estimated mainly on the basis of geological information with some input from other disciplines. Mineral reserves, which are a modified subset of the indicated and measured mineral resources (shown within the dashed outline in the figure), require*

consideration of the modifying factors affecting extraction and should in most instances be estimated with input from a range of disciplines.

10. *Measured mineral resources may be converted into either proved mineral reserves or probable mineral reserves. Measured mineral resources may be converted into probable mineral reserves because of uncertainties associated with some or all of the modifying factors that are taken into account in the conversion from mineral resources into mineral reserves. This relationship is shown by the broken arrow in the figure. Although the trend of the broken arrow includes a vertical component, it does not, in this instance, imply a reduction in the level of geological knowledge or confidence. In such a case, the modifying factors should be fully explained (see also para. 21 for a subdivision of mineral resources).*

IV. General reporting

11. Reports to the Authority concerning a contractor's mineral exploration results assessments, mineral resources or mineral reserves must include a description of the style and nature of mineralization.

12. A contractor must disclose any relevant information concerning a mineral deposit that could materially influence the economic value of that deposit to the contractor. A contractor must promptly report any material changes in its mineral resources or mineral reserves to the Authority.

13. Throughout the reporting standard, certain words are used in a generic sense when a more specific meaning might be attached to them by particular groups within the industry. In order to avoid duplication or ambiguity, those terms are listed in enclosure 1 together with other terms that may be regarded as synonymous for the purpose of the present document.[4]

V. Reporting of mineral exploration results assessments

14. **An exploration target is a statement or estimate of the exploration potential of a mineral deposit in a defined geological setting, where the statement or estimate, quoted as a range of tons and of grade or quality, relates to mineralization for which there has been insufficient exploration to estimate mineral resources.**

15. **Mineral exploration results assessments include data and information generated by mineral exploration programmes which might be of use to readers of the report but do not form part of a declaration of mineral resources or mineral reserves.**[5]

---

[4] The use of a particular term throughout the present document does not signify that it is preferred or necessarily the ideal term in all circumstances. The contractors would be expected to select and use the most appropriate terminology for the commodity or activity reported on.

[5] It should be made clear in reports that contain mineral exploration results assessments that it is inappropriate to use such information to derive estimates of tonnage and grade. It is recommended that such reports carry a continuing statement along the following lines: "The information provided in the present report/statement/release constitutes mineral exploration results assessments as defined in the reporting standard of the International Seabed Authority, in relation to clause 24. It is inappropriate to use such information for deriving estimates of tonnage and grade".

16. This sort of data is common in the early stages of exploration when the quantity of data available is generally not sufficient to allow for any estimates other than in the form of an exploration target to be reached.

17. If a contractor reports mineral exploration results assessments in relation to mineralization not classified as a mineral resource or mineral reserve, then estimates of tonnage and associated average grade must not be reported other than in the form of an exploration target.[6]

18. Reports on mineral exploration results assessments relating to mineralization not classified as a mineral resource or mineral reserve must contain sufficient information to allow a considered and balanced judgement of the significance of the results. Reports on mineral exploration results assessments must not be presented so as to unreasonably imply that mineralization of potential economic interest has been discovered.

VI. Reporting of mineral resources

19. **A mineral resource is a concentration or occurrence of solid material of economic interest in or on the Earth's crust in such form, grade or quality and quantity that there are reasonable prospects for eventual economic extraction.**[7]

20. **The location, quantity, grade or quality, continuity and other geological characteristics of a mineral resource are known, estimated or interpreted from specific geological evidence and knowledge, including sampling.**

21. Mineral resources are subdivided, in order of increasing geological confidence into "inferred", "indicated" and "measured" categories.

22. Portions of a mineral deposit that do not offer reasonable prospects for eventual economic extraction must not be included into a mineral resource.[8]

23. **An inferred mineral resource is that part of a <u>mineral resource</u> for which quantity and grade or quality are estimated on the basis of limited geological evidence and sampling. Geological evidence is sufficient to imply, but not verify, geological and grade or quality continuity.**

---

[6] Descriptions of exploration targets or exploration potential given in reports should be expressed so as not to misrepresent them as an estimate of mineral resources or mineral reserves.

[7] The term "mineral resource" covers mineralization which has been identified and estimated through exploration and sampling and within which mineral reserves may be defined by the consideration and application of Modifying Factors.

[8] The term "reasonable prospects for eventual economic extraction" implies a judgement (albeit preliminary) by the contractor with respect to the technical and economic factors likely to influence the prospect of economic extraction, including the approximate mining parameters. In other words, a mineral resource is not an inventory of all mineralization drilled or sampled, regardless of cut-off parameters, likely mining dimensions, location or continuity. It is a realistic inventory of mineralization which, under assumed and justifiable technical and economic conditions, might, in whole or in part, become economically extractable. Any material assumptions made in determining the reasonable prospects for eventual economic extraction should be clearly stated in the report. Any adjustment made to the data for the purpose of making the mineral resource estimate, for example by cut-off or factoring grades, or the factoring of seabed nodule abundance measurements, should be clearly stated and described in the report.

24. An inferred mineral resource has a lower level of confidence than that applying to an <u>indicated mineral resource</u> and must not be converted into a <u>mineral reserve</u>. It is reasonably expected that, with continued exploration, the majority of inferred mineral resources could be upgraded to indicated mineral resources.[9]

25. The inferred category is intended to cover cases in which a mineral concentration or occurrence has been identified and limited measurements and sampling have been completed, but in which data are insufficient to allow the geological or grade continuity to be confidently interpreted. Commonly, it would be reasonable to expect that the majority of inferred mineral resources could be upgraded to indicated mineral resources with continued exploration. However, owing to the uncertainty of inferred mineral resources, it should not be assumed that such upgrading will always occur.

26. An indicated mineral resource is that part of a <u>mineral resource</u> for which quantity, grade or quality, densities, shape and physical characteristics are estimated at a level of confidence high enough to allow for the application of <u>modifying factors</u> in sufficient detail to support mine planning and the evaluation of the economic viability of the deposit.

27. Geological evidence is derived from adequately detailed and reliable exploration, sampling and testing and is sufficient to assume geological and grade or quality continuity between points of observation.

28. An indicated mineral resource has a lower level of confidence than that applying to a <u>measured mineral resource</u> and may only be converted into a <u>probable mineral reserve</u>.[10]

29. A measured mineral resource is that part of a <u>mineral resource</u> for which quantity, grade or quality, densities, shape, and physical characteristics are estimated at a level of confidence high enough to allow for the application of <u>modifying factors</u> to support detailed mine planning and a final evaluation of the economic viability of the deposit.

30. Geological evidence is derived from detailed and reliable exploration, sampling and testing and is sufficient to confirm geological and grade or quality continuity between points of observation.

31. A measured mineral resource has a higher level of confidence than that applying to either an <u>indicated mineral resource</u> or an <u>inferred mineral resource</u>. It may be converted into a <u>proved mineral reserve</u> or to a <u>probable mineral reserve</u>.

---

[9] Confidence in the estimate is usually not sufficient to allow for the results of the application of technical and economic parameters to be used for detailed planning. For this reason, there is no direct link from an inferred resource to any category of mineral reserves (see the figure in para. 7). Caution should be exercised if that category is considered in technical and economic studies.

[10] Mineralization may be classified as an indicated mineral resource when the nature, quality, amount and distribution of data are sufficient to allow for a confident interpretation of the geological framework and to assume continuity of mineralization. Confidence in the estimate is sufficient to allow for the application of technical and economic parameters and to enable an evaluation of economic viability.

Guidance

32. *Mineralization may be classified as a measured mineral resource when the nature, quality, amount and distribution of data are such as to leave no reasonable doubt, in the opinion of the contractor determining the mineral resource, that the tonnage and grade of the mineralization can be estimated to within close limits, and that any variation from the estimate would be unlikely to affect significantly potential economic viability.*

33. *This category requires a high level of confidence in, and understanding of, the geology and the controls of the mineral deposit.*

34. *Confidence in the estimate is sufficient to allow for the application of technical and economic parameters and to enable an evaluation of economic viability with a high level of confidence.*

35. The choice of the appropriate category of mineral resource depends upon the quantity, distribution and quality of data available and the level of confidence attached to those data.

Guidance

36. *Mineral resource classification is a matter for skilled judgement and the contractor should take into account those items in enclosure 1 that relate to confidence in mineral resource estimations.*

37. *In deciding between indicated mineral resources and measured mineral resources, it may be useful to consider, in addition to the explanations relating to geological and grade continuity in paragraphs 26 and 29, the language in the guideline attached to the definition of measured mineral resources, namely that "any variation from the estimate would be unlikely to affect significantly potential economic viability".*

38. *In deciding between inferred mineral resources and indicated mineral resources, it may be useful to consider, in addition to the explanations in paragraphs 23 and 26 relating to geological and grade continuity, the guideline attached to the definition of indicated mineral resources, namely that "confidence in the estimate is sufficient to allow for the application of technical and economic parameters and to enable an evaluation of economic viability", which contrasts with the guideline relating to the definition of inferred mineral resources, namely that "confidence in the estimate of inferred mineral resources is usually not sufficient to allow for the results of the application of technical and economic parameters to be used for detailed planning" and that "caution should be exercised if that category is considered in technical and economic studies".*

39. *The contractor should take into consideration the style of mineralization, scale and cut-off parameters when assessing geological and grade continuity.*

40. Mineral resource estimates are not precise calculations, being dependent on the interpretation of limited information on the location, shape and continuity of the occurrence and on the available sampling results. The reporting of tonnage and grade figures should reflect the relative uncertainty of the estimate by rounding off

to significant figures and, in the case of inferred mineral resources, by using terms such as "approximately".[11]

Guidance

41. *The contractor is encouraged, where appropriate, to discuss the relative accuracy or confidence level of the mineral resource estimates. The statement should specify whether it relates to estimates that are global (whole resource) or local (a subset of the resource for which the accuracy /or confidence level might differ from that of the whole resource), and, if local, state the relevant tonnage or volume. Where a statement of the relative accuracy or confidence level is not possible, a qualitative discussion of the uncertainties should be provided (see enclosure 1).*

42. Reports of mineral resources must specify one or more of the "inferred", "indicated" and "measured" categories. Categories must not be reported in a combined form unless details of the individual categories are also provided. Mineral resources must not be reported in terms of contained metal or mineral content unless corresponding tonnages and grades are also presented. Mineral resources must not be aggregated with mineral reserves.[12]

43. Enclosure 1 provides, in a summary form, a list of the main criteria that should be considered when preparing reports on mineral exploration results assessments, mineral resources and mineral reserves. These criteria need not be discussed in a report unless they materially affect the estimation or the classification of the mineral resources.[13]

44. The words "ore" and "reserves" must not be used in providing mineral resource estimates, as those terms imply technical feasibility and economic viability and are only appropriate when all relevant modifying factors have been considered. Reports and statements should continue to refer to the appropriate category or categories of mineral resources until technical feasibility and economic viability have been established. If a re-evaluation indicates that any part of the mineral

---

[11] In most cases, rounding off to the second significant figure should be sufficient. For example, 10,863,000 tons at 8.23 per cent should be stated as 11 million tons at 8.2 per cent. There will be occasions, however, where rounding off to the first significant figure may be necessary in order to convey properly the uncertainties in estimation. This would usually be the case with inferred mineral resources. To emphasize the imprecise nature of a mineral resource estimate, the final result should always be referred to as an estimate and not a calculation.

[12] Reporting tonnage and grade outside the categories covered by the reporting standard is not permitted.

[13] It is not necessary, when reporting, to comment on each item in enclosure 1, but it is essential to discuss any matters that might materially affect the reader's understanding or interpretation of the results assessments or estimates reported on. This is particularly important where inadequate or uncertain data affect the reliability of, or confidence in, a statement of exploration results assessments or an estimate of mineral resources or mineral reserves, for example, poor sample recovery, reliance on video or acoustic seabed reconnaissance results, etc. If there is doubt as to what should be reported, it is better to provide too much information rather than too little. Uncertainties in any of the criteria listed in enclosure 1 that could lead to under- or over-statement of resources should be disclosed.

reserves is no longer viable, such mineral reserves must be reclassified as mineral resources or removed from the mineral resource and mineral reserve statements.[14]

VII. Reporting of mineral reserves

45. **A mineral reserve is the economically mineable part of a measured or indicated mineral resource.**

46. **It includes diluting materials and allowances for losses, which may occur when the material is mined or extracted, and is defined by studies at pre-feasibility or feasibility level, as appropriate, that include the application of modifying factors. Such studies demonstrate that, at the time of reporting, extraction could reasonably be justified.**

47. **The reference point at which reserves are defined, usually the point where the ore is delivered to the processing plant, must be stated. It is important that, wherever the reference point is different, a clarifying statement be included to ensure that the reader is fully informed of what is being reported.**

Guidance

48. *Mineral reserves are those portions of mineral resources that, after the application of all mining factors, result in an estimated tonnage and grade which, in the opinion of the contractor making the estimates, can be the basis of a viable project, after taking account of all relevant modifying factors.*

49. *When reporting mineral reserves, information on estimated mineral processing recovery factors is very important, and should always be included in reports.*

50. *The term "economically mineable" implies that the extraction of the mineral reserve has been demonstrated to be viable under reasonable financial assumptions. What may be "realistically assumed" will vary with the type of deposit, the level of study that has been carried out and the financial criteria of the individual contractor. For this reason, there can be no fixed definition for the term "economically mineable". However, it is expected that companies will attempt to achieve an acceptable return on the capital invested, and that returns to investors in the project will be competitive with alternative investments of comparable risk.*

51. *In order to achieve the required level of confidence in the mineral resources and all the modifying factors, studies of pre-feasibility or feasibility, as appropriate, will have been carried out before determining the mineral reserves. The study will need to determine a mine plan that is technically achievable and economically viable and from which the mineral reserves can be derived.*

52. *The term "mineral reserves" need not necessarily signify that extraction facilities are in place or operative, or that all necessary approvals or sales contracts have been received. It signifies that there are reasonable expectations of*

---

[14] It is not intended that the reclassification from mineral reserves to mineral resources, or vice versa, should be applied as a result of changes expected to be of a short-term or temporary nature, or where a contractor's management has made a deliberate decision to operate on a non-economic basis. Examples of such cases include commodity price fluctuations expected to be of short duration, mine emergency of a non-permanent nature and transport strike.

such approvals or contracts. The contractor should consider the materiality of any unresolved matter that is dependent on a third party on which extraction is contingent.

53. *Any adjustment made to the data for the purpose of making the mineral reserve estimate, for example by cut-off or factoring grades, or the factoring of seabed nodule abundance measurements, should be clearly stated and described in the report.*

54. *It should be noted that the reporting standard does not imply that an economic operation should have proved mineral reserves. Cases may arise where probable mineral reserves alone may be sufficient to justify extraction. This is a matter of judgement by the contractor.*

55. **A probable mineral reserve is the economically mineable part of an indicated and, in some circumstances, <u>measured mineral resource</u>. The level of confidence in the <u>modifying factors</u> applying to a probable mineral reserve is lower than that applying to a <u>proved mineral reserve</u>.**

56. A probable mineral reserve has a lower level of confidence than a proved mineral reserve but is sufficiently reliable to serve as the basis for a decision on the development of the deposit.

57. **A proved mineral reserve is the economically mineable part of a <u>measured mineral resource</u> and implies a high degree of confidence in the <u>modifying factors</u>.**

58. A proved mineral reserve represents the highest level of confidence for reserve estimates.[15]

59. The choice of the appropriate category of the mineral reserve is determined primarily by the relevant level of confidence in the mineral resource and after considering any uncertainties in the modifying factors. The allocation of the appropriate category must be made by the contractor.

60. The reporting standard provides for a direct relationship between indicated mineral resources and probable mineral reserves, and between measured mineral resources and proved mineral reserves. In other words, the level of geological confidence for probable mineral reserves is similar to that required for the determination of indicated mineral resources. The level of geological confidence for proved mineral reserves is similar to that required for the determination of measured mineral resources. Inferred mineral resources are always in addition to mineral reserves.

Guidance

61. *The reporting standard also provides for a two-way relationship between measured mineral resources and probable mineral reserves. This provision is to cover cases in which uncertainties associated with any of the modifying factors*

---

[15] The style of mineralization or other factors could mean that the status of proved mineral reserves is not achievable in some deposits. The contractor should be aware of the consequences of declaring material of the highest confidence category before satisfying themselves that all of the relevant resource parameters and modifying factors have been established at a similarly high level of confidence.

considered when converting mineral resources into mineral reserves may result in there being a lower degree of confidence in the mineral reserves than in the corresponding mineral resources. Such a conversion would not imply a reduction in the level of geological knowledge or confidence.

62. *A probable mineral reserve derived from a measured mineral resource may be converted into a proved mineral reserve if the uncertainties in the modifying factors are removed. No amount of confidence in the modifying factors for the conversion of a mineral resource into a mineral reserve can override the upper level of confidence that exists in the mineral resource. Under no circumstances can an indicated mineral resource be converted directly into a proved mineral reserve (see the figure in para. 7).*

63. *The application of the category of proved mineral reserves implies the highest degree of confidence in the estimate, with consequent expectations in the minds of the readers of the report. Such expectations should be borne in mind when categorizing a mineral resource as measured.*[16]

64. Mineral reserve estimates are not precise calculations. The reporting of tonnage and grade figures should reflect the relative uncertainty of the estimate by rounding off to significant figures (see also para. 40).[17]

Guidance

65. *The contractors are encouraged, where appropriate, to discuss the relative accuracy or confidence level of the mineral reserve estimates. The statement should specify whether it relates to estimates that are global (whole reserve) or local (a subset of the reserve for which the accuracy or confidence level might differ from that of the whole reserve), and, if local, state the relevant tonnage or volume. Where a statement of the relative accuracy or confidence level is not possible, a qualitative discussion of the uncertainties should be provided (see enclosure 1 and the guidelines in para. 40).*

66. Reports of mineral reserves must specify one or both of the categories of "proved" and "probable". Categories must not be reported in a combined proved and probable mineral reserve unless the relevant figures are provided for each category. Reports must not present metal or mineral content figures unless corresponding tonnage and grade figures are also given. Mineral reserves must not be aggregated with mineral resources.[13]

Guidance

67. *Mineral reserves may incorporate material (dilution) that is not part of the original mineral resource. It is essential that this fundamental difference between mineral resources and mineral reserves be borne in mind and caution exercised if attempting to draw conclusions from a comparison of the two.*

68. *When revised mineral reserve and mineral resource statements are reported, they should be accompanied by a reconciliation with previous statements. A detailed*

---

[16] See also the guidelines in paras. 32-34 regarding the classification of mineral resources.
[17] To emphasize the imprecise nature of a mineral reserve, the final result should always be referred to as an estimate and not a calculation.

account of differences between figures is not essential, but sufficient comments should be provided to enable significant changes to be understood by the reader.

69. When figures for both the mineral resources and the mineral reserves are reported, a statement must be included in the report that clearly indicates whether the mineral resources include the mineral reserves or are reported in addition to them.

70. Mineral reserve estimates must not be included in mineral resource estimates under a single combined figure.[18]

Guidance

71. The measured and indicated mineral resources are additional to the mineral reserves. In the former case, if any measured and indicated mineral resources have not been modified to produce mineral reserves for economic or other reasons, the relevant details of these unmodified mineral resources should be included in the report. This is to assist the reader of the report in making a judgement on the likelihood of the unmodified measured and indicated mineral resources eventually of being converted into mineral reserves.

72. Inferred mineral resources are by definition always in addition to mineral reserves. For reasons stated in paragraph 24 and in the present paragraph, the reported mineral reserve figures must not be included in the reported mineral resource figures. The resulting total is misleading and may be misunderstood or misused to give a false impression of a contractor's prospects.

VIII. Technical studies

73. A scoping study is an economic study of the potential viability of <u>mineral resources</u> that includes appropriate assessments of realistically assumed <u>modifying factors</u>, together with any other relevant operational factors that are necessary to demonstrate at the time of reporting that progress to a <u>pre-feasibility study</u> can be reasonably justified.

74. A pre-feasibility study is a comprehensive study of a range of options for the technical and economic viability of a mineral project that has advanced to a stage where a preferred mining method is established and an effective method of mineral processing is determined. It includes a financial analysis based on reasonable assumptions with regard to the <u>modifying factors</u> and the evaluation of any other relevant factors that are sufficient for an contractor, acting reasonably, to determine whether all or part of the <u>mineral resource</u> may be converted into a <u>mineral reserve</u> at the time of reporting. A pre-feasibility study is at a lower confidence level than a <u>feasibility study</u>.

75. A feasibility study is a comprehensive technical and economic study of the selected development option for a mineral project that includes appropriately detailed assessments of applicable <u>modifying factors</u>, together with any other

---

[18] In some cases, there are reasons for reporting mineral resources inclusive of mineral reserves and, in other cases, for reporting mineral resources in addition to mineral reserves. It must be made clear which form of reporting has been adopted. Appropriate forms of clarifying statements may be reported.

relevant operational factors and detailed financial analysis that are necessary to demonstrate at the time of reporting that extraction is reasonably justified (economically mineable). The results of the study may reasonably serve as the basis for a final decision by a proponent or financial institution to proceed with, or finance, the development of the project. The confidence level of the study will be higher than that of a <u>pre-feasibility study</u>.

Guidance

76. Enclosure 1 provides, in a summary form, a list of the criteria that should be considered when preparing reports on mineral exploration results assessments, mineral resources and mineral reserves. Those criteria need not be discussed in a report unless they materially affect the estimation or the classification of the mineral reserves. Changes in economic or political factors alone may be the basis for significant changes in mineral reserves and should be reported accordingly.

Enclosure 1

Checklist of assessment and reporting criteria

1. The present table is a checklist that those preparing reports on mineral exploration results assessments, mineral resources and mineral reserves should use as a reference. The checklist is not prescriptive and, as always, relevance and materiality are overriding principles that determine what information should be reported. It is, however, important to report any matters that might materially affect a reader's understanding or interpretation of the results assessments or estimates that are reported. This is particularly important where inadequate or uncertain data affect the reliability of, or confidence in, a statement of mineral exploration results assessments or an estimate of mineral resources or mineral reserves.

2. The order and grouping of the criteria in the table reflect the normal systematic approach to exploration and evaluation. Criteria in the first group (sampling techniques and data) apply to all succeeding groups. In the remainder of the checklist, criteria listed in one group would often apply to succeeding groups and should be considered when estimating and reporting.

Criteria	Explanation
Sampling techniques and data **(criteria in this group apply to all succeeding groups)**	
Sampling techniques	Nature and quality of the sampling (e.g. free-fall grab samplers, box corers, box grab samplers, etc.) and measures taken to ensure sample representativity.
Sample recovery	• Indication of whether the recovery of samples has been properly recorded and the results assessed • Measures taken to maximize sample recovery and ensure the representative nature of the samples • Indication of whether a relationship exists between sample recovery and grade and whether sample bias may have occurred owing to the preferential loss or gain of fine and coarse material
Logging and sample description	• Indication of whether the samples have been logged or described to a level of detail sufficient to support appropriate mineral resource estimations, mining studies and metallurgical studies • Indication of whether logging is qualitative or quantitative in nature and provision of sample photographs
Subsampling techniques and sample preparation	• Nature, quality and appropriateness of the sample preparation technique • Quality control procedures adopted for all subsampling stages to maximize the representativity of samples • Measures taken to ensure that the sampling is representative of the material collected in situ

Criteria	Explanation
	• Indication of whether sample sizes are appropriate for the grain size of the material being sampled
	• Statement as to the security measures taken to ensure sample integrity is recommended
Quality of assay data and laboratory tests	• Nature, quality and appropriateness of the assaying and laboratory procedures used and whether the technique is considered partial or total
	• Nature of the quality control procedures adopted (e.g. standards, blanks, duplicates or external laboratory checks) and whether acceptable levels of accuracy (i.e. lack of bias) and precision have been established
Location of data points	• Accuracy and quality of surveys used to locate other sample sites used in the mineral resource estimation
	• Quality and adequacy of the topographic control (providing locality plans)
Data spacing and distribution	• Data spacing for reporting mineral exploration results assessments
	• Indication of whether the data spacing and distribution are sufficient to establish the degree of geological and grade continuity appropriate for the mineral resource and mineral reserve estimation procedures and the classifications applied
	• Indication of whether sample compositing has been applied
Reporting archives	Documentation of primary data, data entry procedures, data verification, data storage (physical and electronic) for preparing the report
Audits or reviews	Results of any audits or reviews of the sampling techniques and data
Reporting of mineral exploration results assessments (criteria listed in the preceding group also apply to this group)	
Mineral rights and land ownership	• Type, reference name or number, location and ownership, including agreements or material issues with third parties, such as joint ventures, partnerships, overriding royalties, environmental setting, etc.
	• Security of the tenure held at the time of reporting, along with any known impediments to obtaining a contract to operate in the area
	• Location plans of the mineral rights and titles. It is not expected that the description of a mineral title in a technical report should represent a legal opinion but it should be a brief and clear description of such title as understood by the author
Exploration done by other parties	Acknowledgment and appraisal of exploration by other parties
Geology	• Type of deposit, geological setting and style of mineralization
	• Reliable geological maps should exist to support interpretations

Criteria	Explanation
Data reporting methods	• When reporting mineral exploration results assessments, maximum and minimum grade truncations (e.g. the cut-off of high grades) and cut-off grades are usually material and should be stated • The assumptions used for any reporting of metal equivalent values should be clearly stated
Diagrams	Where possible, maps and scaled tabulations of sample results should be included for any material discovery being reported, if such diagrams significantly clarify the report
Balanced reporting	Where the comprehensive reporting of all mineral exploration results assessments is not practicable, the representative reporting of both low and high grades and widths should be applied to avoid the misleading reporting of such assessments
Other substantive exploration data	Other exploration data, if meaningful and material, should be reported, including (but not limited to): geological observations; geophysical survey results; geochemical survey results; seabed photography or sonar results; bulk samples and the size and method of treatment; metallurgical test results; bulk density and the geotechnical and rock characteristics; potential deleterious or contaminating substances
Further work	Nature and scale of planned further work (e.g. tests for lateral extensions)

Estimation and reporting of mineral resources
(criteria listed in the first group and, where relevant, in the second group, also apply to this group)

Database integrity	• Measures taken to ensure that the data have not been corrupted by, for example, transcription or keying errors, between its initial collection and its use for mineral resource estimation purposes • Data verification or validation procedures used
Geological interpretation	• Confidence in (or, conversely, the uncertainty of) the geological interpretation of the mineral deposit • Nature of the data used and of any assumptions made • Effect, if any, of alternative interpretations on the mineral resource estimation • Use of geology in guiding and controlling the mineral resource estimation • Factors affecting the continuity of both grade and geology
Dimensions	Extent and variability of the mineral resource expressed as length (along strike or otherwise) and width
Estimation and modelling techniques	• Nature and appropriateness of the estimation techniques applied and key assumptions, including the treatment of extreme grade values, domaining, interpolation parameters and the maximum distance of extrapolation from data points • Availability of check estimates, previous estimates and mine production records, and indication of whether the mineral resource estimate takes appropriate account of such data

Criteria	Explanation
	• Assumptions made regarding the recovery of by-products
	• Estimation of deleterious elements or other non-grade variables of economic significance
	• In the case of a block model interpolation, block size in relation to the average sample spacing and the search employed
	• Any assumptions behind modelling of selective mining units (e.g. non-linear kriging)
	• Indicate any assumptions about correlation among variables
	• Process of validation, checking process used, comparison of model data to sampling data and use of reconciliation data, if available
	• Detailed description of the method used and the assumptions made to estimate the tonnage (or abundance) and grades (section, polygon, inverse distance, geostatistical or other method)
	• Description of how the geological interpretation was used to control the resource estimates
	• Discussion of the basis for using or not using grade cutting or capping. If a computer method was chosen, description of the programmes and parameters used
	• Geostatistical methods are extremely varied and should be described in detail. The method chosen should be justified. The geostatistical parameters, including the variogram, and their compatibility with the geological interpretation should be discussed
	• Experience gained in applying geostatistics to similar deposits should be taken into account
Moisture	Indication of whether the tonnage or abundance is estimated on a dry basis or with natural moisture, and the method of determination of the moisture content
Cut-off parameter	Basis of the adopted cut-off grade or grades, or quality or quantity parameters applied, including the basis, if appropriate, of equivalent metal formulae
Mining factors or assumptions	• Assumptions made regarding possible mining methods, minimum mining dimensions and internal (or, if applicable, external) mining dilution. It may not always be possible to make assumptions regarding mining methods and parameters when estimating mineral resources. Where no assumptions have been made, this should be reported
	• In order to demonstrate realistic prospects for eventual economic extraction, basic assumptions are necessary. Examples include geotechnical parameters, seabed topography, size of seabed mining area, infrastructure requirements and estimated mining costs. All assumptions should be clearly stated
Metallurgical factors or assumptions	• Metallurgical process proposed and appropriateness of that process to the type of mineralization. It may not always be possible to make assumptions regarding metallurgical treatment processes and parameters when reporting mineral resources. Where no assumptions have been made, this should be reported

Criteria	Explanation
	• In order to demonstrate realistic prospects for eventual economic extraction, basic assumptions are necessary. Examples include the extent of metallurgical test work, recovery factors, allowances for by-product credits or deleterious elements, infrastructure requirements and estimated processing costs. All assumptions should be clearly stated
Bulk density	• Indication of whether the bulk density is assumed or determined. If assumed, basis for the assumptions. If determined, method used, whether wet or dry, frequency of the measurements and nature, size and representativeness of the samples
Classification	• Basis for the classification of the mineral resources into varying confidence categories
	• Indication of whether appropriate account has been taken of all relevant factors (i.e. the relative confidence in tonnage or grade computations, the confidence in the continuity of geology and metal values, quality, quantity and the distribution of the data)
	• Indication of whether the result appropriately reflects the view that the contractor has of the deposit
Audits or reviews	Results of any audits or reviews of the mineral resource estimates
Discussion of relative accuracy and confidence	• Where appropriate, statement of the relative accuracy or confidence level of the mineral resource estimate using an approach or procedure deemed appropriate by the contractor. For example, application of statistical or geostatistical procedures to quantify the relative accuracy of the resource within stated confidence limits or, if such an approach is not deemed appropriate, qualitative discussion of the factors that could affect the relative accuracy and confidence level of the estimate
	• The statement should specify whether it relates to global or local estimates, and, if local, state the relevant tonnage or abundance, which should be relevant to the technical and economic evaluation
	• The documentation should include the assumptions made and the procedures used
	• The statements of relative accuracy and confidence level of the estimate should be compared with production data, where available
Estimation and reporting of mineral reserves **(criteria listed in the first group and, where relevant, in other preceding groups, also apply to this group)**	
Mineral resource estimate for conversion into mineral reserves	• Description of the mineral resource estimate used as a basis for the conversion into a mineral reserve
	• Clear statement as to whether the mineral resources are reported in addition to the mineral reserves or include them
Study status	• Type and level of the study undertaken to enable the conversion of the mineral resources into mineral reserves

Criteria	Explanation
	• The reporting standard does not require for a final feasibility study to have been undertaken to convert mineral resources into mineral reserves; however, it requires that studies to at least pre-feasibility level have determined a mine plan that is technically achievable and economically viable, and that all modifying factors have been considered
Cut-off parameter	Basis of the cut-off grade or grades or quality parameters applied, including the basis, if appropriate, of equivalent metal formulae. The cut-off parameter may be an economic value per block rather than a grade
Mining factors or assumptions	• Method and assumptions used to convert the mineral resource into a mineral reserve (i.e. either by the application of appropriate factors by optimization or by a preliminary or detailed design)
	• Choice, nature and appropriateness of the selected mining method or methods, size of the selected mining unit and other mining parameters, including associated design issues
	• Assumptions made regarding geotechnical parameters (e.g. the seabed floor slope and the topographic conditions)
	• Mining dilution factors, mining recovery factors and minimum mining widths used
	• Infrastructure requirements of the selected mining methods and, where available, historical reliability of the performance parameters
Metallurgical factors or assumptions	• Metallurgical process proposed and appropriateness of that process to the style of mineralization
	• Indication of whether the metallurgical process is a well-tested technology or novel in nature
	• Nature, amount and representativeness of the metallurgical test work undertaken and the metallurgical recovery factors applied
	• Any assumptions or allowances made for deleterious elements
	• Existence of any bulk sample or pilot-scale test work and degree to which such samples are representative of the orebody as a whole
	• The tonnage and grades reported for mineral reserves should state clearly whether they are in respect of material sent to the plant or after recovery
	• Comment on the existing plant and equipment, including an indication of their replacement and salvage value
Cost and revenue factors	• Derivation of, or assumptions made, regarding the projected capital and the operating costs
	• Assumptions made regarding revenue, including head grade, metal or commodity prices, exchange rates, transportation and treatment charges, penalties, etc.
	• Allowances made for royalties payable, international benefit sharing, etc.

Criteria	Explanation
Market assessment	• Basic cash flow inputs for a stated period
	• Demand, supply and stock situation for the particular commodity, as well as consumption trends and factors likely to affect supply and demand in future
	• Customer and competitor analysis, along with the identification of likely market windows for the product
	• Price and volume forecasts and the basis for such forecasts
Other	• Effect, if any, of natural risk, infrastructure, environmental, legal, marketing, social or governmental factors on the likely viability of a project and on the estimation and the classification of the mineral reserves
	• Status of titles and approvals critical to the viability of the project, such as mining leases, discharge permits and governmental and statutory approvals
	• Environmental descriptions of anticipated liabilities
	• Location plans of mineral rights and titles
Classification	• Basis for the classification of the mineral reserves into varying confidence categories
	• Indication of whether the result appropriately reflects the view that the contractor has of the deposit
	• Proportion of probable mineral reserves that have been derived from measured mineral resources, if any
Audits or reviews	Results of any audits or reviews of the mineral reserve estimates
Discussion of relative accuracy and confidence	• Where appropriate, statement of the relative accuracy or confidence level of the mineral reserve estimate using an approach or procedure deemed appropriate by the contractor. For example, application of statistical or geostatistical procedures to quantify the relative accuracy of the reserve within stated confidence limits or, if such an approach is not deemed appropriate, qualitative discussion of the factors that could affect the relative accuracy and confidence level of the estimate
	• The statement should specify whether it relates to global or local estimates and, if local, state the relevant tonnage or abundance, which should be relevant to the technical and economic evaluation. The documentation should include the assumptions made and the procedures used
	• Statements of the relative accuracy or confidence level of the estimate should be compared with production data, where available

Enclosure 2

Generic terms and equivalents and definitions

The reporting standard of the International Seabed Authority uses in a generic sense certain words that might have a more specific meaning attached to them by particular groups in the industry. In order to avoid duplication or ambiguity, those terms are defined below, together with other terms that may be regarded as synonymous for the purposes of the present guidance.

Generic term	*Synonym or similar term*	*Definition*
Cut-off grade	Product specification	The lowest grade, or quality, of mineralized material that qualifies as economically mineable and available in a given deposit. It may be defined on the basis of economic evaluation or on the physical or chemical attributes that define an acceptable product specification
Feasibility study	–	A comprehensive study of a mineral deposit in which all geological, engineering, legal, operating, economic, social, environmental and other relevant factors are considered in such detail that it may reasonably serve as the basis for a final decision by a financial institution to finance the development of the deposit for mineral production
Grade	Quality; assay; analysis; value	Any physical or chemical measurement of the characteristics of the material of interest in samples or product
Metallurgy	Processing; beneficiation; preparation concentration	Physical or chemical separation of constituents of interest from a larger mass of material; methods employed to prepare a final marketable product from material as mined. Examples include screening, flotation, magnetic separation, leaching, washing and roasting
Mineral reserve	Ore reserve	A deposit that has been classified as a reserve. "Mineral" is the preferred term in the reporting standard of the Authority, but "ore" is in common use and generally acceptable. Other terms can be used to clarify the meaning, for instance "seabed reserves"
Mineralization	Type of deposit; style of mineralization	Any single mineral or combination of minerals occurring in a mass, or deposit of economic interest. The term is intended to cover all forms in which mineralization might occur, whether by type of deposit, mode of occurrence, genesis or composition
Mining	Seabed harvesting	All activities related to the extraction of metals and minerals from the earth, whether on the surface, underground or on the seabed

Generic term	Synonym or similar term	Definition
Pre-feasibility study	Preliminary feasibility study	A comprehensive study of the viability of a mineral project that: (a) has advanced to a stage where the mining method has been established and where an effective method of mineral processing has been determined; and (b) includes a financial analysis based on reasonable assumptions of technical, engineering, legal, operating and economic factors and the evaluation of other relevant factors sufficient for a suitably qualified and experienced qualified person to determine, within reason, whether all or part of the mineral resource may be classified as a mineral reserve
Recovery	Yield	The percentage of material of initial interest that is extracted during mining or processing; a measure of mining or processing efficiency
Tonnage	Quantity; volume; abundance	An expression of the amount of material of interest irrespective of the units of measurement (which should be stated when figures are reported)

International Seabed Authority

Council

ISBA/21/C/19*

Distr.: General
23 July 2015

Original: English

Twenty-first session
Kingston, Jamaica
13-24 July 2015

Decision of the Council of the International Seabed Authority relating to the procedures and criteria for the extension of an approved plan of work for exploration pursuant to section 1, paragraph 9, of the annex to the Agreement relating to the Implementation of Part XI of the United Nations Convention on the Law of the Sea of 10 December 1982

The Council of the International Seabed Authority,

Recalling that, pursuant to article 162, subparagraphs 2 (a) and (l), of the United Nations Convention on the Law of the Sea, the Council shall supervise and coordinate the implementation of the provisions of Part XI of the Convention on all questions and matters within the competence of the Authority and shall exercise control over activities in the Area in accordance with article 153, paragraph 4, of the Convention and the rules, regulations and procedures of the Authority,

Recalling also paragraph 2 of its decision of 23 July 2014,[1] in which it requested the Legal and Technical Commission, as a matter of urgency and as its first priority, to formulate draft procedures and criteria for applications for extensions of contracts for exploration, in accordance with section 3.2 of the standard clauses contained in annex IV to the Regulations, for consideration by the Council at its twenty-first session,

Taking into account the recommendations of the Legal and Technical Commission on the procedures and criteria for extension of an approved plan of work for exploration pursuant to section 1, paragraph 9, of the annex to the Agreement relating to the Implementation of Part XI of the United Nations Convention on the Law of the Sea of 10 December 1982,[2] and the recommendations of the Finance Committee,

1. *Adopts* the procedures and criteria for extension of an approved plan of work for exploration pursuant to section 1, paragraph 9, of the annex to the Agreement relating to the Implementation of Part XI of the United Nations

---

* Reissued for technical reasons on 24 July 2015.
[1] ISBA/20/C/31.
[2] ISBA/21/C/WP.1.

Please recycle

Convention on the Law of the Sea of 10 December 1982, as contained in the annex to the present decision;

2. *Reaffirms* that, consistent with its mandate under article 165 of the Convention and paragraph 9 of section 1 of the annex to the 1994 Agreement, the Legal and Technical Commission shall consider whether the contractor has made efforts in good faith to fulfil its obligations under the contract for exploration, but for reasons beyond the contractor's control, has been unable to complete the necessary preparatory work for proceeding to the exploitation stage, or whether the prevailing economic circumstances do not justify proceeding to the exploitation stage;

3. *Calls upon* the sponsoring State or States, in accordance with their obligations, to confirm to the Secretary-General the continuation of sponsorship for the duration of the extension;

4. *Requests* the Secretary-General to communicate the present decision to all contractors with the Authority, and requests the contractors applying for extensions to underscore the proposed modifications and/or additions to the programme of activities.

212th meeting
23 July 2015

Annex
Procedures and criteria for the extension of an approved plan of work for exploration pursuant to section 1, paragraph 9, of the annex to the Agreement relating to the Implementation of Part XI of the United Nations Convention on the Law of the Sea of 10 December 1982

I. **Form and content of application for extension**

1. The holder of a contract for exploration (hereinafter referred to as "the Contractor") may submit an application for extension of such contract in accordance with the procedures set out below. Contractors may apply for such extensions for periods of not more than five years each.

2. Each application for extension of a contract for exploration shall be in writing, addressed to the Secretary-General of the International Seabed Authority, and shall contain the information set out in annex I to the present document. Each such application shall be submitted no later than six months before the expiration of the contract in respect of which the application is made.

3. Unless otherwise indicated by the sponsoring State or States at the time of making the application for an extension, sponsorship shall be deemed to continue throughout the extension period and the sponsoring State or States shall continue to assume responsibility in accordance with articles 139 and 153 (4) of the Convention and article 4 (4) of annex III to the Convention.

4. The fee for processing an application for extension of a contract for exploration shall be a fixed amount of $67,000 or its equivalent in a freely convertible currency, to be paid in full at the time of the submission of an application.

5. If the administrative costs incurred by the Authority in processing an application are less than the fixed amount indicated in paragraph 4 above, the Authority shall refund the difference to the Contractor. If the administrative costs incurred by the Authority in processing an application are more than the fixed amount indicated in paragraph 4 above, the Contractor shall pay the difference to the Authority, provided that any additional amount to be paid by the Contractor shall not exceed 10 per cent of the fixed fee referred to in paragraph 4.

6. Taking into account any criteria established for this purpose by the Finance Committee, the Secretary-General shall determine the amount of such differences as indicated in paragraph 5 above and notify the Contractor of the amount. The notification shall include a statement of the expenditure incurred by the Authority. The amount due shall be paid by the Contractor or reimbursed by the Authority within three months of the final decision by the Council in respect of the application.

II. Processing of an application for extension of a contract for exploration

7. The Secretary-General shall:

(a) Acknowledge in writing the receipt of every application for extension of a contract for exploration, specifying the date of receipt;

(b) Notify the sponsoring State or States of the receipt of the application and of the requirement set out in paragraph 3 above;

(c) Place the application, together with the attachments and annexes thereto, in safe custody and ensure the confidentiality of all confidential data and information contained in the application;

(d) Notify the members of the Authority of the receipt of such application and circulate to them information of a general nature which is not confidential regarding the application;

(e) Notify the members of the Legal and Technical Commission and place consideration of the application as an item on the agenda for the next meeting of the Commission.

III. Consideration by the Legal and Technical Commission

8. The Commission shall consider applications for extensions of contracts for exploration expeditiously and in the order in which they are received.

9. The Commission shall consider and review the data and information provided by the Contractor in connection with the application for extension of the contract for exploration. For the purposes of the review, the Commission may request the Contractor to submit such additional data and information as may be necessary regarding the implementation of the plan of work and compliance with the standard clauses of the contract.

10. In discharging its duties, the Commission shall apply the present procedures and criteria and the rules, regulations for the specific mineral resource and procedures of the Authority in a uniform and non-discriminatory manner.

11. If the Commission finds that an application for extension of a contract for exploration does not comply with these procedures, or the Contractor fails to provide data and information requested by the Commission, it shall notify the Contractor in writing, through the Secretary-General, indicating the reasons. The

Contractor may, within 45 days of such notification, amend its application. If the Commission, after further consideration, is of the view that it should not recommend approval of the application for extension of the contract for exploration, it shall so inform the Contractor, through the Secretary-General, and provide the Contractor with a further opportunity to make representations within 30 days. The Commission shall consider any such representations made by the Contractor in preparing its report and recommendation to the Council.

12. The Commission shall recommend approval of the application for extension of the contract for exploration if it considers that the Contractor has made efforts in good faith to comply with the requirements of the contract for exploration but, for reasons beyond the Contractor's control, has been unable to complete the necessary preparatory work for proceeding to the exploitation stage, or if the prevailing economic circumstances do not justify proceeding to the exploitation stage.

13. The Commission shall submit its report and recommendations to the Council at the first possible opportunity, taking into account the schedule of meetings of the Authority.

IV. Consideration by the Council

14. The Council shall consider the reports and recommendations of the Commission relating to applications for extension of approved plans of work for exploration in accordance with paragraphs 11 and 12 of section 3 of the annex to the Agreement relating to the Implementation of Part XI of the United Nations Convention on the Law of the Sea of 10 December 1982.

15. Upon approval by the Council, a contract shall be extended by the execution by the Secretary-General and the authorized representative of the Contractor of an agreement in the form set out in annex II to the present document. The terms and conditions applicable to the contract during the extension period shall be the terms and conditions in force as at the date of the extension, pursuant to the relevant regulations.[3]

V. Transitional provision

16. In the event that an application for extension of a contract has been duly submitted in accordance with the present procedures, but the contract would otherwise expire on a date after the next scheduled meeting of the Legal and Technical Commission but prior to the next scheduled meeting of the Council, the contract and all rights and obligations under the contract shall be deemed to be extended until such time as the Council is able to meet and approve the report and recommendations issued by the Commission in respect of that contract. In no case shall the application of the present provision result in the extension of the contract beyond a period of five years, or such shorter period as may have been requested by the Contractor, from the date on which the contract would otherwise have expired had it not been extended in accordance with these procedures.

---

[3] Except where otherwise indicated, references to "the Regulations" are to be read as collective references to the Regulations on Prospecting and Exploration for Polymetallic Nodules in the Area (ISBA/19/C/17, annex), the Regulations on Prospecting and Exploration for Polymetallic Sulphides in the Area (ISBA/16/A/12/Rev.1) and the Regulations on Prospecting and Exploration for Cobalt-rich Ferromanganese Crusts in the Area (ISBA/18/A/11).

Appendix I

Information to be contained in an application for extension of a contract for exploration

1. An application for extension of a contract for exploration shall consist of the following:

(a) A statement by the Contractor of the grounds upon which an extension of the contract for exploration is sought. Such statement shall state the duration of the extension sought (up to five years) and shall include either:

(i) Particulars of the reasons beyond the Contractor's control that have rendered it unable to complete the necessary preparatory work for proceeding to the exploitation stage; or

(ii) An explanation of the reasons why the prevailing economic circumstances do not justify proceeding to the exploitation stage, including an explanation as to whether the economic circumstances in question refer to global market conditions in general or to a feasibility assessment regarding the Contractor's own project;

(b) A detailed summary of the work carried out by the Contractor during the entire period of the contract to date and the results obtained measured against the approved plan of work for exploration. Such summary shall include:

(i) An estimation of mineral resources and/or reserves according to the reporting standards for the specific mineral resources as established by the Authority, and their spatial distribution within the exploration area;

(ii) A table summarizing all environmental baseline data collected in relation to the environmental variables listed in the relevant recommendations for the guidance of contractors;[a]

(iii) A complete list of all reports submitted to the Authority pursuant to the contract for exploration;

(iv) A complete inventory of all data and information submitted to the Authority pursuant to the contract for exploration;

(v) All data that have been requested by the Authority following the review of annual reports pursuant to the contract for exploration or that otherwise should have been submitted to the Authority pursuant to the contract, and that have not yet been supplied or have not been supplied in the format requested by or acceptable to the Authority;

(vi) A breakdown of expenditure pursuant to the contract for exploration, in accordance with the relevant recommendations for the guidance of contractors issued by the Legal and Technical Commission pursuant to the Regulations,[b] and identifying any deviation from the anticipated yearly expenditures during the period of the contract;

(vii) A summary of training provided pursuant to the contract for exploration;

---

[a] ISBA/19/LTC/8.
[b] ISBA/21/LTC/11.

(c) A description and a schedule of the proposed exploration programme during the extension period, including a detailed programme of activities, showing any proposed modifications or additions to the approved plan of work for exploration under the contract, and a statement that during the extension period the Contractor will complete the necessary preparatory work for proceeding to the exploitation stage;

(d) Details of any proposed relinquishment of any part of the exploration area during the extension period, as may be necessary;

(e) A schedule of anticipated yearly expenditures in respect of the programme of activities for the extension period;

(f) A proposed training programme for the extension period in accordance with the relevant recommendations for the guidance of contractors issued by the Legal and Technical Commission pursuant to the Regulations.[c]

2. All data and information submitted in connection with the application for extension of the contract for exploration shall be submitted in hard copy and in a digital format specified by the Authority.

---

[c] ISBA/19/LTC/14.

Appendix II

Agreement between the International Seabed Authority and [Contractor] concerning the extension of the Contract for Exploration for [mineral resource] between the International Seabed Authority and [Contractor], dated [date]

The International Seabed Authority, represented by its Secretary-General (hereinafter referred to as "the Authority"), and [Contractor], represented by [...] (hereinafter referred to as "the Contractor"), agree that the Contract for Exploration for [mineral resource] between the Authority and the Contractor signed on [date] at [place] for a period of 15 years from [date of entry into force of original contract], together with related annexes, is extended for a period of [...] years to [date], subject to the following amendments.

1. Schedule 2 of the Contract shall be replaced by the programme of activities attached to this agreement as annex I.

2. Schedule 3 of the Contract shall be replaced by the training programme attached to this agreement as annex II.

3. The standard clauses referred to in operative paragraph 1 of the Contract shall be replaced by the standard clauses attached to this agreement as annex III,[a] which shall be incorporated into the Contract and shall have effect as if set out therein at length.

Subject to the above amendments, the Contract shall continue in all other respects with full force and effect. This amendment will enter into force on [date].

IN WITNESS WHEREOF the undersigned, being duly authorized thereto by the respective parties, have signed this agreement at [place] this [date].

---

[a] In relation to the contracts due to expire in 2016 and 2017, this is a reference to annex IV to the Regulations on Prospecting and Exploration for Polymetallic Nodules in the Area, adopted by the Council on 22 July 2013 (ISBA/19/C/17, annex), as amended by ISBA/19/A/12.

www.ingramcontent.com/pod-product-compliance
Lightning Source LLC
Chambersburg PA
CBHW081142180526
45170CB00006B/1901